Mary King

Mary King is married with two children and lives in Devon.

Kate Green, who worked on this book with Mary King, is managing editor of *Country Life*. She has been an equestrian journalist for twenty years, reporting on all the major championships, and has written eight books, including one with Pippa Funnell.

Mary King

THE AUTOBIOGRAPHY

An Orion paperback

First published in Great Britain in 2009
by Orion
This paperback edition published in 2011
by Orion Books Ltd,
Orion House, 5 Upper St Martin's Lane,
London, WC2H 9EA

An Hachette UK company

1 3 5 7 9 10 8 6 4 2

Copyright © Mary King 2009

A CIP catalogue record for this book
is available from the British Library.

ISBN 978-1-4091-0280-9

Typeset by Input Data Services Ltd,
Bridgwater, Somerset

Printed in the UK by
CPI Mackays, Chatham ME5 8TD

The Orion Publishing Group's policy is to use papers that
are natural, renewable and recyclable products and
made from wood grown in sustainable forests. The logging
and manufacturing processes are expected to conform to
the environmental regulations of the country of origin.

www.orionbooks.co.uk

To my late father Michael, my wonderful mother Jill, my supportive and understanding husband David, and my beautiful children Emily and Freddie, who make my life complete

CONTENTS

ACKNOWLEDGEMENTS

First I would like to say a huge thank you to Kate Green, who enthusiastically did all the hard work. The book has taken shape with enormous help from her, and from years of scrapbooks which my dear mother has methodically kept, plus her own daily diaries dating back to 1963!

Also, thank you to Susan Lamb and Orion for asking me to write my autobiography, and for all the people at Orion who have been part of its production.

The list of people I would like to thank is endless: the vets who have helped and advised me over the years, notably John Fowler, Sue Dyson and Grant & Partners; Clive Evans, my brilliant farrier; my owners and sponsors past and present on whom I am totally reliant – with a very special mention for a very special person, Gilly Robinson. Thank you to all my hardworking grooms who I have had over the years – thank you for your part in helping me achieve my dreams. Annie Corbin, née Collings, worked for me for ten years and we had some great times together. Thanks also to Sheila Willcox, for the broad base of knowledge which she instilled in me, on which I built my career; my trainers Ferdi Eilberg, Lars Sederholm, Kenneth Clawson, Yogi Breisner, and all the other people who have helped me to improve over the years.

The support of the local people in the Sid Valley has been fantastic, and I would especially like to thank all the kind farmers who turn a blind eye when I sneak into their fields to work the horses.

Thank you to all my friends and relations and supporters.

But my biggest thank you goes to all the wonderful horses that I have been privileged to ride.

CHAPTER 1

Childhood

Drama surrounded even my arrival into the world, for it came just six months after the horrific accident to my father, Michael Thomson, which was to change our family's whole way of life for ever.

My father was then a young lieutenant commander in the Royal Navy working within the supply and secretariat department, and he, my mother, Jill, who was three months pregnant with me, and my brother Simon, aged two and a half, were based in Scotland. One winter's night, my father was found unconscious in the road, having fallen from his motor scooter on the way home from an evening game of squash. No one knows to this day what happened, whether he was hit, or whether he swerved to avoid an animal, but he had suffered terrible, personality-changing head injuries.

I was born, an inconvenient three weeks late, at 6 a.m. on 8 June 1961, in Winthorpe, near Newark in Nottinghamshire, where my mother's parents lived. My grandparents were retiring and moving to Guernsey, so within hours of my birth the removal men arrived to label all the furniture, and my mother and grandmother had to pack us up and drive all the way to Kilmington, East Devon, to introduce my father to his new-born daughter.

I

Having spent six months in Haslar, the naval hospital in Portsmouth, my father had gone to stay with his parents in Kilmington where he could have the total peace and quiet he needed. Our first encounter was not a great success, because he promptly suffered one of his many daily fits. And then I was whisked off to board the afternoon ferry to Guernsey, my carry-cot perched on top of all the luggage in the back of our Morris Traveller.

Recounting this, I now realise that what my mother had to do was extraordinary, especially considering that, in addition to all the practicalities, she was facing up to the fact that the dashing, sporting, naval officer she'd married was changed for ever. She has always been so uncomplaining and relaxed that I sometimes forget her heroics were not normal by other people's standards.

My mother knew she couldn't cope with two tiny children and a recuperating husband, so we stayed in Guernsey with my grandparents for a few months, waiting for my father to get better. Daddy didn't want to be parted from his family's local GP, Dr Parkinson, and would only travel to Guernsey to see us if the doctor would go with him, but when Mummy went to meet the ferry, there was no sign of Dr Parkinson – the poor man had suffered terrible seasickness and wouldn't have been any help to my father at all if he'd needed him.

As if my mother didn't have enough to worry about, I had been born with a hole in my heart and was prone to go blue, especially when cold. I had to be closely observed when swimming in the sea, and later it became a good excuse for getting out of games when it was very cold. The doctors were concerned that the hole would grow as I got bigger, but it didn't, and eventually we stopped worrying about it because there was enough else to think about.

When I was ten months old, it was decided that the time had come for us to try and begin family life on our own. Our first home was a cottage in Bath, which belonged to Tim White, a naval captain. Though I was oblivious to it, life for my mother must have been pretty harrowing. Daddy wasn't really with it. He had regular fits and would wander off, resulting in the neighbours ringing each other up to ask, 'Who on earth is this fellow running around?' He got more and more worked up over his obsession about being near Dr Parkinson and would often lose his temper.

There was a blow-up one day when my mother was trying to get him to sit down and have lunch, because he wanted us all to go to church and pray – religion was to become a focal point of our family life. My mother persuaded him to sit quietly and pray with her at the table and, miracle of miracles, the phone suddenly rang and it was Granny Thomson telling us there was a cottage to rent in Membury, near Kilmington, for £5 a week.

We spent the next eighteen months there, before moving to a farm cottage that came rent-free in return for Daddy helping on the farm. I was very keen on the animals and, aged two and three-quarters, escaped one day into a field of cows. My mother suddenly spotted me in the field, surrounded by heifers, but apparently I wasn't at all frightened, and bopped one of them on the nose with my doll.

Life was still pretty difficult. As a result of Daddy's injury, he couldn't bear any noise, so Simon and I had to learn to be good little babies, which wasn't always easy. Daddy couldn't, and wouldn't, do anything to help my mother; the only way to get him out of bed in the morning was to ply him with cups of tea so he'd need to go to the loo, then when he was out of the bed she would strip it so he couldn't get back in. He once chucked petrol on the fire to make it go, causing a mini explosion, and one day, when he'd gone out for a run and Mummy was just thinking how blissfully peaceful it all was, she realised he'd left the bath running and water was pouring down the stairs and through the ceiling.

The great tragedy of my father's life was that he longed to be ordained but although he was extremely well-read on the subject of religion he was never well enough to pass the theology exams. Before the accident, he'd been brilliant at sports and had a great mathematical brain, but the injury left him unable to concentrate. Over the years, he grew frustrated at not being used very often as a lay reader, but this was because he would lose the thread of what he was talking about. He could also be incredibly rude, which wasn't the best thing for a career in the church. When I was starting out as a rider, many of my friends were nervous of ringing up in case he answered the phone, and messages left for me got lost. He used to walk past the post box on his way to unlock the church each day, and I'd give him letters to post. One day he came back saying, 'I found this in the vestry, do you still want it posted?' It was an envelope with all my entries for an event. Luckily the horse was lame so we couldn't go to the event anyway!

Eventually, my father's fits subsided, but his brain never recovered. He had to have complete peace and quiet – we couldn't get a television until after he'd died – and a strict daily routine. He would have his tea out of the same cup every day – leaves, never bags – before listening to the 8 a.m. pips on the radio, after which, without fail, he would go to the loo. If we had visitors, they were barred from the bathroom at that time. He hardly went anywhere for the rest of his life; a trip to Sidmouth four times a year for a haircut was considered a major outing, and he went out for dinner three times a year – his birthday, my mum's birthday, and their wedding anniversary and always to the local pub, The Blue Bell, one mile away.

The turning point – and saving grace – in our lives came when someone spotted a job advertised in the *Pulman's Weekly News*. It was for a verger at the church in Salcombe Regis, a beautiful East Devon village set in a steep valley running down to the sea east of Sidmouth. The post, which had a salary of £50 a month, came with a rent-free cottage, albeit a freezing, damp one, with no central heating and an outside loo. When Mum wasn't spending her time scrubbing off the dark damp – all sorts of interesting new species of fungus appeared every year – she had jobs painting, gardening, cleaning and looking after old people in the village, though everything had to revolve around getting my father's lunch at one o'clock on the dot.

With the move to Salcombe Regis came my first chance to ride a pony. No one in our family rode, except for Aunty Betty, who took me for my first gallop when I was nine, on Aylesbeare Common. My mother, who was frightened of horses, had given up after three lessons. However, I was absolutely fascinated by them, and would spend hours sitting on gates staring at horses in fields. I longed for a pony of my own, but there was no hope, as we had neither land nor money. My mother says if she hadn't had me at home in bed, she would have thought the hospital had given her the wrong baby.

On Wednesdays at school – Manor House in Seaton – there

were optional extras, such as elocution, ballet, or riding, and I instantly chose the latter. But I was hopeless – it took me a whole year to learn rising trot and the first time Mum and Dad came to see me, I was riding with my thumbs in the air, because no one had taught me any differently.

The vicar of Salcombe Regis, Donald Peyton-Jones, whose brother, Loftus, was Speaker in the House of Commons, was a real character and very popular. He would ride around the village on Magpie, a hairy, sturdy 14 hh piebald cob, rounding up the parishioners and visiting the pub or betting shop, leaving the cob tied up outside.

He also had a rather beastly little white pony, Silver, who nipped, but if Mummy could find someone to tack him up, she would nobly lead me around the lanes, despite the fact that he once bit her in the stomach.

When I was six, amid great excitement, I took Magpie to my first gymkhana, hacking there in pouring rain. My first competition was the bending race. The judge said, 'Ready, steady, go,' and I kicked and kicked, but nothing happened. Then someone said, 'Stop kicking, she's spending a penny.' I was mortified and said, 'Oh, sorry,' and stood up in my stirrups. But the whole gymkhana was so chaotic that I somehow finished second in the race anyway, and went on to win another four rosettes, which was thrilling and fired me up to want to do more.

My first proper show was near Seaton, six miles away, with Magpie, even though I must have looked strange on her. I had no idea how to turn a pony out, apart from what I had gleaned from books. I had one called *The Show Pony*, which contained pictures of exquisite show ponies that were a far cry from dear Magpie.

I didn't understand what it meant by 'pulling a tail', so I just chopped the hair off the top in an attempt to tidy it up, then I snipped off Magpie's feathers and vaguely attempted to plait her mane. I came last in the class, but I didn't really mind too much, as I was so pleased just to be doing it.

Everything was about ponies. If I saw one in a field, I would beg for the car to be stopped so I could get out and stroke it. When Mum bought a piano for a pound (it cost four pounds to be tuned), even though I eventually got as far as Grade IV on it, the only piece I really retained was 'The Galloping Horseman'. I collected stamps, preferably with horses on them, and endlessly drew horses on my jotter at school. As we didn't have television, most of the children's programmes of the day completely passed me by – I often felt a bit left out when my schoolfriends were discussing what they'd seen the previous night – but I always contrived to be at someone else's house when *The Virginian* was on.

I joined the Axe Vale Pony Club, going to rallies on my bicycle and trying to find out if there was anything I could borrow to ride. I even borrowed a donkey once and attempted to 'school' it. I managed to get it doing circles, and I can remember clearly the peculiar feeling of riding something with such a short neck.

I had friends – April Currell and Diana Kindersley – whose ponies I rode when I went to stay, but my best friend, Rosina Hurford, a farmer's daughter, didn't have a pony either, so we used to ride the dairy cows. We were constantly jumping things on our feet, building jumping grids down the cattle lines and leaping over hay-bales while we fantasised about being on a horse.

One day, some ponies turned up nearby, having escaped from a country park. We managed to catch one with a rope and rode it bareback; worryingly for our parents, it was discovered afterwards that they were unbroken two-year-olds!

When I was seven the Greenhills, a farming family, lent me a pony and I won my first ever cup on him at the Axe Vale Pony Club hunter trials at Trinity Hill. I'd had lots of stops but I was still the best branch member and couldn't believe that I'd won the members' prize.

I had a bit of a breakthrough when the Arkwright family lent me their 14.2 hh pony, Tomahawk. He was too big for their children, but I was tall for my age with long legs. I rode him after school and borrowed him for shows, winning a few classes and taking him to my first Pony Club camps, great fun old-fashioned affairs with the ponies in stables made up of hurdles and the children sleeping in army tents.

Getting to all these rallies and shows and hunter trials wasn't easy, because we didn't have transport – there was no hope of the Morris Traveller towing anything. But by the time I was ten, I'd found a way round this, going through the *Yellow Pages*, phoning hauliers and then ringing around other children with no transport so we could share the cost.

Gillian Macfadyen, who is now a British eventing junior coordinator and who then bred and competed show ponies, was very helpful to me, giving tips on how to trim a horse's feathers with a comb and scissors instead of just hacking across the hair.

When the Arkwrights grew old enough to take over the ride, it felt like the end of the world, though it turned out that, by another miracle, I was soon to have a pony of my own.

CHAPTER 2

Butterboy

When I was twelve, my maternal grandfather gave us £500 to buy a pony.

We had a new vicar by this time, Michael Courtney, who was happy to let me use his stables, and there was a paddock available about a quarter of a mile away. Gillian Macfadyen came with us to look at ponies and we found Butterboy, who had been advertised in the Axminster paper, *Pulman's Weekly News*.

Butterboy, who was owned by Mr Cox at Dalwood, was a lovely pony, very nice-looking, and had only just been broken. We thought he was 14.2 hh, but he turned out to be just over 14.3 hh, which was a blow as I wouldn't be able to jump him in 14.2 hh classes. However, there was a good working hunter pony category for up to 15 hh and we were able to specialise in that.

Our relationship began disastrously when, due to the pair of us being green, he started refusing. I took him to Chepstow with the intention of selling him, but fortunately he didn't get his £500 reserve so we brought him home with us. It was an instructor called Gillian Sutton who got me back on track; she still follows my career and often turns up to watch me, although she's very modest and says she doesn't want to interrupt. She recalls that if she told me something back then, I always took it on straight away. Right from the early days, I've always wanted my riding to be analysed, and I like to have reminders; I have never minded criticism, because it's always driven me to try and get better.

One day, I was going for a hack on Butterboy and decided, for some reason, to sit on his bottom like a circus rider. He was quite a flighty pony – you had to be careful putting his rugs on and off – so I don't know why I thought it was a good idea. He took off and I fell backwards on to the road. For a while I lay in the ditch crying, but I had to stop because no one was around to hear me.

Definitely a bit concussed, I wandered along a farm drive and turned up at the Greenhills' house. I could hear a radio playing so went upstairs and found Margaret in the bath. I knocked on the door and said, 'I've fallen off!' Apparently I was covered in blood and looked quite a mess.

Mum had to be got out of choir practice and eventually we found Butterboy on a corner, grazing. She told me to get back on, or I'd lose my nerve. I didn't dare tell anyone what I'd done because I was so embarrassed (it wasn't until Mum read this book that she found out what I'd done). The worst part was that the fall happened the day after my first ever proper haircut – normally, Mum would give me awful pudding-basin haircuts at home – but I had to have stitches in my head and that was the end of my smart hairstyle.

I hunted Butterboy with the Axe Vale Harriers, and can remember being blooded when I was thirteen – I've still got the brush I was given. Mum was adamant that I couldn't go hunting unless I'd done my school work, and she was firm that my pony had to be exercised in the week to get him hunting fit. So I'd get up at 5.30 a.m., strap a little torch to my leg, and ride before school. The tack was hidden in a box in the corner of the field. Then the night before hunting I'd keep Butterboy in, though in my ignorance I used to over-feed the poor pony and he seized up a couple of times.

One summer, we went to Lychett Minster for a working hunter pony qualifier. Somehow, we crashed through the practice fence, landing in a heap. I felt rather battered myself, and depressed at not winning, but I was even more uneasy about Butterboy. Usually, he'd go straight to the grass verge and eat, but when we got home he didn't seem to be able to chew, and it turned out that he'd broken his jaw. Our vet, Don Attenborough, came to see him and advised that it would have to heal on its own and we'd have to feed him liquid gruels to keep him nourished in the meantime.

So while I was at school, Mum had to take Butterboy regular meals of boiled linseed and beg him to eat. Unsurprisingly, he lost a lot of condition until, one wonderful day, I found him nibbling grass. Eventually, I started riding him again with just a rope halter and did a few shows in a hackamore (bitless) bridle. I missed all competitions during the summer holidays while he was recuperating, but the good thing was that we had a heatwave so I got to spend lots of time down on the beach.

Butterboy turned out to be a great little pony; he was good-looking and very successful in working hunter pony classes. One year we won five qualifiers for the BSPS championships at Peterborough, and went to the final, where I was way out of my depth. I had thought I must be brilliant to have got there, but I soon realised that the West Country qualifiers were a far cry from the real thing, and I got eliminated at the third fence.

The outcome was similar when I won the regional Pony Club inter-branch eventing competition and travelled to Stoneleigh in Warwickshire for the championships. I was fourteenth after dressage but had a run-out across country and then fell off in the show jumping warm-up.

My exploits with Butterboy meant that we needed proper transport. An old lady that Mum had looked after died and left us, as promised, £250. Mum went straight to the library to look at the advertisements and found an old-fashioned, bull-nosed petrol lorry. It was an old South West Electricity Board vehicle that had had a wooden back put on it. I was quite embarrassed by its ramshackle appearance, and would make Mum park it at the end of the field at shows, but though it was in a rotten state and regularly broke down, it got us around. Mum didn't trust it to go beyond a twenty-mile radius, but I was always trying to persuade her to edge further and further afield, to places like Bridport and Melplash.

Meanwhile, school was going well. Having passed my Eleven-plus exams, I went to the grammar school, King's School in Ottery St Mary. Unlike Simon, who was more like Mum – relaxed and practical, always preferring to carry the stretcher rather than play rugby – I was quite competitive. I was good at the hundred metres and high jump; I represented East Devon in both.

Simon was good at art but struggled academically, so he was sent to a crammer to help him into the boys' public school, All Hallows, where he was a weekly boarder. When he was away, Mum took in foster children. We turned the bathroom into another bedroom and had a shower instead, which was a rather dribbly, half-outside affair with a scalding towel rail. I took great pride in telling other children that I hadn't had a bath for years!

Over the years, Mum fostered thirty-six children. Some came from awful homes, and were even deformed from malnutrition. I particularly remember three-year-old twin boys who had been shut up in a bedroom with just an apple while their mother went off hitch-hiking for days, and they couldn't talk. Another boy, during his stay with us, set fire to a barn then rushed back into the house and tuned in to the police radio. He then went up and helped the firefighters, until they cottoned on that it was him who had started it.

Many of the children were shocked at coming to a house without television, but they'd learn to play the piano and join in with games like Monopoly and cards, which we did a lot of as a family. I became very attached to some of them, and was never resentful of even more calls on my mother's time, perhaps because I was always out being busy with my pony.

Eventually, when I left school, Butterboy was advertised in *Horse & Hound* and bought by the Hines, now a well-known polo family, as a hunting pony. Although he'd been great for me and I loved him dearly, I had no qualms about selling him because I knew what I wanted to do. I was going to leave school at sixteen and get a job in a yard.

The teachers thought I was mad; I'd got seven out of my eight O-levels, so was quite brainy, but Mum and Dad were very supportive. My friend's mother, Mrs Kindersley, had given me the address to write to the famous event rider, Sheila Willcox, and I wrote to her to say that my ambition was to be the top female event rider like her.

To begin with, I was only vaguely aware of the sport of horse trials and of the famous names in it. But then at the age of eleven I went to Badminton with the Axe Vale Pony Club, and suddenly I realised there was another world and another level of riding out there.

I was fascinated by what I saw. I couldn't understand how people could be so brave, to jump these huge fences. But they all seemed to be so rich; both the riders and the horses looked amazingly smart and sleek. It was a whole world adrift of what I was doing back in Devon, but I managed to grasp that this was what I should be aiming at, even though we had no knowledge and no money, and it all really, deep down, seemed impossible.

Every year I collected the Badminton programme and studied the fence names – Tom Smith's Walls, Luckington Lane, Normandy Bank – and dimensions. Lucinda Green (then Prior-Palmer) was my heroine, followed by Ginny Elliot (then Holgate) and Mark Todd. These were the three I followed. I thought they were terribly glamorous; I can still remember Lucinda wearing this elegant long skirt at a trot-up and looking marvellous.

When it came to decision time at school, I realised that eventing was what I wanted to do and competing at Badminton was the completely impossible ultimate aim that I would pursue to achieve my dreams.

CHAPTER 3

The Sheila Willcox Years

Sheila Willcox was probably the most important influence on my career. Her teaching has proved invaluable to this day, and I owe her a huge amount, but I have to admit that the time spent in her yard was probably the hardest of my life.

Sheila was really the first truly professional event rider – certainly the first woman – and in that way she was the forerunner to the likes of Lucinda Green and Ginny Elliot. In her day, the fifties and sixties, she was a glamorous, enigmatic and sometimes controversial figure, especially where her non-selection for the 1968 Olympics was concerned. She had studied German methods, and took a far more technical approach to both flatwork and jumping than other riders of her time, raising the bar in terms of preparation and professionalism.

Like me, she didn't come from a traditionally 'horsey' background, but was determined to get to the top. In 1957 she became the first woman to win the European Championships, and she went on to become the first rider to win Badminton three times, which she did in succession and is still a record. She was, however, bitter that the third time her name appeared on Badminton's Whitbread Trophy, it was in her married name, Waddington. The marriage didn't last, and even at my interview she advised me to have as much fun as I could before getting tied down.

Sheila didn't normally take students, but I didn't know any better than to be hopeful, and went to the interview wearing my best T-shirt. Mum worked in the local Oxfam shop, but this was one of the few garments I owned that wasn't from a charity shop.

The yard, at Stanton, near Broadway in the Cotswolds, was far smarter than anything I'd seen before. When I arrived, a girl was working an immaculate horse in the outdoor school, and there were lots of stables and barns. The whole thing was something out of a dream for me.

Straight away, Sheila told me to get my hat and boots as I was going to ride in front of her. The horse provided was about 16.3 hh and I looked around for a mounting block, but Sheila said, 'Oh no, you get on from the ground.' Fortunately, I was quite tall and athletic and managed to get on in a reasonably dignified fashion.

I'd never ridden a big horse before, but I must have managed not to do anything too awful. When Mum came to pick me up three days later, she asked Sheila's companion, Keith Higgs – a nice but not terribly practical man who I later realised was awfully henpecked – how I'd got on. He said, 'I think Sheila's quite pro her,' but I didn't know what that meant.

Fortunately for me, Sheila was short of a rider at the time. A horse had reared up and come over backwards with her head girl, who had broken her pelvis. I was young and raw, and I think Sheila saw me as someone she could mould. She couldn't compete any more, having broken her back badly, but I think at that stage she hoped she could continue her competition career through me.

My days would begin at 5.30 a.m. and, before I even got on a horse, I realised that the stable management was extraordinarily thorough. Mucking out was a very strict procedure; the floor had to be 'clean enough to eat from' and you had to move the straw back completely. The finished bed had to be absolutely flat and perfect. The bedding in the stable doorways had to be square and swept back, and no more than one pile of poo was allowed in a stable at any time. Windows were Windolened inside and out once a week and there mustn't be a cobweb in sight. Sheila Willcox was a perfectionist who left no stone unturned.

Horses had their own individual grooming kits, including face flannels. You always started grooming on the left, at the side of the horse's neck, using your left hand, and then your right hand for the right side. You used a soft dandy brush first; then a body brush and curry comb scraped together in the old fashioned way.

Then we had to get out the horse's individual stable rubber, make it into a thick square and, using your right hand on the left side of the horse, strap twenty times on the neck muscle, twenty times on the muscle above the elbow, while looking to the back of the horse, then twenty times on the quarters. The whole process was then repeated on the other side. It not only built up the horse's muscles and crest, but also your own – I developed whopping muscles!

Then you fetched warm water and wiped the horse's eyes, nose, mouth and inside the ears, followed by the dock and sheath area, always rinsing in between. The hooves were oiled inside and out, and then the rugs, which had to be folded in a particular way, were put back on. If a horse came out of the stable with straw in its tail, you had to put ten pence in a box.

Horses were never allowed to be untied in the stable if they didn't have bandages on with a layer of gamgee underneath, and they were always worked with white bandages on. Sheila was very particular about this. All bandages and summer sheets were washed once a week. The summer sheets had to be ironed, along with the stable bandages and even the tapes. Then you folded the tape inside the bandage before rolling it up. Tack was cleaned every day. It was all very new to me – I'd never even used rugs and bandages before.

I'd never clipped a horse, either, and I remember Sheila praising me after my first time, as I had managed to get a good finish. She seldom said 'well done', so when she did, it meant so much. If she walked by your stable, and kept going without saying anything, that could be considered praise in itself. But if she spotted a bit of straw in the gravel, which we raked regularly, she'd just point silently and disapprovingly, and you'd scuttle along and pick it up. The awful thing was that, if she was critical of someone else, you couldn't help but be relieved that you were getting a break. I once lost what I believed was a gold stock pin of hers, and fretted for months feeling sick whenever I thought about telling her. When I eventually confessed, she said, 'Oh, that doesn't matter. It wasn't real gold.' The feeling of relief was enormous.

It was, essentially, a high-class dealing and producing yard, and if, for instance, German clients happened to be around and rang to say, 'Can we be with you in an hour?', Sheila knew that we would always be ready to show the horses off at their best. The presentation of the horses in hand was a serious procedure, and one that had to run like clockwork.

While the other girls would be getting rugs and bandages off and leading the horses out, I was the main presenter and trotter-up. It took me ages to learn to do this properly. The horses had to be 'stood up' in front of the clients very correctly and the horse's head had to be exactly at the right carriage, and you had to run to the same footfall to the horse. I still do it now.

At Sheila's, I didn't speak until I was spoken to and always did as I was told without arguing. My two and a half years there turned out to be fantastic training and the broad base on which I have built my career. Nowadays, a lot of riders start off in their own yards; as a result, they reach the top of their pyramid too early and don't really go any further.

I was lucky in that I got a lot of riding at Sheila's, though I was never allowed to ride a horse in the school without her being there, and she was constantly critical. My local teenage successes had led me to think I must be pretty good, but soon after my arrival at Sheila's the reality hit home that I was, in fact, hopeless. I took me a week to learn to ride a twenty-metre circle in trot as she wanted, and soon I was permanently in a state of upset at my inability to get anything right.

I'd be frustrated that I found it so hard to get horses to work soft and 'through'; and then Sheila would get on with her paralysed leg and within minutes the same horse would be going beautifully. I wasn't naturally a good jumping rider; I couldn't see a stride and had no natural grasp of placing a horse at a fence. I'd forever miss my jerk and Sheila would be furious. She'd call for Mark Phillips or Richard Walker to get on the horse, and I'd watch helplessly as they cantered rhythmically and arrived at the same spot every time in a way that was completely elusive to me.

I got to know the great showman Robert Oliver, who came over regularly, and I still have a soft spot for him because he would actually come up and say if you'd ridden well. Sheila, by contrast, never held back from criticising me in front of potential clients, and I had to just take it. There were many tearful nights because I was permanently frustrated that I wasn't good enough for her, but I was determined never to let it show.

Sheila bought a lot of horses from sales, like Ascot and Doncaster, sometimes coming back with nothing and other times with three, and this was the fun part, as it was exciting waiting to see what she would bring home. She always went for a similar stamp; she liked big horses with good natural paces, and she never bought anything that didn't move well.

Often, the horses would be unbroken or barely broken, and some were quite naughty, but that didn't deter her. The procedure was to tack the horse up, then I would put on a skull cap and body protector, and be given a leg-up, after which we'd see what happened. Sometimes the horses were fine, but many were nappy.

Sheila would say, 'Don't you dare fall off!' and the fact that I was much more scared of her than I was of a rearing and bucking horse made me stick on. It was very educational.

In those days, a lot of horse people used the method of curing a rearer by pulling it over backwards, and Sheila would make me do it. I learned that you held off pulling until a horse got up high, almost to the point of no return, and then you then dragged it over backwards before quickly sliding off and getting out of the way. Sheila would be furious if I missed the moment and let the horse go down frontwards.

When the horse was down, I had to sit on its neck and growl

at it to make it understand that it was stuck, to teach it a lesson. Usually the horse would never rear again, but it was a drastic cure which most people, including myself, disapprove of nowadays when it is generally accepted that riders should work with a horse, rather than dominating it.

I've kept in touch with a couple of the girls there, including Mandy Cox, but no one else from Sheila's went on to compete and some of the girls lasted literally only a day. Sheila, who was never anything but immaculately turned out herself, could make cutting personal remarks – she never minded telling girls if they had BO or greasy hair – and some of them just couldn't take it.

After about six months, I became head girl, and eventually Sheila let me compete. My first affiliated horse trials was Dauntsey in Wiltshire, and I was beside myself with excitement. I did quite poor dressage tests on both horses, but because I'd had Sheila's training it was still superior to everyone else's and, though she was extremely critical, I didn't mind because I was in the lead on one horse.

We probably didn't go to enough jumping classes for these young horses, and I can remember having a couple of fences down on both horses, probably due to my own inability to see a stride.

But I was clear across country twice, finishing second and third, and was so elated because it seemed incredible to have done that at my first affiliated event. Sheila, however, was furious I hadn't won. She said, 'You just looked like a pony clubber.' I sat in the back of the lorry in disgrace on the way home as she drove at her customary irritable speed.

I did a few more horse trials before Sheila decided I wasn't good enough and handed over the horses to Richard and Mark to ride. At least she was unbelievably critical of them, too, albeit behind their backs. In a way, I was relieved, but the episode nearly broke my competitive spirit for ever.

Even though I'd never been away from home before, I don't recall being homesick. I would go to the phone box once a week to talk to Mum, but the rest of the time I was very well looked after. The quarters were nice and we had a housekeeper, Susan Howard, who cooked us delicious suppers, which was a far cry from girl grooms who had to cook their own baked beans.

Although the competing dream was clearly over for the time being, I carried on working for Sheila and made quite a bit of progress on other fronts. I was doing lots of breaking in and schooling, producing young horses until they were bought and taken away. There was one good in-hand three-year-old which made it to Wembley, and I was involved with that. Again, standards had to be perfect. The horse finished reserve champion; as you can imagine, that wasn't right either.

I did manage to have a bit of independent life. On my day off, I'd go shopping in Cheltenham or to see my father's brother and his family in Worcester. Uncle John, a naval commander, and Aunt Pat, were really good to me. They used to describe Sheila as a 'tartar', although I wasn't sure what the word meant then!

I also took up woodwork – I made a stool – and pottery classes. A friendly potter called Danny Finnegan would take us to the pub and we'd play darts. Sheila approved of the classes but not the pub and, when I had my first taste of romance as a result, that got me into quite a bit of trouble as well.

I fell madly in love with Andrew Cole, who played in the band at the pub. He was tall, blond and dashing and, having worked in Saudi Arabia, bronzed. There were a lot of late nights while I waited for him to finish playing his Bob Dylan-type music, and Sheila was quick to spot my drooping eyelids next day.

Eventually, I decided that it was time to go my own way, and, somewhat nervously, told Sheila of my plans. She made me feel guilty, saying, 'I've put all this work into you and now you should repay me,' but part of me still wanted to compete, even though I had no idea whether it would ever be possible.

We played cat and mouse for a while, with me handing in my notice and Sheila persuading me not to go, but eventually I gave her a deadline. This was probably a mistake, because the final month was awful. Sheila was obviously annoyed by my presence now and I couldn't stand up to her, which was perhaps a bit weak – but then I was only eighteen.

The day I left I took her a big bunch of flowers, but she wasn't interested. It left me very shaken, and I dreamed about Sheila's yard every night for quite a long time. But I have come to realise that I'd had a start in my riding life that probably no other person of my generation had been privileged to share, and it toughened me up in a way that has stood me in good stead ever since.

CHAPTER 4

Getting Started

When I left Sheila Willcox, I had a terrific urge to travel. I knew horses were to be my ultimate future, but seeing the world was also a priority, and I particularly loved the sea. If horses hadn't worked out, I would probably have worked with boats instead. My maternal grandparents, the Holes, lived in Guernsey and were 'boaty' people. My cousins, Christopher and Sally Ann Hollis, and Simon and I had some wonderful summer holidays staying with them. This led to a trip with the Sail Training Association on one of their tall ships, the *Sir Winston Churchill*.

Through our old Salcombe Regis vicar, Donald Peyton-Jones, I applied to the Sidbury Trust for a sailing bursary and joined a crew of other girls aged between eighteen and twenty-one on a voyage that took us from Southampton to France, back to Land's End, the Scilly Isles and Swansea. I loved it. After working for Sheila, all-night watches, climbing the masthead and clinging on in a rough sea seemed nothing. It was just a challenge. I was invited back the following year as a Watch Leader.

I'd also decided that learning to cook would be a useful extra skill in earning my living and, as my parents had paid school fees for Simon (who had gone to Allhallows School before going to Tiverton Technical College to do an HND in mechanics – cars were his thing, including racing a frog-eyed Sprite), they didn't mind funding my cordon bleu course. In the meantime, there was a gap before the cookery course started, and I decided to take the £1,500 from selling Butterboy, which had been sitting in the bank, gaining interest, and in the twelve-week window see whether I could make some money. It was time to find out whether I'd really learned anything from Sheila.

Clissy Strachan (now Bleekman), a member of the British eventing team who lives in Devon, was advertising a horse for sale. She'd been sent a scatty five-year-old Thoroughbred to sell. It wasn't in great condition and had mud fever, but, after my time with Sheila, I was sure I knew what to do.

I asked a local farmer, Will Davey, if I could use one of his cowsheds as a stable, and signed up to membership of British Dressage and the BSJA to get some dressage and jumping points with the horse, which was aptly named Ferrari. In those days, mid summer was the off-season for eventing, due to the hard ground, and, anyway, Ferrari would have been far too green to do novice horse trials, the lowest point at which you could start back then, long before pre-novice and intro classes came into being.

When the twelve weeks were up, I succeeded in selling Ferrari for £4,000, to Michael and Angela Pinder, who were later to become my first eventing owners. Sally Wigglesworth rode Ferrari for them, taking him to advanced.

Then it was off to Evendine Court, near Malvern, for my three-month cordon bleu certificate course. To be in bed by 9.30 p.m., in the warm, having had my food cooked, was luxury. Lots of girls were moaning about the hard work, but I'd think, *You have no idea what hard work is!*

I was probably a bit more assured than the other girls, and one day I challenged a teacher who was telling us about whisking egg whites. I suggested that if you used a wind-up hand whisk instead of an electric whisk – I'd watched Mummy making meringues, for which she was renowned – surely it would be quicker. The teacher said, 'Right, we'll have a race.' I was sweating a bit by then, and rather regretting being cocky, but I won by miles. I felt awful, but the teacher forgave me.

I also took the lead in the traditional end-of-term prank, and that threatened to have more serious consequences than I'd foreseen. I had the bright idea of putting food colouring in the milk at breakfast, but instead of getting the amused reception I'd anticipated, the headmistress, Mrs Burt, went ballistic, and said, 'Whoever did this will get expelled.'

I'd been such a goody-goody that the other girls were rubbing their hands with glee and making the situation worse by saying 'Ugh' and refusing to drink the coloured milk. I knew they were all listening at the door when I slunk in to see Mrs Burt. 'I'm so sorry, it was me,' I confessed, 'I thought it was a harmless joke.' But she just smiled and said, 'Oh, don't worry, Mary.'

It was the first time I'd heard the expression 'the sun shines out of your arse!' and I finished with a cordon bleu distinction – an A pass in the theory and a distinction in the practical.

My next ambition was to do a ski season, so I applied to Supertravel. The company was then one of the smartest of the ski companies, owned by David and Di Lewthwaite, whom I was later to get to know when they owned Pippa Funnell's Badminton winner Supreme Rock.

I set off for the interview – my first visit to London on my own – with my mother issuing all sorts of instructions about

London being a shocking place and how I should keep my money in separate pockets, etc.

I was on a crowded tube when I realised that my handbag had gone. Feeling very helpless, I got off at Knightsbridge, as planned, and went to see the ticket collector about my stolen bag. He sent me to the ticket office upstairs and, as I was going up the escalator, I heard a commotion which seemed to be about a boy who had a cape over his shoulder, which I realised was concealing a load of handbags under his arm. He was also brandishing a flick knife.

As he ran past me, I leant back out of the way, but the American tourist next to me grabbed at the boy, who promptly turned and, quick as a flash, cut the man's throat. I said, 'Are you all right?' which was pretty foolish, as the man had sunk to his knees with blood spouting everywhere. He managed to gurgle 'No!' and I saw, to my horror, that he was breathing through a hole in his neck. It was all quite surreal. I stayed with him for a while, even though I felt pretty helpless.

Soon, other people took over looking after him and, somewhat shaken, I staggered off towards my interview. As I was looking for Hans Place, where Supertravel's office was, an older gentleman said, 'Are you lost?' Then he handed me a card and said, 'Do come round to my hotel room afterwards.' I was beginning to wonder what else might happen!

The Supertravel people were rather grand, and not sure whether to believe my tale of being robbed, witnessing an attack and being propositioned all in an hour, but then the story of the knifing came on the radio news. The police were asking for witnesses, including 'the girl who'd stayed with the wounded man'. My interviewers changed their attitude then. They said

Mary King

they were impressed with my calmness, and offered me a job, even though they didn't normally take people as young as me.

I got called back for the court case halfway through the ski season – annoyingly just when the best guests were staying: a group of gorgeous Welsh farmers bearing crates of whisky. Mum came to meet me at the airport, but unfortunately picked the wrong one. She was at Heathrow and I came in at Gatwick. It was before the days of mobile phones, and there was quite a lot of confusion, but the police were waiting for me at passport control and sorted it out.

When I got to court, there was a black boy in the dock and the awful thing was that I couldn't tell whether it was him or not. I was also quite unprepared for the nightmare of giving evidence. I thought it had been a straightforward incident, but the defence lawyers tried to twist everything I said and suggested the police had just picked this boy up for the sake of it.

In the confusion, I had agreed to do an identity parade, but when they asked me to do so six months after the event I had to say no, because though I'd had the incident clear in my mind at the time, I knew I wouldn't be able to identify the boy so much later. I never found out the outcome of the case, but at least the poor man who had his throat cut survived.

I loved Zermatt. Being a chalet girl is hard work but, again, after my time with Sheila Willcox, it didn't seem that arduous. I was in a three-floor chalet, which I shared with two other girls: Sarah Gerald, who is now my regular hostess for Badminton, and Sarah Dick-Read, who became one of my closest friends.

Sarah Gerald was in charge, and did the accounts, while Sarah

28

Dick-Read was as mad keen as I to get out on the slopes as often as we could, so we got a good system going. One night one of us would do the starter and cakes for all, the next night the main course, and then the pudding, and so on.

One of my guests was Sue Harry-Thomas, now a well-known eventing judge. I told her that the cooking was only a temporary job and that I really wanted to be an event rider and go to Badminton. She tried to put me off, and we laughed about it when, many years later, she was judging me there.

It's amazing how you can keep going in the Alps. In those days, chalet girls ate and socialised with their guests, and it was like holding a dinner party every night. I had quite a repertoire of party games, and then it would be drinking and dancing, and popping the Pro plus pills to keep the eyes open. It made me grow up, learning to talk to people and cope with different personalities, and I found it surprising how close you would become to people in just a week.

During my time in Zermatt I went out with a Swede called Gregor Bengesson, who was also out there for the whole ski season. Gregor was a brilliant skier and trying to keep up with him on the slopes really improved my skiing! He went back to Stockholm when the season ended, and though we kept in touch and I visited him in Sweden, the relationship fizzled out as I became absorbed in starting my eventing career.

On my return to England, I'd said to Mum and Dad, 'Right, I'm going to be an event rider now.' They just said, 'Yes, but how?'

It was a good question. I had nowhere to keep a horse even if I owned one.

The first enormously lucky thing to happen was that Will

Davey, who had been unsuccessful in getting planning permission to turn his old flint farmyard into holiday lets, agreed that I could take it over.

There was a lot to do. It was a square yard, full of scrap metal – the left-hand side was an old tool shed, cobwebby and fascinating – and with Mum's help I cleared it all out and turned three of the cowsheds into liveable stables. I had to share with the farmer's pigs, which meant that sometimes there were rats eating with the pigs at the troughs, not to mention the slurry.

The idea was that I would have three horses on the go, to break, school and compete, one of which would always be for sale to raise funds that would keep the enterprise going. Three horses was a manageable number, allowing me to have other jobs to make ends meet.

For three years I did a butcher's delivery round twice a week – Mum took it on afterwards – I dug gardens, cleaned campsite loos, cooked for people's deep freezers on our temperamental Raeburn, picked soft fruit and apples at a fruit farm at Newton Poppleford, and, pre-Christmas, worked for the nearby Donkey Sanctuary, which involved being in a nice warm office sorting their mail.

I had incredible beginner's luck with my first event horse, Humphrey. He was advertised, with some novice points, in the *Horse & Hound*, and sounded suitable for me to start off. I bought him from Posy and Tadzik Kopanski, using the money I made on Ferrari, plus some from Mum and Dad. Tadzik ran the Pony Club and had been chef d'equipe of the British team; Posy competed, and had started eventing Humphrey. He failed the vet first time, because he made a noise in his wind when he galloped, but I knew that I didn't really have too much choice as my budget was tight, so I went ahead and bought him.

He wasn't great on the flat because he'd get excited, and I wasn't too brilliant at the show jumping phase, but he was a good cross-country horse and that experience made him ideal for me to start.

Amazingly, I had almost immediate success. This was mostly entirely due to the fact that Sheila had trained me so well in the dressage; I was a real novice at jumping. It helped that I had no fear, which wasn't necessarily a good thing, because I'd go flat out across country, jumping out of what would now be terrifyingly long strides and somehow getting away with it.

I won three intermediate classes in a row, at Frensham, Powderham and Taunton Vale. This was both thrilling and scary, because I knew I was going much too fast for my ability. In those days, you could make up a lot of ground in a competition by going fast and, in my ignorance, all I cared about was winning. I was obviously hungry for success but, on a more basic level, I needed the prize-money, and it all seemed terribly easy.

My first advanced competition was at Goodwood in October 1981, and I won, beating Jane Starkey on Topper Too and Sue Benson riding Monacle, both international combinations who had represented Britain. I'd been equal fifth after dressage, dropped further in the order with a show jump down, but then had the fastest cross-country time to win.

When I came away with the Vera Howse Trophy for the best under-20 rider, I thought I had it made.

CHAPTER 5

Divers Rock

I rounded off the 1981 season by finishing second in my first three-day event, Osberton, to the New Zealander Mark Todd. We'd travelled as a family up to Nottinghamshire in our lorry, which was an old ice-cream van. It didn't have any proper living quarters, but we still slept in the back, and cooked on a Gaz stove. We didn't have any lights, and I didn't want to run the battery flat, so I worked out my cross-country times, kilometre markers and roads and tracks times by torchlight, using Sheila's book, *The Event Horse Guide*, to help me. Despite not having a clue what I was doing, and not really understanding about asking someone to help me, I was third after cross-country and remember feeling hugely satisfied that my enterprising efforts had paid off.

It was also my first experience of a trot-up (horse inspection on the last day), and I didn't leave nearly enough time. I had a headache from washing my hair in cold water, Humphrey was stiff, and I got behind on the plaiting. But I had some more luck, as whoever it was in the lead got eliminated in the show jumping and we all went up a place. Mum went up to Mark and said, 'Shame you didn't come to England next week!' I nearly died of embarrassment.

*

After such a successful start, I was way too confident in the following spring. *Here we go*, I thought, as I charged off to my first
event, Hagley Hall. But I had a crashing fall, breaking a rib,
banging my head and springing my collarbone. It didn't sober me
up one bit; I had no idea that my riding was really quite dangerous.

I was still eligible for the Young Rider (under-21) team and
the selectors had indicated they were quite interested in me. I'd
been invited to a training session at Gill Watson's Aston Farm,
and set off on my own, with Humphrey and a young horse, and
all their feed, plus my bicycle, crammed into the old ice-cream
van. On my way up to the training I competed at Stowell Park
Horse Trials near Cirencester.

'Make sure the people you park next to know you're on your
own . . .' said Mum.

Again, I took off like a madwoman across country, and
stupidly galloped straight at an upright white gate in a hedgeline. Humphrey chipped in a stride and hit the gate hard. I flew
off and hit my head. When I woke up, in the ambulance on
the way to Cheltenham Hospital, all I could do was repeat
confusedly, 'I'm on my own, I'm on my own.'

I'd been parked next to Jancis Yeo, who then lived in Tavistock, and she and her mother kindly drove my box home. They
must have had a nightmare journey, as they didn't know how
to work the lorry's somewhat unique starter motor and ended
up doing the entire journey in third gear.

I, meanwhile, was throwing up blood in hospital, due to a
broken nose. The same evening, Mum got a call from Simon in
Durham – he was in hospital too, having fallen off his Vespa and
broken his leg. At that point, Mum decided that her accident-
prone daughter shouldn't go to any more events on her own.

I recovered enough to ride at Bramham in June 1982, in the national Young Rider section, and if I did well enough there was still an outside chance of selection for the European Championships. Simon came down on his crutches to watch, and my Aunty Betty came. We all slept in the lorry, but I didn't get a wink of sleep. There was a huge electrical storm, Simon was sleep-talking, Aunty Betty was snoring, and Mum was making the annoying clicking sound she makes when she breathes in while she is sleeping.

I was also terribly nervous, as by now I was aware that two heavy falls in two outings was not a great statistic, and I was on the verge of being quite scared. In addition, it was very hot weather and the organisers were worried about horses collapsing on the course – some horses did come in really tired and had to be on drips, which was all a bit of an eye-opener for me. I went clear, but didn't complete the competition because Humphrey lost a shoe and went lame. He was sound again by the time I got home, but by then the selectors had lost interest.

Eventually, Humphrey had a recurring tendon problem, which never recovered, and it was suggested that I have him put down. It was a very hard decision, and made me realise that this eventing career wasn't going to be plain sailing.

Among the horses I bought and sold during this period was King Rollo, who came from Lady Inchcape's Addington sale. I was staying nearby with my skiing friend Sarah Dick-Read, so I thought I'd go and look. I fell completely in love with Rollo. He was Irish, a big chestnut five-year-old, probably three-quarters bred, and with good movement.

At that stage, the one area where I was ahead of the game was in the dressage – others have caught up now! – thanks to my time with Sheila, and I was quite successful with Rollo in pure dressage competitions. Our eventing career was less successful, as he used to stop at ditches. He then became rather 'footy' and navicular was diagnosed.

As I'd only had him for a year, I went back to the vet who'd inspected him, but I couldn't prove that he'd been negligent. There was no alternative but to have the horse put down and to take the insurance money for him. It was a steep learning curve. I now know that bad shoeing and confirmation need to be taken into account, but we knew less about the disease then.

Undoubtedly the star buy of my early dealing career – although people thought I was mad at the time – was Divers Rock, whom I saw advertised in *Horse & Hound*. He'd been a successful show horse with Roger Stack, but wasn't settled enough in his mind to win at the highest level and, though he'd got to advanced level in pure dressage with the Olympic rider Jennie Loriston-Clarke, he was too sharp to cope with *piaffe-passage*. He'd been hacking for a year with a girl in the New Forest, but she was going to the USA, which is why he was for sale.

Known at home as George, Divers Rock was the most beautiful, big, 17.2 hh horse with perfect conformation and terrific movement. I couldn't believe he was only £3,000 and that I could afford him. When I asked to see him over a fence, the girl said, 'You can, but not with me!'

I soon found out why she was reluctant. She had an outdoor arena with one cavaletti in it, and when I came round to jump it, Divers Rock bolted over and broke it. But I so loved him, his presence and the way he moved, that I decided to risk my money, not thinking for one moment that this might not be the most suitable event horse.

It took a long time to get his jumping settled. I didn't have an arena, or any proper fences, so I'd go down to the beach and find driftwood, which then had to be carried up 120 steps and across five fields. There must have been a shipwreck because I found some perfect two-by-two rails which, along with some old barrels and deckchairs, had to suffice as show jumps because I couldn't afford anything else.

I would spend hours trying to get the horse to jump quietly out of trot and, once we got over his initial fear and his tendency to gallop at fences, he took to it. We were perhaps helped by the fact that I was naïvely quite brave then, despite my falls, and would let him gallop on, but he was soon taking to the jumping very easily.

He was such an impressive-looking horse that I had a few offers for him, which I was tempted to accept. Jim Fox, the gold-medal Olympic pentathlete, offered me £10,000, which I knew was a lot of money. I wrestled with the idea for a while, but in the end I said no, I'd rather be famous than rich. I was sure this was the horse who would take me to Badminton.

I had a good year with Divers Rock in 1984. I was second at Windsor, in terrible wet weather, to Fenella Fawcus on Blue Max. Sarah Dick-Read, my chalet girl friend, and Mandy Cox, whom I'd worked with at Sheila's, came to support me and I won £300, a bottle of champagne and – despite the fact that I hadn't even cleaned my tack after the cross-country – the turn-out prize.

Divers Rock went on to win the Horse Trials Group's Calcutta Light Horse trophy for the horse with the most points that season, and I competed abroad for the first time.

Clare Mason offered me a lift to Boekelo in Holland. She was based at Waterstock, the renowned centre in Oxfordshire run by Lars Sederholm. I borrowed some knee pads and hock boots. Unfortunately, these made Divers Rock sore – he wasn't used to wearing knee and hock leg protection, because I didn't have any – and so he arrived at Boekelo with sores. He also had a lot of other suspicious little scabs, because I'm ashamed to say that he also had ringworm, which I didn't dare tell Clare about. When she reads this, she'll understand how she managed to get ringworm! I do hope she didn't though!

It was my first proper international event and my first real experience of the partying side of the sport, and I loved it. We stayed in a hotel – another first – and I was amazed to look out of my bedroom window and see two well-known riders cavorting about starkers. *So this is what it's all about!* I thought.

I was thrilled to be put in the British team for the informal team competition, along with Lucinda Prior-Palmer on Village Gossip, Rachel Hunt on Piglet – who eventually finished second – and Richard Walker on Accumulator – third. The team won and I finished sixth individually, so all in all, it had been a triumph.

The journey home, however, was less cheerful. Clare and I had started as equal forty-sixth after dressage, but her weekend had gone wrong and I felt I had to suppress my elation, especially as she and her father, David, a great supporter of the sport through his MacConnell-Mason Gallery, had been so kind – they wouldn't accept any travel money from me because they knew things were desperately tight.

I'd begun to build up quite a bit of business, gradually converting more cowsheds into stables, but even so I was surviving only because I paid a very minimal rent to Will Davey. When he announced after I'd been there three years that the yard was going on the market, I knew I had to make a major decision about buying the place. With the price going up and up, it seemed an insurmountable problem.

We knew the Daveys well – they went to church at Salcombe Regis – so the situation could have been awkward, but in the end my desperation overcame any squeamishness about being pushy. A solicitor advised that I had 'squatters' rights' and should offer to pay what I felt I could afford. Mum and Dad helped me and, thankfully, our offer of £18,000 – which seemed huge at the time – was accepted.

Once the yard was ours, Mum and I went to town, hiring a drill to knock out the concrete pillars of the milking parlour, and plastering and pointing the walls, painting on bitumen and mending the guttering. I've always loved doing practical things, and the woodworking classes proved worthwhile, as I chopped up wood to make doors and partitions and put on hinges (I felt quite sad some years later when my sponsors, Ascot Timber Buildings, replaced my old doors). The scrap lorry came about five times, moving rubble and old cars and trailers. We concreted inside the stables and Mum built a ramp so we could get the wheelbarrow up into the back yard.

It was around this time that the Carphone Group sponsorship began. It was all thanks to the Kopanskis, who had followed my progress since I bought Humphrey off them and knew that I was struggling for money. Posy's brother was accountant to the Carphone Group, and so they knew that the owners, Graham and Gill Thomas, were interested in sponsoring an event rider. They actually wanted someone higher up the scale, like Lucinda, but the Kopanskis kept plugging away, partly because Posy wanted sponsorship for her Grade-A show jumper!

I got a portfolio made up, setting out my plans and my results so far, and tried to make it look as professional as possible. The lady at the Donkey Sanctuary kindly typed it and I laid out my best photographs. I've still got it, and it looks rather rough and ready now, but at the time I thought it was the last word in professionalism.

Knowing that Gill was an animal lover, I stuck in a picture of myself with a little gosling, which I thought looked rather good. Apparently it really helped, because when Gilly saw it, she said, 'Oh, this girl obviously loves animals. I'd like to meet her.'

The Kopanskis kindly hosted a dinner party to introduce me to the Thomases. I couldn't believe I was having dinner with people who might be sufficiently interested to give me money to do what I wanted to do, and was quite nervous. Graham was a tall, larger-than-life person, and Gilly was immediately very kind and welcoming.

Unfortunately, though, her first question was how the gosling – 'Gregory' – was doing. My heart sank, because we'd eaten him for Christmas. It crossed my mind that this could mean an early end to my chances of sponsorship, and I debated whether to lie, but then I burst out, 'I'm afraid we've eaten him.' After looking rather shocked, Gilly roared with laughter and we've been the best of friends ever since. I think she thought that, if nothing else, I was at least a truthful person.

Gilly and Graham agreed to take on funding Divers Rock for one year. They put boards on my little old Bedford TK lorry which said, 'The Carphone Group, sponsoring Mary Thomson and Divers Rock' and I felt so proud. *Badminton, here we come*, I thought.

CHAPTER 6

Dawn of the Kings

In the spring of 1985, all my focus was on Badminton. I couldn't think about anything else, and it was hard to believe that at last I was actually going. People would ask if I was frightened by the idea, but there was no way I was scared. I was just so excited to finally be achieving a fourteen-year ambition that started as a pony clubber's dream.

Everyone was so friendly, and I felt completely overcome to be doing all the things I'd dreamed of since I was a pony clubber – attending the cocktail party in Badminton House, jumping those famous fences, appearing on television and being, if not exactly on an equal footing with the likes of Ginny and Ian Stark, at least sharing the same stage with them in this historic event.

I wore my best dress to the cocktail party to meet Graham and Gill Thomas, who were so thrilled by the whole experience, including being in the same room as Princess Anne, that Graham said afterwards, 'We're enjoying this [Badminton] so much we'd like you to look for two young horses to buy.' I went rushing back to Mummy who, like Cinderella, was boiling her kettle on the Gaz camping stove in the back of the lorry, and said, 'You'll never guess what!'

It was the start of a wonderful weekend. My dressage test wasn't that amazing – I scored 81! – but even Ginny Holgate only scored 59 on Priceless, which put my effort in perspective. This was before the days of flashy dressage marks, even for the best; Ginny was at that time a dual Olympic medallist and on the verge of winning the Europeans.

Realising that it was important not to let my advantage in this phase slip, I was having regular dressage lessons with Ferdi Eilberg – one of the benefits of my sponsorship with Carphone. German-born Ferdi had trained with Dr Reiner Klimke, who'd won more medals than any other dressage rider in the history of the sport, and who I remembered had worked with Sheila Willcox at one stage. I had first started with Ferdi in 1982 as a result of winning £200 in Mark Phillips Range Rover Scholarship at Sherborne Horse Trials, and he was to become a crucial part of my future success.

Divers Rock had turned into a fantastic cross-country horse, which was just as well, because I was still making loads of mistakes. My stirrups were too long, my legs would slip back and my upper body and weight would be too far forward, but, fortunately, George took no notice of my failings; he just kept galloping and jumping no matter what I did on his back.

He was one of those rare horses who was a complete natural across country. He had upgraded very quickly, and he always felt safe and bold. I loved riding him and was lucky to have a horse like this at my first Badminton.

Bruce Davidson, who'd been World Champion twice for America and is one of the most experienced and wise people around, was particularly kind to me. He knew it was my first time, and came up to me and said, 'Look, Badminton is like no other course. You've just got to kick on.' It was such good advice, and I took it.

I think it's fair to say that 1985 was a big year at Badminton; the cross-country fences included jumping off the awesome Badminton Drop, followed by three strides to a bounce of large rails, and there was a huge footbridge where a few people crashed. It also snowed on cross-country day, which was bizarre, considering I'd got sunburned arms on dressage day.

The thrill of clearing these famous fences was indescribable, ticking the evocative names off in my head one by one: the Quarry, Huntsman's Close, the Lake, Luckington Lane, Tom Smith's Walls, the Normandy Bank, and even the terrifying Vicarage Vee, which George flew. Many of these fences don't exist any more, having been replaced by perhaps more technical but certainly less awe-inspiring challenges, so I now feel privileged to have gone clear at Badminton at such a time in the sport's history.

The course caused a lot of problems and, amazingly, only three horses completed the whole of endurance day (including the two roads and tracks phases, A and C, steeplechase, phase B, and cross-country, D) without penalties. Two of those finished first and second – Priceless, giving Ginny her first Badminton victory, and little Charisma, Mark Todd's wonderful Olympic gold medallist. The third, unbelievably, was Divers Rock.

I had one show jumping fence down and finished seventh at my first Badminton, earning my first little silver horse (for finishing in the top twelve). The Queen presented me with the Whitbread Spurs as the best under-25 rider. Lucinda Prior-Palmer (now Green) was in the collecting ring afterwards; she was my absolute heroine whom I tried to copy in every way, even down to wearing the same breeches! My day was made when she came up and said, 'Well done, Frances, you rode so well.' *Frances?!* I was so pleased that she had congratulated me, I didn't even mind that she'd got my name wrong!

Best of all, when I came out of the arena, I was handed a white envelope with a letter from Henrietta Knight, the chairman of selectors, telling me that I had been longlisted for the European Championships which were taking place at Burghley that September.

Sadly, in the first of several frustrations and disappointments I was to suffer in the course of my career, my euphoria turned out to be extremely short-lived. On my return from Badminton I discovered that George wasn't sound. My vet, John Fowler, advised me to take him to Sue Dyson at the Animal Health Trust in Newmarket. I drove him up in the little tin lorry, towing a caravan behind to sleep in, and it felt a long journey not knowing what would happen at the other end.

To make matters worse, the lorry broke down. I had to knock on someone's door in the dark, and they kindly phoned the rescue people, who eventually got me to Newmarket in the middle of the night.

Sue Dyson diagnosed navicular. It was a massive blow. I sat in my caravan, exhausted and weeping my eyes out. First Rollo, now George. I was sure that it must be down to something I was doing wrong with my horses. The only upside to the whole saga was that Sue and I went on to become good friends, and through her I've learned a lot about horses' soundness.

We tried George on the drug warfarin and then Sue asked if she could use him for a new operation that she'd only tried a few times, in which the ligaments which suspend the navicular bone are cut so that the bone moves, thereby relieving the pressure.

This did improve the lameness a bit, but he still wasn't 100 per cent right. The poor horse then went violently lame. Due to an infection he was in so much pain that he was breathing in great panting blows and I knew it was no good, so I called the vet. Then I went home to the village and put my hands over my ears, but I could still hear the bang when he was shot.

What was particularly gruesome was that the Animal Health Trust wanted to look at his hooves for research purposes. This meant that I had to keep them in the deep freeze, and it was very unsettling as, for some reason, I had a compulsion to open the box and have a look. I resisted it though. Later it was found that George had been suffering from a huge abscess which was eating away at his hoof.

I felt at rock bottom, with my dreams shattered and my wonderful four-star horse dead, but the Thomases, although shocked by the turn of events, remained philosophical and supportive, and kept to their promise to support some young horses. One of these was to be King Boris, whom I'd bought with David King.

I first met David through a mutual friend, Bimmy Derrick, whom I knew through working hunter pony classes. I sometimes went with the Derricks to shows. Bimmy and I passed the time on the long journeys by playing games, one memorable example of which was earring races, the winner being the fastest to take them out and put them in again! David was going out with Sarah, Bimmy's elder sister, and I first clapped eyes on him at a New Year's Eve party. The Derrick family had taken a table at the Combe House Hotel for a smart do, and, as Bimmy didn't have a boyfriend at the time, I went to make up numbers.

We all met up first in the Derricks' house in Ottery St Mary; it was all rather smart and John Derrick, who was very successful with show hunters, was a larger-than-life character. I remember feeling slightly overawed, and when David arrived, late, it felt like a breath of fresh air. He had a lovely open face, not handsome but friendly, and even though, for one reason or another, it was quite a stressful evening, I found myself watching him. He seemed oblivious to any undercurrents, and was just enjoying himself. I thought what a nice chap he was, but as he was with Sarah I didn't think anything would come of it.

The next time we met was at Bimmy's twenty-first. Again, I thought how nice he was, but then I went off him because he got massively drunk! However, at the end of the evening we were all in the kitchen and he started talking about a racehorse he owned a share in that was running in a race. Next day, I found myself tuning in to the race on television, though the jockey fell off before the start.

When Sarah got a job in Geneva, the relationship waned, but the Derricks kept in touch with David and a group of us, including Bimmy, used to go out regularly as a foursome. Gradually, the dynamic changed until, one day, David invited me out for dinner on my own. I was so nervous about what I was going to talk about that I became obsessive and wrote myself a list of topics. But there was no need to worry, as David never runs out of things to say and, even if he does, like lots of Devon farmers, he just starts again!

He worked on his family farm, at Exminster, near Exeter, and ran a business with his father. They'd had a sad time, because his mother, who was Dutch, had died suddenly from a blood clot when David was sixteen and his sister, Carina, only fourteen, and they'd been looked after by a series of housekeepers.

We'd been dating for a while when I found Boris in the spring of 1985. He was advertised in *Horse & Hound*, and was in a showing yard with Geoffrey Buckingham-Bawden, near Worcester. He was four, by the Thoroughbred Rapid Pass out of a hunter mare, Miss Mandy II, and had been shown successfully in-hand at county shows but hadn't matured quite well enough to be successful under saddle. He was a hefty, show-conditioned horse, but I loved his face and huge ears. He was so interested in everything, with a rather bossy, purposeful way about him, and so obviously had a big heart.

He hadn't done any jumping, but was kind and eager to please, and at our first event – two competitions in one weekend at the Wiegersma family's place in Penzance – we were first and second. Boris had got halfway to intermediate in two days!

Although David had been keen on racehorses, they hadn't been that successful, and he was happy to pay for half of Boris. He'd been shown under the name Ramsgate Rampus, but I'd always liked the name Boris – it's what I called the old horsebox – and seeing that David King was half-owner I thought it sounded good with a King in front of it, which is how the King prefix started.

I introduced Boris to Gilly and Graham at Portman Horse Trials. Boris was a very friendly horse, and he went up and snuffled Gilly, which she loved. She ended up buying David's half-share, which made David a nice profit, as by that stage Boris had gone up easily to intermediate level.

He was a stuffy galloper at first, because he was rather overweight, and also on his forehand, mainly because I didn't know enough. As a result, he was reliant on my hand, so I was lucky to get such a forgiving horse at that stage of my career, when I was still on a big learning curve.

I made a terrible mistake with him at the end of my first season. It was at Osberton, our first three-day event together, and I was going too fast – again. We wheeled around a corner to what I thought was a straightforward steeplechase fence, but it had an apron in front of it. I asked Boris for a long stride, but he didn't like that idea and banked it. I fell off and, more seriously, Boris got a splinter of wood in his knee. It gave him so much pain that he suffered colic but, miraculously, there was no long-term damage.

In the meantime I'd found two young horses for Gilly and Graham: King Arthur, who had come over to the Kopanskis from Ireland, and King Max Max originally came to my yard because the owners were going away, but I liked him and bought him.

They were good two-star level horses, who helped get my name around. Arthur, who had the potential to go to the top, gave me my first three-day wins, at Windsor and Osberton, and he won a two-day event at Tidworth. Max won the Breda three-day event in Holland, which was when I got my first dressage mark of 10, for an extended trot, from the German dressage judge.

I sold Max to a junior, as he was only 15.2 hh and three-star level was really beyond him. Arthur's career ended sadly. He was being hacked up the road by a young lad who worked for me and spooked at some plastic bags. In that one swivel round, he incurred a tendon lesion on a hind leg which never came right. Despite box rest, the injury deteriorated and he had to be put down.

After Divers Rock was put down, the Thomases generously said they'd buy me an advanced horse, which was how I got

King Cuthbert. He was competing with Bernice Cuthbert, who knew him as Metz until I renamed him as part of my 'King' stable. To a certain extent, he was the first 'made' horse I had, and he was fast, but he had a tendency towards over-excitement which I never managed to curb completely.

We had an alarming somersaulting fall as the result of a disagreement in front of a fence at King's Somborne, and he once jumped out of the start-box too soon in the steeplechase phase at Bramham. We had to go back and start again, but still made the time!

And then there was Silverstone, who was coming up through the grades. He was an attractive grey thoroughbred owned by the Pinders, who'd bought Ferrari; they'd phoned up and asked me if I would take the ride on as their son, David, didn't want to carry on with him.

It was around this time I took on my first employees. Tina Court was a lovely local girl, who had trained at Bicton Agriculture College and was working as a groom. We'd met at a Young Farmers event in 1984, where I was giving a demonstration, and she asked me if she could work for me, but at the time I didn't have enough horses and owners to employ anyone. Tina then introduced me to Annie Collings, who was to stay with me for ten years. Annie had trained at Porlock and been working for Martin Salter, master of the Axe Vale Harriers, and I knew her and her family from Pony Club days – her older sister Julie was my age. I used to see Annie driving about and one day she went by waving and I thought, *If ever I employ someone, I'd like it to be her*. She had a lovely smiley face.

Thanks to the Carphone Group, I was now able to employ them both.

CHAPTER 7

Trials and Tribulations

Having acquired a taste for eventing, the Carphone Group decided they would like to extend their support by taking on a group of riders. In 1986 they took on Rodney Powell in a major way, plus Katie Parker, Jon Evans, Duncan Douglas and Sarah Cotton. They also assumed title sponsorship of Bramham Horse Trials, and the whole team decamped there to make a big thing of it. Graham and Gilly were incredibly generous with their hospitality, and I remember it as a particularly happy time in the sport.

For me, it was a personal triumph, as I finished first and second on King Cuthbert and Silverstone, beating Lucinda Green on Brass Monkey. It was a Bramham record which lasted for several years until William Fox-Pitt came along and smashed it! It was also the first time anyone had scored a one-two at a three-day event. Of course, the following year Mark Todd went and did it at Burghley, and Ian Stark achieved it at Badminton in 1988, but at the time it was very special, and it meant that I was in the lead in the Horse Trials Group's spring points table, with Ginny Leng in second place.

Silverstone was a Thoroughbred, the first one I'd competed. He was a good cross-country horse and could produce middling show jumping and dressage performances, though I wouldn't ride him now because he tended to be rather 'hangy' with his front legs. I have a picture of Silver jumping a fence with them crossed, which is disconcerting. I had a few tumbles with him, but this was before the days of heightened awareness of safety and, anyway, I couldn't afford to be fussy about what I rode.

King Cuthbert, a chestnut with a white face, was a jolly character. He was a cheeky monkey, sometimes quite annoyingly so. He once did an awful test at Gatcombe and then finished by coming up the centre line beautifully, halting so still and square that I could have murdered him. In comparison to Silver's luxurious galloping stride, Cuthbert tended to beetle along. He was an Irish Thoroughbred cross who constantly had to be on a diet because he was plump and a good doer; I felt mean restricting his feed, but he was like a pony who'd got laminitis.

Cuthbert was the first really good jumping horse that I had; sharp and tidy, and capable of jumping lots of clear rounds. Divers Rock hadn't been ultra tidy and Max and Arthur were both a bit ordinary. Boris was also a pretty good jumper, plus he was very forgiving and he always tried. His style was steady, because he was a heavy horse and it was hard work for him, but he was naturally rhythmic and didn't pull so you could keep coming forward, and he taught me a lot about smoother riding. He was such an easy horse that I finished ninth at my first Burghley, in 1987, when he was only an eight-year-old.

Although I still wasn't the greatest cross-country rider, by now I'd had enough good rounds to have gained confidence.

I was getting quite a bit of publicity locally by this time, especially from the local papers, who have always supported me, and when *Songs of Praise* was filmed at Sidmouth, I was put forward to be interviewed by Cliff Michelmore. I remember getting rather tongue-tied when he asked about my religious beliefs. Although the church, and a belief in God, has always played an important part in keeping my life on an even keel, I am not particularly interested in talking about it and I found it hard to articulate my feelings on the subject.

In 1988 the television cameras were there to capture another uncomfortable moment. Having finished first and second at Brigstock, the traditional pre-Badminton advanced competition, on Cuthbert and Boris, I was one of the favourites for Badminton. But it all went terribly pear-shaped when I had a horrendous fall on Boris at Badminton's Normandy Bank and, as a result, wasn't allowed to ride Cuthbert.

Falls are usually the fault of the rider, not the horse, and on this occasion I made a serious mistake. Instead of condensing the horse and riding forward on to the bank so that he had enough power to jump up and bounce over the rails that topped the bank and off into space, I had steadied him too much by being restrictive with the reins. This meant Boris didn't have the freedom of his head, which was up in the air, and his hindlegs slipped underneath him on the bank. He tried to put in a stride, tripped over the rails and dramatically turned turtle, landing on his neck. Fortunately, his legs went down into the ditch, or he would have broken his neck.

Because I'd been first out on the course, the television cameras had no one else to show, so they apparently focused on me lying in an unconscious jerking heap, which was horrible for my mother. She didn't even bother running for the fence but just made her way to the first-aid tent to see what state I was in.

Colonel Frank Weldon was the director of Badminton. He was a great character, and a formidable horseman and course-designer who inspired both huge respect and terror among riders. They don't make them like that any more, which is both a pity and a relief! It was his last year at Badminton, and he certainly went out with a bang. Lucinda was following me out on course and she, poor thing, was stopped just in front of the Normandy Bank, which is a pretty daunting fence to jump in cold blood. She was also in full view of the fuss surrounding me being stretchered into the ambulance, which must have been rather demoralising and, perhaps unsurprisingly, she fell there too. It was dramatic all round, as that was also the year Ginny fell from Murphy Himself when he launched off the Ski Jump, and she snapped her ankle.

I had Silverstone entered for Punchestown in Ireland the following week, but the doctors would only pass me fit to ride on condition I had a brain scan. I went to Bridgewater 'Brainwave' unit where they slotted me into this claustrophobic tube for forty minutes. They said they'd pull me out if I shouted but, because I was so tired, I fell asleep. Apparently I was the first person to fall asleep in a scanner. Fortunately, everything looked normal and they gave me permission to ride at Punchestown, but I fell off there too, when Silverstone floundered out of the water complex.

Cuthbert finished second at Bramham, but by then the Badminton fall had put paid to any chance of selection for the Seoul Olympics.

*

My chances of making the British team in 1989 were looking good when I finished second at Badminton on Boris. He had a tail-swishing habit; his tail swirled all the time, whatever he was doing, and it was generally considered rather endearing, except on this occasion. One judge put him first after the dressage, the other second, but the Irish judge Patrick Conolly-Carew placed him thirty-third because of it.

Only three horses got the cross-country time; with five penalties, I came in fifth fastest, because Boris was so rhythmic that what he lost in speed he made up in manoeuvrability and the way he could knife around the corners.

It was a terrific line-up that year. Mark Todd was third, having taken the ride on Rodney Powell's The Irishman at the last minute, due to Rodney being injured, and Ian was fourth and fifth on his great greys, Glenburnie and Murphy Himself. I ended up losing to Ginny on Master Craftsman by just 0.2 of a penalty.

In the prize-giving, Patrick came up and said, 'I'm so sorry, I didn't realise he swished his tail all the time.' It was big of him to apologise, but it was still pretty frustrating!

My next opportunity to show the selectors what I could do came when I took Boris to Stockholm, where there was a test event for the 1990 World Equestrian Games. By now I was getting into the swing of regularly competing abroad, but things did not go well when I made a mistake across country with poor Boris. I saw a bad stride and he tried to take off too far out from a big spread parallel going into some woods and landed heavily on his stifle. I flew off the front end. I remounted and we completed the cross country, but poor Boris was very sore and couldn't show jump the following day.

I was furious with myself afterwards, and spent a miserable night in my room in tears. I'd gone and let the horse down and, out of the British squad of Ginny, Jon Evans and Rachel Hunt, I was the only one to muck up. But your fellow riders don't let you sulk for long, and I soon bounced back.

Toddy won the event and, straight away, he and I flew on down to Le Touquet with his fellow New Zealand rider Tinks Pottinger. When we landed, I saw Tinks's mother, Tiny, taking what I thought was my bag off the carousel and, thinking, *How kind*, strolled out of the airport without my bag. In fact, it was her own bag, so I now had no clothes.

Mike Vacher, our chef d'equipe, kindly collected it from the airport the following day. The weather was hot, we were being put up at a hotel – which was often the norm at events in those days, to provide accommodation for riders – and we were in for a big partying event at the seaside. I was especially looking forward to it, as this was during a phase when David and I weren't getting on all that well, and I fancied a German rider, Theo Leuchter.

I led the dressage on Max and became even more relaxed when, with an early draw, I was still in the lead after cross-country, secure in the knowledge that no one could overtake me. Annie Collings, my groom, had been enjoying herself so much that she was sick twice while getting the horse ready for cross-country – when I got back from the steeplechase I couldn't see her, until she emerged, looking green, from behind a bush.

We all went to a nightclub that night, wearing swimming costumes underneath, as we planned to swim in the sea after-wards. Toddy and Andy Pottinger disappeared into the gents to put on their Speedos, for some reason deciding it would be funny to mummify themselves in loo paper as well.

Mercifully, the final trot-up wasn't until 11 a.m. the next day, and Gilly Thomas decided to have a Bucks Fizz breakfast party first. Lots of the French riders came; we sat around on her sunny balcony and all got pretty light-headed. I think it's the only trot-up I've done inebriated. They announced: 'Here's Mary Thomson for Australia,' which puzzled me until I looked down and realised that I was wearing an Australia sweatshirt.

Unfortunately, show jumping wasn't Max's forte and I was probably still too relaxed. We had three fences down and dropped to fifth, but I didn't mind because it had been such a good time.

I came back to earth with a bump on English soil, at Gatcombe, with a crashing fall on Cuthbert which was to more or less end my season and put me out of contention for the European Championships.

I was being competitive, as usual, in the British Open and having a great round. I had a lot of trust in Cuthbert and we'd done most of the difficult fences, like the water and the steep drop at the top of the park bowl. Turning for the coffin, there was a choice of cutting inside a tree to jump a rail before a ditch. I already had Cuthbert fired up and when I ducked to avoid the low branches it made him accelerate even more so that he dived at the rail and tipped over.

He landed on me, but I was saved from serious injury – or worse – by the saddle, because I landed under the curve of it. But I had one foot still in the stirrup and, as Cuthbert got up, my groin muscle tore. Luckily, my foot came out of the stirrup, and I ended up sitting on the edge of the ditch in a rather ungainly way, feeling squashed.

Again, poor Mum saw the whole thing on telly, but at least this time they showed me getting into the ambulance and smiling and waving to someone. I phoned Mum to say that I was fine, but at that moment I had this excruciating feeling that my insides were moving around of their own accord – and had to put the phone down dramatically.

After a few weeks of hobbling around, I did get back into the saddle to take Cuthbert to the three-star three-day event at Rotherfield Park in Hampshire. I won the prize for the Best Groom – but as I had gone on my own, I was groom. The prize was a bottle of whisky which I willingly swapped with my father for my first wheelbarrow. Until then, I'd mucked out into a sheet.

I experimented with Cuthbert in the dressage, partly because I wanted to try something out before the next year's Badminton. He was tricky to settle for dressage, because the more you worked him, the more excited he would get, bouncing around like a kangaroo, and you could never get to the bottom of him. So this time I stayed in the lorry, dressed, until the person before me was in the dressage arena.

Willing myself to keep calm, I walked him down to the arena on a long rein. It was perhaps a rather unprofessional approach, but it worked and he did a very nice test.

We finished second, behind Ginny on Griffin, but it brought it home to me how important it is to be fit. I'd been riding for just two weeks, and he was the only horse in the stable; I felt like a real amateur at the end of the course, so floppy in the saddle.

During the time I'd been unable to ride, I had to find another way to make money, so I drove HGV lorries at night. It was good money, but I hated it. One of my shifts was in a big articulated Volvo milk tanker, in which you could feel the skim moving around disconcertingly and unbalancing the vehicle. It had about sixteen gears, which I struggled to change, and every time I missed my jerk, the skim would slop to the back of the lorry.

One night I was trying to change down while going up a hill, but I missed and had to stop, and put it into crawler gear. The wheels started to spin, so I had to edge backwards downhill in the dark and start again from the bottom. When I eventually arrived at the milk depot, an elderly man came out to greet me and said, 'I've been working here for sixty years and never seen a lady drive one of these!'

I also drove a St Ivel's refrigerated artic lorry full of yoghurts, milks and butters. One night, I arrived at Somerfields in Yeovil, backed into the docking bay, and found a notice on the door saying: 'Don't disturb at lunchtime' – which I ignored. I'd forgotten it was lunchtime for the nightworkers! I heard loads of swearing, but they did a double-take when they saw me and came out and helped me unload.

At the end of every season, I'd save my prize-money and go travelling. This time I went to Australia with Melanie Hawtree. We visited my cousin, Sally-Anne Copp, just outside Sydney – she had married Brad Copp, an Australian, who she had met while travelling – and then we bought a kangaroo pass which took us to Alice Springs, where we saw the Pope and climbed Ayers Rock, before heading on to Perth to watch the Americas Cup and Ian Botham playing cricket.

Then we made our way to Brisbane where we met up at David Green's parents with David and Lucinda, Chris and Sam Hunnable and Rodney Powell, plus a group of other British and

Australian friends of David's. We did an initial dive course in their swimming pool, and then drove to Gladstone where we joined our dive boat and motored out through the night to Swain Reef. It was glorious; sunbathing, swimming and fishing filled our days. Diving twice a day, I completed and passed my PADI open divers exam, and we also did some night dives. We didn't see another dive boat for a week and had some exciting encounters with reef sharks and manta rays.

We also all went out to Jim and Sue Gunn's cattle station at Gundiwindi, where Lucinda's world champion horse Regal Realm came from. They were very hospitable, and took us off 'roo' and boar-shooting, and mustering on an amazing cattle drive.

David and I were having one of our 'off periods' and I fell for David and Lucinda Green's best man, Nick Lee. He was an excellent diver, and we went on a romantic dive. He grabbed the tail of a wobabong (a type of shark) which then grabbed his leg – when we shot to the surface, sure enough, he had needle marks through his wetsuit.

Nick and I carried on going out for a while, alternating between him coming to England and my going out to Australia again the following winter, which was just as enjoyable as the first time. He wanted me to go to Australia and settle down with him but, as much as I adored him, I was completely selfish about my ambitions.

Nick was a great sportsman and eventually became a pilot. One day, years later, when flying a light aircraft, the engine failed and he was killed, leaving behind a wife and baby. It was such a waste of a lovely, talented person.

*

I was convinced that 1990 would be the year I'd finally get into the team. Boris and I were third at Badminton, behind the surprise winner Nicky McIrvine on Middle Road, who was a three-quarters bred type, and the New Zealander Blyth Tait, who seemed to have sprung from nowhere and was second on Messiah.

It was the year of the notoriously off-putting bright white rails into the Lake, and I was one of the riders to fall off there, with Cuthbert. But Boris was his consistent self. He always did a competitive dressage test, would get near the cross-country time, and jumped a reliable amount of clear show jumping rounds.

Unfortunately, the selectors were all into their Thoroughbreds at the time, although they did longlist me and, as a result, I went to my first team training session at Badminton. I absolutely loved it; the horses were stabled near the house and we lived above the dog kennels, each with our own old-fashioned bedroom, and were looked after really well, with Lucinda Hanbury cooking for us. I found it all a great treat, especially being able to watch television and catch up on riding videos.

It was a fantastic experience and I loved getting to know the other riders, Ginny, Rodney Powell and Karen Dixon, plus Ian Stark, who was always huge fun. He was a great ringleader, always one for saying after training, 'Let's go off jet-skiing,' or whatever.

I also saw it as a great opportunity for some free training. I had my first lessons with Pat Burgess, who was helping with the jumping. She was the person who really brought it to my attention that I had a weak lower leg position and sorted out the problem.

I really thought my chances of being selected were good this time, partly because one of the listed horses, Lorna Clarke's Fearliath Mor, had a soundness problem. But it wasn't to be; they went and I didn't.

Gilly was very disillusioned with the selectors and couldn't understand why I hadn't been chosen, and I did wonder what on earth I had to do, considering mine had been the best Badminton performance that year. It was especially frustrating when Fearliath Mor didn't even run in the end, as he was lame when out in Stockholm.

The team won silver, despite the fact that Ian, who deservedly won individual silver, was the only one to go clear across country. I found this result pretty hard to swallow, considering Boris's consistency, but the episode did serve to fuel my desire even more.

Instead, Boris and I went to the British Open Championships at Gatcombe, and we won. It was my first major British win, my first title, and it was shown live on BBC, and I felt that Boris really deserved it.

The cross-country at Gatcombe is run in reverse order of merit, so I'd had to spend a long time waiting in the lorry, feeling terribly sick, but it was all worth it. There's a shot of me coming through the finish flags, punching the air because I could hear Annie screaming in the background as the loudspeaker announced: 'Mary Thomson, British Open Champion.' Revenge would be the wrong word, but I certainly felt a deep satisfaction.

CHAPTER 8

King William's Reign

The only upside to not getting into the British team in 1990 was that it spurred me on to a roll of success, which made me feel I was finally breaking into the big time and riding better, and surely couldn't be overlooked again.

In autumn 1990, I finished second and fourth at Burghley with King Boris and King Cuthbert. I had been lying first and third after cross-country, but, unbelievably, I managed to have the last show jump down on both horses. It was an awful mistake to make, and I felt frustrated for a long time, but it was still great to be up there. The winner was, yet again, Toddy, this time on Face the Music.

I retired Cuthbert after this, his finest hour. He had a lot of miles on the clock, and I had begun to feel that it was unfair to put the sort of pressure on him that was necessary if I was to get a reasonable dressage test out of him.

Annie had always been mad about Cuthbert; she felt he was in the shadow of Boris, whom Gilly and I both adored the most, and she was thrilled when Gilly decided that she should be given him. They took a while to cement as a partnership, as Annie found him buzzy to jump, but they had great fun in riding club events and going hunting.

Meanwhile, I was quietly excited about a young horse called King William that I'd found and Gilly had bought in 1988 as a five-year-old. He was one of three horses that I got from Bernice Alexander (now Strong) at Chievely, near Newbury, and William had been particularly recommended by Geoff Orrock, a friend of Karen Dixon's, who had been looking out for horses for me.

I fell for William the moment I saw him. He was a beautiful, striking, big, dark bay horse with a white blaze, who looked so alert, purposeful and light on his feet. However, his presence belied his poor conformation, and that did cause me concern and prevented me rushing headlong into a purchase. He was slightly back at the knee, pigeon-toed and tied in below the knee. He also had curbed hocks, and I thought, *As lovely as he is, I can't buy a horse like this because he'll never stay sound.*

I was embarrassed to even ask Peter Scott-Dunn, the former British team veterinarian, to vet the horse, but he was very open-minded and said, 'Well, he has got poor front limbs, but he's a lovely horse and if you want him, go ahead and buy him.'

William was difficult to shoe, as he had shallow heels, but he turned out to be one of the soundest horses of all time. He ran on all sorts of ground and I always rode him competitively, even at one-day events.

When I got him, he hadn't been across country, only show jumping, and I decided to do just one event that autumn, a novice section at Lulworth, to see how he would go. He was as green as grass and yet so mature in the way he went across country. The course was causing lots of problems, but he cruised along with his ears forward and we won. And, looking back, that was the start of everything good.

Even though David and I weren't together at that stage we were still great friends, and he didn't mind that I had got in the groove of calling my horses 'King' this and that. Gilly and Graham paid for William, so he was their horse. They remained terrific owners, who always made me feel looked after. Graham would invariably take over in a crisis. Once, there was a problem with the lorry they'd bought me through Carphone. It was our first outing with it and Mum and I were driving past Wincanton with only Boris on board when I heard quite a bit of noise. When I went into the back to investigate, I found him with his bottom lip wobbling, which he'd do when he was worried. I peered over the partition and, to my horror, saw he was holding a hindleg up over a hole in the floor, through which I could see the road and the wheels going round.

I shouted to Mummy to stop the lorry. She said, 'I can't, we're on a dual carriageway.' Eventually I managed to make her understand that we had to stop. I rang up Graham and told him what had happened and he was absolutely furious because he adored Boris. He phoned up the lorry company and threatened to sue them if they didn't sort it out in twenty-four hours.

Sadly, however, things started to go wrong for the Thomases. Their marriage split up – Graham went to Australia – and the Carphone Group was sold to Cable & Wireless, who weren't interested in sponsoring eventing. But Gilly was amazing. She'd been a major shareholder in the company and received a windfall, so she continued to support me, off her own bat, for another three years, until she couldn't do so any longer and I was lucky enough to be taken on by the insurance group Frizzell, through Richard and Barbara Matthews. They also gave me title sponsorship for three years, and supported the British team.

Gilly has continued to be a great owner. She has always gone with the flow, with whatever horses I've bought. She is wonderfully generous and sporting, and she famously loves a party. If something goes wrong, she'll say, 'Never mind' – and still open a bottle of champagne – and she is always perfectly happy with my decisions about when and where to run horses. She has been incredibly supportive, a dream owner.

King William did her proud in 1990 when he was seven years old, finishing seventh at Bramham and third at the new horse trials at Blenheim, so Badminton in 1991 seemed a natural progression, even though he would only be eight. Now it's rare to take an eight-year-old to a four-star, not just because it is considered too young, but because increasingly complicated qualifying procedures have made it a near impossibility.

William had done the big French two-star at Le Lion d'Angers as a six-year-old, which you wouldn't normally do until seven these days. There was none of this faffing around with pre-novice classes or one-star level then; you just had to get on with it. Horses progressed that bit quicker, which suited some of them, and it probably suited the professional riders too, but the current system does give amateurs and some horses the chance to progress more slowly and safely.

We had an amazing cross-country round at that Badminton, but we were early to go on quite slippery ground, and as we came out of Huntsman's Close to make the turn to the big trakehner, William lost his hindlegs and slipped over on his side. It was in the days of penalty zones around fences – they don't exist now – and so it counted as 60 penalties because it was inside the fence's surrounding zone.

I leapt back on and cantered straight on over the huge trakehner. William's ability to pick up and jump such a big fence straight off was extremely impressive, and I knew I had a horse about which I could be really excited.

This was timely, because it was to be Boris's last major event. He was fourteen by now and, having done a good test, I did harbour thoughts that we might win. But he had suffered a ligament injury and during the recovery I took him to an equine pool to swim him. After this he became a bit hesitant jumping into water. He always went in, but very cautiously and slowly, and that was our undoing. He lurched into the Lake slowly, over the rails, his girth caught on the rails and the whole jump moved with him, so he was temporarily stuck.

I fell on my feet into the water and Boris ended up standing next to me. My first thought was 'Shit!' But then I felt so sad for the horse. I owed him so much because he had been such a forgiving horse while I was learning.

We kept going, somewhat intentionally, because I only intended to jump one more fence to restore confidence, but I couldn't find a gap in the string along the course and so found myself keeping going. And Boris was again his forgiving, obliging self, and kept trundling around. But that night he was lame, having damaged a suspensory ligament.

I did a few more one-day events with him, but knew it would be kinder to retire him. Boris had been placed at seventy-five out of his eighty-five events – an amazing record – and he was the first horse to earn more than 1,000 horse trial points. This puts him up among the very best horses, because then you only earned major points for doing well at four-star level, which illustrates how consistent his record was.

I gave him to Paula Lee, a young rider based in Devon who looked after him impeccably and had fun doing mainly dressage competitions with him.

My next outing after Badminton was Punchestown, which turned into another chaotic trip, so much so that I can't remember what horse I was riding or where I finished. The weather was terribly windy and the ferries weren't keen to load horses, but the event sponsor, Heineken, was determined that British-based riders should be there, so they offered to fly us from Stansted.

Mum drove me up to David and Lucinda Green's near Andover where we transferred to their lorry, but, going up the A303 in David Green's horsebox, we heard an ominous knocking noise; the big end had gone. Luckily, mobile phones had been invented by now so we phoned Mum. We unloaded everything into the lay-by and waited for Mum to pick us up, leaving the knackered lorry abandoned on the side of the road.

Punchestown was a fantastic event. We had a mega party in Andrew Nicholson's lorry early in the week, so much so that Tiny Clapham fell backwards out of the window while Greeny and Nicholson pinned me to the floor and 'drenched' me with neat gin. Next day, I couldn't do up the girth without nearly passing out. I'd like to think riders still party like that, but I'm not sure they do these days.

I took William to Gatcombe that year, to try and defend my title. He was in the lead before cross-country, with Ian Stark lying second on Murphy Himself. As we circled near the start,

I was sick with nerves, not least because I knew William was a special horse and I didn't want to let him down.

I said to Ian, 'I feel really sick.' He replied, 'You can't be as bad as me, and I warn you, the older you get, the worse the feeling gets.' I couldn't believe it, because he was always so daring across country, which is why he was known as the Flying Scot, but it's true. You never really stop being nervous.

Our marks were close and I didn't think I'd be able to beat him, but it was to my advantage that Ian lost control of Murphy. He jumped the string into the crowds and lost several seconds, which gave me the leeway to win.

By now, I was starting to get fan mail. It started after I first won at Gatcombe and built up to hundreds the next year. I've always tried to be good and answer the letters myself, so I got a word processor and organised a standard letter, which I'd then top and tail personally.

Soon after Gatcombe, we were travelling to Thirlestane with Simon Putt, a young lad from Sidmouth who came with me to events. We were sitting in the back of the lorry, engrossed in sticking down envelopes and listening to *Jack and the Beanstalk*, when suddenly Mum said, 'We're going past Gretna Green. Anyone want to get married?' No one answered. Miles passed and an hour later I asked Mum where we were and was horrified to find we were very near Glasgow. We should have turned off at Gretna Green for Edinburgh, so we'd added an extra hour to our journey, but the scenery was magnificent!

Gatcombe proved to be the start of an extraordinary run, when I won five international events in a row, continuing that autumn with wins at Le Lion d'Angers on King Samuel, who had also come from Bernice Alexander, and Loughanmore; a two-star event in Northern Ireland, with King Alfred. He was a lovely grey Irish-bred, by Sky Boy, whom I eventually sold to Italy through the brilliant 'horse finder' Susie Pragnell.

But first there was the momentous occasion of gaining my first Union flag, and my first medal. However, I didn't achieve either in the manner in which I'd hoped.

Despite William's slip-up at Badminton, he had proved he was a true four-star horse and attracted the selectors' attention. It was a dream come true to be stitching on that Union Jack – once you've got it, you've got it for life – but it was ironic. A year ago the selectors hadn't wanted Boris, one of the most consistent horses in the world, yet they were prepared to take an eight-year-old to the European Championships at Punchestown.

This time I was fairly sure I'd be going, and when Ginny's Master Craftsman went lame, I got her slot on the team with Ian – Scotty – on Glenburnie; Richard Walker, whom I'd known in my Sheila Willcox days, on Jacana; and Karen Dixon with Get Smart. I was particularly pleased, because Karen was a good mate by then and Katie Meacham, who rode as an individual on her lovely grey, Montana Blue, was one of my best friends.

We arrived with a couple of days spare and it wasn't long before Scotty was feeling restless. He suggested we went water-skiing. Karen could be quite wild, and was always brave, but to my amazement she said she didn't want to risk it, which was quite unlike her. I went, of course, and looking back, it was an incredibly stupid thing to do.

Obviously, we didn't tell Patrick Beresford, our chef d'equipe – we told him we were going shopping! – and we had a great time. Katie hadn't done much water-skiing, but we managed to get her up on her skis, with her bum stuck out. She was getting on very well when she became fixated with two buoys in the water, and started lining up for them. It looked as if disaster was inevitable, but at the last moment, she opened her legs wider and the buoys shot between them!

Next day was the first day of dressage, and I felt very stiff and extremely silly but, fortunately, under Ferdi Eilberg as team dressage trainer, no one was any the wiser and William did a great test which put me into the lead individually and the team in gold medal position.

The Irish course designer, Tommy Brennan, had built an extraordinary masterpiece. The Stockholm cross-country course had, by all accounts, been striking, but this was arguably the first of the properly themed and stunningly executed tracks and it looked different from anything we'd ever seen before.

Every fence had an Irish theme; there were even stuffed donkeys, the Crannogs – thatched peat huts, the 'Book of Kells', plus a huge bank with white rails on the top, a massive slide and water complexes with stone and replicas of historic waterfalls.

The course was enormous and caused loads of trouble, especially one water complex, where you jumped down a huge sheer drop into the water. Several horses stopped on the edge of the drop and most other nations gave team orders to take the alternative route. Not the British, though!

When I came back from the roads and tracks phase, I was told I could do the direct route, which I didn't question, as we all did as we were told in those days. Richard Walker, who was our trailblazer, had gone well and clear and team officials instructed me to make sure I kept riding to the edge of the drop.

Sadly, that was unfortunate advice for me because William was so bold and tended to gallop on naïvely.

I was having a great ride until we got to this fence; I was up on the time allowed and William was making mincemeat of the course. As we approached the big drop, I shortened him up, but remembered the instructions to keep riding. William literally cantered off the edge of the drop and landed, splat, in the water.

Even now, watching the footage, I cannot believe I did this. I should have come back to trot and let him lower his head to see where he was going, because he would never have stopped. Instead, his head was too high, and down he went.

In the confusion, I didn't realise that William had trodden all over me, and that I'd wrenched my knee. I got back on, soaked and uncomfortable, and finished the course. Next day, I could hardly walk. I had torn some ligaments in my knee. Ian trotted up William for me, but once we knew we had three horses through to the show jumping, I withdrew.

The team went on to win gold, and my team mates won all three individual medals. Ian rode an amazing round on Glenburnie, who pulled his arms out, to win a thoroughly deserved gold medal, Richard took the silver and Karen the bronze, despite a stop, which just showed how influential the course had been.

I limped on to the podium to collect my first team gold medal, but it felt a hollow victory. Terrific celebrations followed, involving Ian haring off in a Land Rover that had been lent to us and crashing into someone's garden wall, but underneath I felt incredibly humiliated and tearful; I couldn't believe that I'd been so close to winning an individual gold medal and had thrown it all away, and I felt I'd really let the side down.

It took me a while to get over what had happened, but that autumn, I went on a trip which put everything in perspective.

Lucinda Green had started a charity, Riders for Romania, to help the lost children abandoned in orphanages. The orphans' plight had received a lot of publicity after Ceauşescu was shot; Lucinda's children were still young and it really got to her. We had several meetings at her home and she was incredibly organised, getting together lorryloads of supplies which she kept in a warehouse, and phoning round a number of riders to see who would go with her on a mercy mission.

This appealed greatly to me, especially as event riders don't often do things for other people because you get so focused on your own life, and it was the first of three consecutive trips I did to Romania.

We took my lorry, plus Mark Phillips's and Robert Lemieux's, and had two drivers per lorry. Among the people who went were my friend Sarah Dick-Read, Annie, the Swedish event riders Erik Duvander and Anna Hermann, Moysie Barton, William Fox-Pitt, Anna Hilton, the show jumper Barry Fox and the dressage rider Dane Rawlins, with whom I played a lot of backgammon.

We had to be careful, as we'd been warned that some of the orphanage staff were corrupt and would pinch supplies. Puffa gave us old clothing stock, Toddy's sponsor, Kimberly-Clarke, gave us tampons, we took things like sugar, clothing and medical supplies, and we got WI groups to make bags and knit teddy bears, and we'd make up goody bags with Mars Bars, notepads and pencils.

Giving out the goody bags was as satisfying as anything. The conditions were horrific. The children slept on rough little basic beds in dormitories with broken windows, despite freezing temperatures. The washroom had a long cattle trough; the children stood under a pipe with holes in it.

These children, who had shaven heads to prevent lice, were little, thin, cold and dying. Their faces were expressionless. Some of them took their goody bags and hid them under the mattresses; they didn't even know how to open a chocolate bar. Some rocked and banged their heads. When you left, they clung to you. It was heartbreaking.

Due to appalling government policy, Romania had a major AIDS problem. In their enthusiasm for creating a 'master race', each married woman had to have five children and, if she couldn't, she had to pay extra tax. Blood was imported in the belief that this would help strengthen the children and any child who appeared slightly weaker and not up to scratch would be given a transfusion. The problem was that much of the blood imported was cheap and hadn't been screened for AIDS.

The hospital had cots full of sick children, with one nurse to about thirty babies. It would be eerily quiet as these children were past crying. One little yellow baby, who had a bottle hanging limply out of its mouth, died right in front of me.

We were invited to watch an operation, a poor man having brain surgery. We all robed up, but there was no sterilisation or anything like that. We filed into the operating theatre to see a man on a stretcher; they'd peeled back his scalp, but his feet were twitching. The nurses were smoking, the surgeon had open-toed shoes on and it was all so grubby.

After that first trip, when we went to nine orphanages, we focused for the next two years mainly on just one orphanage. On one run we took out a tractor, a generator and large commercial fridges. As time went by, it became more and more difficult to organise, as the government wanted to control everything that came into the country. This was partly understandable because some nations were bringing in out-of-date drugs. Then, due to a new law stating all incoming supplies had to be unloaded at warehouses, it grew harder to maintain personal contact with the orphanages and know that what you had taken went to the right places. Still, I like to think that we made a difference.

CHAPTER 9

Becoming an Olympian

In the spring of 1992, I had a good lead-up to Badminton with King William. He was always consistent at his one-day events – he nearly always won everything for which he was entered, and he jumped a lot of clear rounds.

At Belton, one of the main preparation events for Badminton, he won the advanced class on his dressage mark of 20, which is an amazing score on which to win at this level.

A few weeks earlier, I'd had a letter from a little girl called Emily Graham. She was about six and wrote that she lived near Belton, and would I like to come and stable at her house. She was thrilled when we accepted her invitation, and we've stabled there every year since. Emily hadn't told her mother, who was rather taken aback when we phoned to accept her daughter's offer!

William did another beautiful dressage test at Badminton, and we were in the lead. After my disaster in the European Championships, it was very much on my mind that I really had to get the next part right, but when I woke up on cross-country day, the weather was horrendous, lashing rain and wind.

I was 38th to go and Mark Phillips, who was helping me, said he would keep an eye on how the cross-country was riding while I was out on the roads and tracks and steeplechase phases. When I came into the ten-minute box, before the start of the cross-country, he delivered me the worrying news that no one had gone clear so far.

He tried to cheer me up by telling me that the mistakes were everywhere, rather than at one particular fence, but he said, just as Bruce Davidson had back in 1985, 'Everyone's being cautious, and you cannot ride Badminton cautiously. You must kick on and ignore the mud.'

While I was on the roads and tracks, I had vaguely heard that Mark Todd, who was first to go, had had a fall at a fence which none of us liked anyway. This meant that the fence had been altered so we now had to run across the bridge and jump a little hunting gate. Fortunately, I didn't know that Mark's horse, Face the Music, who had beaten me at Burghley in 1990, had broken his leg and had to be put down.

I didn't like the big upright rails at the Lake either; it was one of the few cross-country fences that has ever turned me cold. When I was at Badminton earlier in the spring, doing a dressage competition, some of us had sneaked out on to the course and had a look, even though we weren't meant to. It probably served me right, because the Lake fence worried me all spring, and I had already decided that I'd be doing the alternative route there.

William Fox-Pitt had had a bad time at the Lake. Briarlands Pippin had broken his neck in a terrifying fall and he, too, had been destroyed.

Ginny had had a horrible slipping fall at the Waterloo Rails on Welton Houdini, and conditions were getting wetter and wetter.

I was aware enough of the nervous atmosphere that I prayed, 'Please God, look after William.' I felt guilty, putting him through what was coming, and so responsible for his safety.

But William wore the biggest studs in his shoes that I'd ever used, and, because I was buoyed up by Mark Phillips's words, I rode him confidently so that he galloped on over the mud and didn't slip.

He had amazing reserves of stamina and, when we got to the end, felt as though he could do it again; he was a naturally strong, powerful horse and had made it seem easy. It was a wonderful feeling to come through the finish with the first clear round of the day, but more importantly, I was thinking that I must have done enough to be selected for the Olympics.

It was a difficult evening because I couldn't help feeling so elated, but I had to keep quiet because there was a terrible atmosphere in the stables. Not only had a lot of people gone badly, but a third horse had died, American rider Karen Lende's Mr Maxwell, who had broken a bone in his neck.

Going into the final show jumping phase, I was reasonably confident. I knew Ginny Leng was breathing down my neck on her second ride, Master Craftsman, but I had a fence in hand and William had never done anything too awful in the show jumping phase before.

He rubbed nearly every fence and each time we touched one, the crowd gasped, and so did I. William was an awkward horse to ride in that atmosphere; he would shorten in his neck, flatten his back and be very nervous of the crowds. He would also jump to the left, but none of this, as yet, had become a major issue, and we just had the one fence down.

I still feel that winning that first Badminton in 1992 was the best moment of my life; it was the event that I'd dreamed of as a child but felt was an impossibility. Winning Badminton is in a league of its own; it's like a jockey winning the Grand National – virtually everyone in the world has heard of this occasion, and it's your big, famous moment.

I was in a complete daze, surrounded by photographers and crowds and flashing cameras. Sadly, I now realise that the moment of triumph was the beginning of William's undoing. He became fraught and started to lash out in fright, so Annie took him back to the stable while I was swept off into press conferences.

When I got back, he was going batty in the stable, whizzing around, weaving, sweating. The fuss had really got to him mentally and I said that we must get him home.

Mum, Annie and William went on in the lorry, with David and me following. We were on the M5 when, suddenly, I saw a woman standing on the hard shoulder. It was pouring with rain and she had a coat with a hood, but I recognised Mum's red jumper and shrieked at David to stop. She was standing at the turning to Sedgemoor Services, but we'd gone past.

I persuaded David to reverse up the slip road into the services, which he hated doing. We found William very unsettled, weaving all over the place, almost colicky, and in a state of collapse. Mum had flagged down a policeman and asked him to get a vet, but he had told her that they must get to the next service station. After unloading him and walking him around, he calmed down. Annie travelled in the back of the lorry and scratched William's neck all the way home. He had settled by then, but, although I didn't realise it, this was going to be the beginning of our problems. Despite his bold presence, William was a sensitive soul.

When we got home, people in the village had put up congratulatory banners outside the stable yard, and we arranged a party at The Blue Ball in Sidford.

Early Monday morning, the phone rang, and it was Sheila Willcox. It was the first time I'd spoken to her since I'd left her yard in 1980, and she was slightly miffed at reading in the papers that I was the first rider to have led Badminton from the start to the finish because, of course, she'd done it herself in the 1950s.

My heart nearly stopped with fright – despite the twelve years that had passed, I was still terrified of her – but to give Sheila her due, she said, 'Well done, Mary,' and I knew she was sincere. But she couldn't resist adding: 'At least you can see a stride now!' and 'What a lovely horse to carry you around!' which slightly spoilt it!

Windsor, which I won on King Kong a few weeks after Badminton, completed my quintet of straight victories, apparently something of a record at the time.

I nearly made it six, as I decided to take King Samuel to Pratoni del Vivaro, south of Rome, for my first visit to Italy. It was a three-star championship for young horses aged eight and under with decent prize-money and I thought it might not be too demanding and might suit him.

I flew out after Windsor with Robert Lemieux, and Annie and Sammy travelled by lorry with the Irish rider Mark Barry. Gilly came too, the sun shone and we got a great welcome with the Italians pleased that we'd made the effort to come such a long way.

Sammy did a great dressage test which put us in the lead and we were galloping around the cross-country, which was causing lots of trouble, when we came to the penultimate fence. It involved jumping on and off a bank, but I made the mistake of approaching with a lack of power, and Sammy hesitated on top and took a step backwards. His little dither was something and nothing, but we incurred 20 penalties. That was infuriating, but we were still lying third.

Sammy had started to get into the habit of putting in dirty stops and, while warming up for the show jumping, he suddenly refused. I fell off into the dirt and dust and he took off with his tail in the air and stirrups flying. Annie, impractically clad in shorts and flip-flops, took off on a two-pronged chase with Mark Phillips. Time went on, and I was on the verge of being eliminated for not taking my turn in the show jumping, when Annie and Sammy cantered over the hill.

She legged me up and I galloped straight into the arena, thinking that I mustn't let him stop again. He jumped clear, which moved us up to second. We won £7,000, which wasn't bad for a stop and a fall!

Pratoni is always surrounded by wild dogs roaming the hills, mostly after having been dumped from Rome, and, of course, Gilly had to fall in love with one. It was a pretty little young bitch that was in season and was being mobbed by the other dogs. Gilly swept it up in her arms and looked after it for the rest of the week, and decided to go through all the quarantine regs and bring it back to England in Mark Barry's lorry. 'Bella' as she was christened, became a regular on the horse trials circuit after that and lived a privileged life with Gilly until the age of nineteen – what a lucky dog!

Sammy had begun to get into the habit of refusing because he was reaching the limit of his capabilities. Although he came from Ireland, he definitely had a bit of 'foreign' blood and lacked courage. He was very sharp and would suddenly throw down the anchor, which was a bit unnerving. Twice he stopped at Blenheim when we should have won, once becoming distracted by a pile of ticker tape beside the fence and hitting it so hard that I fell off.

I took him up to Bramham where, despite jumping all the big fences, he suddenly stopped at a plain gate on the way to the stables. I knew we'd reached the end of the road with him, and this was where Gilly was wonderful; she never put me under pressure to get lots of money. Her main aim was always that her horses should have a nice home. We sold Sammy for much less than he was worth; he could have been a good Junior horse, but instead he went on to do pure dressage from a wonderful home near Faringdon, where the owners had black swans on their lake, and he had a lovely life.

The next big deal in my life – and it was a huge one – was the Barcelona Olympics. The team was only decided right at the last minute, as Ginny's Master Craftsman went lame literally within days of flying. This let in Karen Dixon on Get Smart, but it was so last-minute that we didn't even have a reserve horse as, by that stage, Owen Moore, who would have been reserve, had turned his mare Locomotion out in the field.

Poor Ginny was completely prepared to the last detail, with a hairdo and tinted eyelashes. In fact, Karen and I looked pretty smart as we'd been visited during team training at Badminton by a beautician who had waxed our legs and bikini lines!

So the team would be the same as for the Punchestown Euro-peans, except that Ian would ride Murphy Himself instead of Glenburnie and, considering we were fielding the current Badminton champion plus the three reigning European indi-vidual medallists, we were obviously hot favourites. Ian had a legendary partnership with Murphy; Karen and Get Smart were a brilliant pair, and Richard, who was making a comeback to the big time, was one of the most experienced horsemen there.

Although we were completely different types of people, we all got on well, and it was a happy quartet. Richard could not have been more of a contrast from Ian; he was so neat and tidy and particular that he folded his clothes up into little piles, and you could see your face in his boots. He was beginning a romance with his groom, Louise, at the time (Annie was my informant!) and they are now married. Karen had recently married Andrew Dixon, but I was confident that that would not stop her being up for partying!

David came out to Barcelona, as he has done since for all my Olympics, and Mum and Dad, although poor Mum had terrible food poisoning and spent most of cross-country day lying under a tree clutching a bottle of water. The Barcelona trip wasn't a good one for friends and relatives and some of the admin-istration left a lot to be desired. They missed the opening ceremony and both trot-ups. Nowadays, owners and family are much better looked after.

It was the first time that William had flown and, rather unnervingly, the horses had to jump off the plane on arrival, as there was no proper ramp. He slipped on the tarmac, which was a nasty moment. That and his too-small stable were not good for his nerves and, right from the start, he was not at his best.

The Olympic Village, however, was everything I'd dreamed of. The food hall, which was open twenty-four hours a day, catered for every nation's preferences, with walls full of fruit and long lines of fridges.

There was a man-made beach where, although the water was pretty grotty, there was an incredible celebratory atmosphere, and endless fit bodies everywhere. I spent a lot of time body-watching!

There was also a brilliant party at the end. As we weren't allowed alcohol in the Village, I thought it would be boring, but then they started squirting this foam on the dance floor; soon we were hip-deep in it, almost floating, an extraordinary sensation which was better than drinking and great fun.

I was adamant that I wanted to go to the opening ceremony but, exciting as that is, I have since discovered that there's an awful lot of hanging around. Karen already knew some of the athletes, especially the pentathletes who had trained with her mother, Elaine, so it was fun meeting other British athletes as we waited our turn to parade.

The best part was when, dressed up in our team kit and waving flags, we ran down a chute and out into an arena surrounded by roaring crowds. We knew the TV cameras would be on us when we emerged, and had to be prepared to do lots of waving and smiling, but this is something I have always enjoyed! Then everyone, from every nation, ended up in a big crowd in the middle, and a huge Olympic flag was draped over us. I loved the whole thing – it was an awesome experience.

After that, we went straight into our competition. For the dressage and cross-country phases, we moved up to a golf course in the hills called El Montanya, with an outdoor swimming pool, which was very sociable.

William, who was by now nine, had matured and he felt good, but I had a hard job to settle him in his new surroundings. It was the first time riders had been allowed 'arena awareness' – working around the arena in which we would perform the dressage – but it didn't really work for me. The electronic scoreboard was flicking over and over and William was really scared of it. I couldn't get him anywhere near it and it made him nervous and on his toes.

He was fourth after dressage, but it certainly wasn't his top test and I hadn't dared to ride him as forward as I would have liked because he was so tense. However, Ian was second, Karen third, Jacana had done the best test of his career and the team was in gold medal position, having usurped the Germans, who used to be dominant in this phase. Britain was going through a good patch in the dressage, under Ferdi Eilberg. Unfortunately, our promising start was too good to be true.

William seemed quite settled on Phase A, the first roads and tracks, but when he saw the crowd waiting to watch him at the steeplechase course, his eyes came out on stalks and his head up like a giraffe. Disconcertingly, I realised that he was, for the first time, ignoring the pelham bit and that I had little control, which did not bode well.

The cross-country course twisted around the undulating golf course, and the tracks were narrow so the spectators were closer to you than normal. They were also much noisier and less inhibited, as enthusiastic Continental audiences tend to be. This can make for a fun atmosphere, but it was a disaster for me on this occasion.

William was wearing his usual vulcanite pelham bit, in which he'd been so good at Badminton, but nerves made him strong and he was running through the bridle. I could barely hold him and he was trying to go flat out. It had been a long time since the days when I used to think it was normal to gallop flat out, and I knew this wasn't how it should be. He felt, terrifyingly, like a strange horse to me.

There was a bank complex at which I had intended to go straight, but I knew he would charge through and would easily fall, so had to take a long route, and then again at the next water complex, all the time losing precious seconds which would cost us medals.

We took the straightforward fences at terrifying speeds. When I look at the video now, you can see how horribly strong he had become. I was annoyed later on when people said, 'Why didn't you let him go?' If I had, we'd have had a serious accident.

I became more and more tired in my upper body so at one point I just had to let him go, and he took off like the wind. I had an almighty fight to get him back for the end of the course, and when I finally slid off him I was so weak and wobbly that my legs gave way. William was quite unfatigued, but I felt as though I might collapse. We'd had a clear round, but it was not at all how I'd envisaged the glorious finish to my first Olympic cross-country ride.

Britain's day had been deteriorating subtly. Richard, who was again first out, having done such a fantastic job in Punchestown, tipped off Jacana when he put in a stop at rails on the top of a mound. Karen went clear, but slowly and, under team orders, over some slow routes, about which she was very disgruntled.

This had put the pressure on Ian and me, and now it all

hinged on Ian. He did go clear, but Murphy became tired in the heat. He hit a rail out of the water horribly hard with his front legs and skewed alarmingly. Ian stayed on, but it was an ominous sight.

However, the team was still in gold medal position, with three clear rounds, and I was still in individual bronze position, although others who'd gone faster had risen dramatically through the ranks. The Australian Matt Ryan was in the lead after a beautiful round on Kibah Tic Toc, and New Zealand's Andrew Nicholson with Spinning Rhombus, riding for their lives, had come from nowhere after dressage.

The next morning was terribly deflating. Murphy wasn't sound, having ignited an old injury. Ian was desperate not to trot him up, but he was made to because the gold medal was at stake. Of course the horse failed the horse inspection, which was a tragic end to his career, and Ian was distraught and clearly longed to be far away from Barcelona.

The rest of the team was then demoralised because we now had to count Richard's score and that meant we were out of the medals. Nevertheless, I went off to work on my jumping, which was to take place in the main stadium in Barcelona.

I was worried about the bitting by this stage, but continued to jump William in the pelham, which seemed fine. However, when we got in the arena we went completely flat, and so did the fences. I couldn't do anything to rectify the situation and had a humiliating six fences down which dropped me to ninth place and the team to sixth, way out of reach of any medals.

It was heartbreaking, and I was acutely aware that somehow this week had gone badly wrong. As I came out of the arena, a group of people were waving and cheering — it was a group from the Axe Vale Pony Club, and so I waved and smiled back. If I hadn't, I'd have been in floods of tears, but my gesture led to a huge rocket from the selectors, especially Mike Tucker, because it looked as if I didn't care that I'd just chucked away an Olympic medal.

The habit of covering my feelings and being polite, no matter how great the disappointment or the provocation, has been instilled in me from childhood. I know that the reaction can make some people disapproving, but I was drilled to be sporting from a very early age, and just because I don't throw a public tantrum doesn't mean that I'm not absolutely devastated inside.

Back at home, we were in huge disgrace, the first British team since 1964 to come home empty-handed from an Olympics. We were absolutely slated by the press, who were appalled at the sequence of events and couldn't believe the gold medal had slipped away from us. Michael Clayton, the editor of *Horse & Hound*, described us as 'hypnotised by our own cleverness' at leading the dressage, and bewailed the lack of British spirit in our cross-country riding, an unfavourable contrast to the medal-winning Aussies and New Zealanders who 'unhindered by team orders' had kicked on gloriously.

I came in for the heaviest criticism. Why hadn't I let William go on the cross-country? Why had I been so ridiculous as to pat the horse when he'd flattened six show jumps? Didn't I take it seriously? Even our team training was criticised, because, with only one horse apiece to ride, we'd had the brass neck to make use of the Duke of Beaufort's tennis court and swimming pool at Badminton.

I stayed out in Barcelona for the second week of the Olympics

Family group: my parents, me (with a dreadful haircut and dress, love from my mum) and my brother, Simon.

Me winning a skipping race on Sports Day at Manor House School, aged eight. I was determined to win from the start!

Below: The pony who started it. Me aged five on Silver (left) at a rogation service.

Donald Peyton-Jones's Magpie with
my friend, Miriam Pile.

Tomahawk at the Axevale Hunter
Trials, 1973, when I was 12.
(*Bryan Smith*)

Butterboy, the first pony I ever owned – in 1973.

Going . . .

going . . .

gone!

King Max and me at Locko Park – this was due to me being too much in front of the movement in those days.

Divers Rock at my first Badminton, 1985.
He really looked after me and did me proud.

The Queen presents me with Whitbread Spurs for
Best Under-25-Year-Old Rider, 1985.

My first and very loyal helpers: Annie Collings and Tina Court.

Above: Silverstone, one of the stalwarts of my yard in the 1980s. (*Sandra Langrish*)

Chalet girl year – Sarah Dick Reed in 1980.

Girls on tour: Mel Hawtree, Annie Collings, Kerry Spencer and Tessa Spencer, British Virgin Islands, 1998.

Another winter holiday – with Katie Meacham at Susan Barrantes' estancia in Argentina.

Drama at Badminton on King Boris in 1988 – miraculously we
both survived unscathed.

What a difference a year makes! Boris on his way to second place at
Badminton, 1989. (*Equestrian Services Thorney*)

and had a wonderful time, getting to know the rowers and watching other sports, but that wasn't right either, because I was deemed to be using the place as a holiday camp.

Above all, it seemed such a long time to the next Olympics, and a chance to rectify this disaster.

CHAPTER 10

Golden Girls

Eventually travel and the company of good friends puts things a little more in perspective. As in previous years, come the winter, it was time to blow some of my prize-money on travelling. The aim was always to do as much as possible on as little money as possible.

This time, it was a particularly memorable trip to South America with Annie, Katie Meacham and Mel Hawtree. We flew into Rio de Janeiro, then travelled on to Paraguay, Uruguay, and then flew to Lima in Peru, where we met the Norwegian event rider Ivar Storli, after which we went by train through the Andes to Bolivia, via Lake Titicaca and the floating islands, Machu Picchu and white-water rafting. That was *Hawaii Five-O* stuff – we wore life-jackets over our bikinis, while in the distance there were snow-capped mountains and an electrical storm. It was amazing.

It was good to have Ivar with us in the more scary, drug-running areas. A man tried to cut the strap of Katie's camera with a knife while we were at a train station in Puno, but I ran at her and pushed her out of the way, which took him by surprise as I don't think he knew anyone was watching.

We ended up in La Paz, where our hotel room was burgled

and our fake Rolexes taken. It was a fascinating town, with llama foetuses hanging up in market stalls and people practising 'witchcraft'.

There was a ski resort near La Paz, but the taxi taking us there conked out in the thin air. We thought we were fit girls and could walk to the top, but it was terribly hard work and the ski resort was closed anyway. We also went to Iquitos in Peru and up a tributary of the Amazon, where we spent three days experiencing jungle life, thrashing through the undergrowth, looking at alligators – you could see their evil eye in the dark – and canoeing up the river, feeding lumps of raw meat to piranhas. We caught and cooked some, but they were rather bony.

As it was incredibly hot, we were told we could swim in the river. Although it was brown, we couldn't wait to get in, but the moment I leapt in, the shout 'Piranha!' went up and I was scrambling out as fast as I could. I could feel them against my legs, which was horrible.

We flew back to Argentina, where Patrick Beresford had arranged for us to spend five days on the estancia belonging to the Duchess of York's mother, Susie Barrantes. Her husband Hector wasn't well then – he died of cancer shortly after – and was away, but Susie was so kind. I think she was desperate for news of England and the eventing world, and she seemed to really enjoy having us.

We were allowed to do some stick and balling on their polo ponies and they held a big barbecue when they killed a sheep and we girls all ogled the Argentine players.

Back in England, my problems with King William had not evaporated. At Badminton in 1993, we were right up there after dressage and cross-country, but the show jumping was yet another disaster: five fences down and right back down the order.

We were a write-off, as far as most people were concerned, and I knew there wouldn't be an envelope from the selectors on this occasion. Sure enough, Bridget Parker, who had taken over from Jane Holderness-Roddam as chairman, came up to me looking worried. Bridget is a good friend, and she was in tears as she said, 'I'm really sorry, Mary, but we feel it's the right thing not to select you this time and let you work on your show jumping.' She was so upset that I became weepy, too.

My problems with William attracted a lot of attention. I received all sorts of funny suggestions, including one from a woman who volunteered to cast a spell on him, and lots of other useless advice. Steve Hadley, the former show jumper and BBC commentator, was very helpful, and so was Mark Phillips, but in the end it was Lars Sederholm who helped me the most.

Lars was famous for his way of getting inside horses' and riders' minds, and almost anyone who was anyone – Richard Walker, David O'Connor, Yogi Breisner and show jumpers like John and Michael Whitaker – had gone through his school at Waterstock in Oxfordshire. Ian Stark, who had a similarly bad show jumper in his grey horse Stanwick Ghost, was also getting help.

Lars phoned up and said, 'Mary, I really think I can help you. If ever you're coming up, stop by and I'll talk to you about what I think.'

Eventually, I managed to find an excuse to be passing. Lars and his wife Diana were really friendly and invited me to supper. I'd had a couple of drinks by the time he asked, 'Have you got your jodhpurs?' He phoned through to his staff and asked them to bring a horse into the school, where he said he was going to do a 'little exercise' with me.

There were two horses, wearing bridles but no saddles. He got a young lad to do some bareback jumping on one, and then he explained to me that he thought one of my problems was that I was leaning too far forward with my upper body, which was encouraging William to accelerate, making him jump too fast and flat. He told me that I must learn to keep my upper body weight back and allow the horse to take off without my weight coming forward.

He put me up on the other horse which, fortunately, was quite steady. I cantered towards a fence and, blow me, it refused. Lars said, 'This horse only stops when the rider leans forward!' And he was right; whenever I leaned forward, it would stop. It was a really good way to get it into my head that's what I was doing wrong.

Lars worshipped the Brazilian show jumper Nelson Pessoa, and would make me watch videos of him which showed his upper body remaining so still. I realised that it was definitely a fault of mine; watching Barcelona on the video, I could see how unstable I was in the saddle then.

Lars was a great help and support. William never became an amazing show jumper, but he did improve a bit, and I learned a lot. Lars had lots of exercises, which he called his 'tools'. He was so well organised that all the exercises would be laid out for when I got there.

He was very much into working with the horse's mind, and his training philosophy came from an intellectual basis. His aim was to get William to believe in himself, because having fences down scared him and the worry would make him switch off.

As I was uninvited to the European Championships that September, I thought I'd go to Burghley instead and show everyone what we could do. It seemed a great opportunity and, in fact, turned out to be William's only visit there, as he was always required for teams in the autumn after that.

It turned out to be a disaster. We were warming up for the dressage down by the Lion Bridge. It was quite wet and, just before I was due to go in the arena, we were standing still when a car went by quite fast, splashing us. William jumped sideways, treading on himself, and the stud sliced down the inside of his hind pastern. There was a clean slice in the flesh and blood gushed out.

We mopped it up hastily and, as he was perfectly sound, carried on. He did a beautiful dressage test, which left us in second place behind Lucinda Murray (now Fredericks) on Just Jeremy.

Stupidly, in the press conference afterwards, I blurted out, 'I'm so lucky – William cut himself just before going into the arena!'

Obviously, that made a good story and all the journalists wrote about it for their Saturday papers.

I thought nothing about it; went back and cleaned up the wound and got the vet, Andy Bathe, to staple it. Next morning, we iced the wound but William had full flexibility and no bruising. I wasn't worried about him knocking it because it was on the inside. I was going to put black Vetwrap around it, plus his usual hind XC boots.

I'd just finished doing the bandages in preparation for Phase A, and was feeling happy, organised and excited when I heard over the tannoy a call for me to go to the horse trials office. They said the ground jury (judges) wanted to see me.

The judges said they were sorry but, having read the papers, they couldn't allow me to run across country. I was gob-smacked; it never occurred to me that they'd stop me and, obviously, I cared about the horse as much as anyone.

I said, 'Do you really mean it?'

They explained, 'It's in the public eye that the horse has been cut; if it comes open when you're galloping along, it will look so bad.'

I was devastated, but there was nothing I could do. It was just very sad, and, although it was no one's fault, it taught me that it wasn't always a good idea to be so open.

That winter, Katie, Annie, Mel and I went off on another adventure, and Tessa Spencer came too. We flew to Antigua with a package through which you can fly to five different islands. The inter islands airline was known as 'LIAT' – 'Luggage In Any Terminal' because they're so chaotic.

First, we descended on Sarah Dick-Read's uncle in Tortola, then we went to the Dominican Republic, St Kitts and St Lucia, and Annie and I finally wound up in Guadeloupe scrubbing the decks on a super yacht on which my godmother's son, Mark Coxon, was a skipper.

We used to book into hotels as one person and then all pile into the same room. Breakfast was a banana off a tree, we'd try and wangle a free lunch, and if anyone got a date, we all had to go too. The result was that we lived pretty cheaply!

They were great days. Another one of our girls' trips (plus Ivar!) was to South Africa, where we travelled, somewhat unwisely, from Durban through a dodgy area called Transky on the Garden Route. Highlights included riding in an ostrich race – most of us fell off – and having my first oysters, in a floating restaurant on a lagoon at Nisna.

We drove from Capetown to Johannesburg, through the rough areas, which we found horribly fascinating, and were woken by the police one night to tell us that our hire car had been broken into. They'd caught a black youth, whom they put in a cage in the back of their van. It didn't feel terribly safe, but we then ended up in the Kruger, which was the other extreme. We went to a rather touristy area so it felt a bit like a zoo – all tarmac roads and tame wild animals, but fantastic to see all the same.

William and I were reinstated on the British team in 1994. We still had trouble at Badminton in the show jumping, dropping from third to eleventh place with five fences down, but the selectors obviously thought that William's soundness and ability in the first two phases meant he was worth taking.

I was pleased, too, because I had always felt that, despite the show jumping problems, he was a more than useful team horse, and I have to admit to feeling vindicated when the team had failed to shine at the 1983 Europeans. Although Tina Gifford saved the day with individual silver, the team didn't complete, the first time a British squad has suffered that ignominy at a European Championships.

The Achselschwang disaster compounded the Barcelona one. British eventing was at a low. British riders were continually being compared unfavourably with the Antipodeans, who were all the rage at that time, and the New Zealanders, having been first, second and third at Badminton in 1994, were hot favourites to win gold at the World Equestrian Games in The Hague.

My team mates were Karen on Get Smart, Tina on General Jock, and Charlotte Bathe, who had gone clear at the Europeans the year before on The Cool Customer. Individuals were Helen Bell on Troubleshooter and Caroline Casburn on The Ghost-hunter. The press made a big thing out of the fact that we were an all-girl team, and they didn't think we had a hope of bringing home a medal.

Unusually for Dutch organisation, The Hague was completely chaotic. When we arrived, the stadium was barely finished, and the cross-country facilities were basic, to say the least. To add to the confusion, Holland had been hit by an unexpected heat-wave; the weather was boiling and sticky.

Annie is always cheerful, no matter what the conditions, and enjoyed herself in The Hague, going out on the town with the Irish – one day, I found her lying fast asleep in a trunk outside William's stable, in which he was only semi tied up! But a lot of the other grooms complained vociferously about their conditions and it was pretty hard on them. The accommodation wasn't great and the loos were simply revolting – we only had one between all of us on cross-country day.

Our team outfit for the horse inspections was brown-and-white gingham tops, with narrow brown linen skirts. As I tried to keep up with William's big trot, as I'd been taught by Sheila Willcox, my skirt ripped right up to my hip and flapped open as I ran.

I didn't mind being first to go for the team because the quiet arena would be ideal for William. On the first day, we established an eight-point lead over America's Karen O'Connor (formerly Lende) on Biko, and we were still in the lead going into cross-country.

The drive to the cross-country course on the previous day took two hours because all the lorries were made to go in a slow, tedious convoy. William had sweated quite a lot on the journey and became unsettled. He didn't like his cramped stable and, we now realise, had probably continued to sweat all night. He must have been very dehydrated, but the hot weather had taken everyone by surprise and we were rather ignorant of that sort of thing then.

It was a scruffy cross-country course, twisting around heathland, which had deep sand on the tracks. The roads and tracks phases were hard, and probably took their toll with a number of horses.

William felt quite normal around three-quarters of the cross-country, but then it was as if someone had flicked a switch, and his legs had gone to jelly. It was a horrible feeling. All I wanted to do was pull up, but I had team responsibility and I told myself there were only a few more fences to go, so I urged him on as gently but persuasively as I could.

He felt very laboured, and our jump over the penultimate fence, a bank complex, was terribly laboured. I was in tears at what I was doing to my horse, especially when I had to give him a smack to get him over the last.

As I leapt off him at the finish, he spied a water butt, and just dragged me to it, where he drank immediately. The poor horse was desperately dehydrated, but after a rapid influx of electrolytes, he was all right and recovered quickly, so the rest of the team horses were given fluids with electrolytes before starting out, and they were all fine.

After all the hype about the other nations who were going to thrash us, the tables turned on cross-country day. It was Britain's day, the only team to have four clear rounds. We were absolutely ecstatic.

The New Zealanders fell apart when Blyth Tait had to pull up Delta because she was struggling. Andrew Nicholson and Toddy both fell off in the same water complex and only Vaughn Jefferis went clear.

All that stood between Britain and a gold medal was America's anchorman, Bruce Davidson on Eagle Lion, and I'm sorry to report that when he fell off in the final water complex at the end of the day, it was hard not to be excited.

We'd risen to second place after cross-country and, next day, when an American team horse was lame, we were suddenly in gold-medal position, with five fences in hand over the French. William and I were lying in individual bronze medal position, behind Australia's Prue Cribb on Navarone and Vaughn Jefferis on his brilliant little Thoroughbred, Bounce.

I told the team that all the five fences in hand were mine! But it didn't quite work that way, as between them they got rid of three, and, as everyone knows, two fences in hand is not usually enough for King William. The French thought they virtually had the gold medal in their grasp, and poor Steve Hadley, who was helping me, was in a terrible lather.

I had Lars's words ringing in my head. He had advised me to trot into the ring, allowing William to have his head up and get a good look at what was around him. He told me not to dominate the horse, but to let him make his own way, and to have an outside counter bend around the right corners, which would help the horse keep his balance and prevent him drifting out to the left.

But Lars wasn't in the practice arena, and William was jumping badly. I don't know if I've ever been in a greater state of nerves. Fortunately, David Broome, one of the most successful ever British show jumpers, was watching and stepped in. He could see that William was lacking confidence, so he pulled the ground rail of the practice fence right out to help the horse get a better jump. William felt much better, so I, too, felt marginally more confident when it was our turn to go into the ring.

It was nearly all over when William accelerated through the treble and had two elements of that down. Our allowance was gone! Previously, the problem had been that, once William had knocked fences down, he would panic and go faster and faster. Fortunately, though, here the next fence was on a turn and it was quite big and spooky. This made him back off and listen to me, and somehow we scraped home clear over the last few fences.

It was a wonderful moment, knowing that I hadn't let everyone down. I was so relieved that I took off on an impromptu lap of honour, much to the bemusement of the Dutch audience who couldn't understand why someone who had lost an individual medal could be so happy!

As a team, we couldn't believe we'd done it either, and the icing on the cake was when Karen won a deserved individual bronze medal, behind Vaughn Jefferis and America's Dorothy Trapp. We went mad, shrieking and leaping around like St Trinian's schoolgirls. I had, indeed, lost my individual medal – I was fourth – but I was thrilled.

In complete contrast to Barcelona, we returned home as heroines – the 'golden girls' – and I had finally won a gold medal in my own right.

*

That winter was my last 'girly' holiday. The usual gang went, this time, to San Francisco, from where we travelled down the West Coast, via Disney World, Los Angeles, Hollywood, to San Diego and Mexico, before flying to Hawaii and meeting up with the faithful Ivar. None of us was much good at surfing the big waves there, but we had great fun trying, and Ivar suffered terrible sore nipples from lying on his board!

I then went on to New Zealand, where, along with some other international riders, I'd been invited to compete in a two-star 'celebrity' CIC at Puhinui, the country's main three-day event, on provided horses – and after the event we flew down to Queenstown – south of the South Island, and then drove north.

David came out to join me, and spent a lot of time looking at the way of farming out there. I also did my first bungee jump, in South Island. I was quite worried about wrenching my back, but my mind was made up when I saw this girl who was so elated at having done it. She was small and plump and, I'm sorry to say that I thought, if she could do it, so could I. Actually, it was OK; there was no wrenching or flicking about as I'd feared, just a gentle spongy feeling.

It was the first of three such trips to New Zealand, all of which were great fun, and I got to know a lot of my fellow riders better, including Pippa Funnell. But it was the last time I travelled as a single woman – life was about to change.

CHAPTER 11

Marriage, Motherhood and Medals

David and I announced our engagement in the spring of 1995. I can't say that it was exactly a romantic proposal – it was more a matter of both of us saying, 'Come on, isn't it about time?' – but it was a very happy period.

We both knew we wanted to have children, and had always agreed that we'd get married when the time was right to try and have a family. I'd also vowed that I wouldn't marry David until we could live together on a farm and have the horses there (David's farm is too near a roundabout and the Exeter ring-road), but we hadn't managed to find anywhere and I had accepted by then that I'd just have to commute the sixteen miles to my yard.

The date was set for 14 June, and David got me a beautiful diamond ring that I'd spotted in a jeweller's shop in Sidmouth; it had belonged to an old lady who died, and was similar to the one my mother wears, which is what I'd always wanted. I've never taken it off since.

I was having a good time on the horse trials front, too. King William was brilliant at the spring one-day events. We ran away with an advanced section at Belton, winning by 14 points on a score of 18, which is an incredible achievement, and a fortnight later we won at Brigstock as well.

Badminton, however, did not go to plan. To my horror, William started playing up in the dressage, a phase that had always previously been our banker. The arena was buzzing, with a lot of people taking photographs and he didn't even want to go in, the first time he'd ever tried to refuse to do anything.

In the test, he halted nervously, ran backwards and then, to gasps from the audience, did a bit of a rear. It was quite unlike him, but showed that his nerves were not getting any better. I managed to pull parts of the test together, and he scored well for some movements, but we ended up with a mark of 54, easily his worst ever, and which would put us out of any chance of a top placing.

We were clear across country, of course, but had an igno-minious 21 penalties in the show jumping and finished four-teenth. I felt that everyone would be thinking, 'Here we go again, why does she bother?' It was so embarrassing, and I started to feel reluctant to go through it again, building my hopes up and then having them dashed so publicly. It seemed a waste of nervous energy.

But, yet again, the selectors decided that William's virtues outweighed his vices, and they gave us our third championship chance, this time to the Open European Championships in Pratoni del Vivaro. I couldn't really believe my luck but, then, we had played a major part in the world gold medal the year before and I suppose it was worth a gamble that we could do the same again.

Meanwhile, wedding preparations continued. It was to be on a budget, as I've never seen any point in spending thousands of pounds on something that lasts only a few hours. Getting married in the church with which our families had such a close connection and in front of all our friends was what mattered, and I felt we could still do a special party.

I borrowed my dress and shoes from Zoë House – a good friend who is part of my Monday night tennis gang – knowing they would go with a beautiful family veil, plus her brides-maid's dresses and shoes. The marquee for the reception was to be set up on my arena; I made my own cake – which I was still frantically decorating the night before – and Mum and her sister, Rea Hollis, did all the flowers, which were wild, including masses of foxgloves and ox-eyed daisies everywhere.

My brother, Simon, would be involved in the service, too, and his children, Andy and Claire, were to be page and bridesmaid.

Simon had found fame, too, in a somewhat different way. He had suffered back pain ever since an accident where he hit his head. Over the years he had five major back ops and eventually both legs became paralysed and he spent two years in a wheel-chair. With my Badminton winnings, I'd paid for him to go to a Harley Street specialist to try and sort it. The doctor had prepared Simon for the prospect of never walking again, telling him that he might be better in ten years' time, but the pain would make him prefer to be in the wheelchair – which wasn't much of a prognosis.

Then something extraordinary happened. He'd been asked to be lead singer at a prayer weekend at Lychett Minster and, during the weekend, the pain began to ease. Then he had a vivid dream, in which he was told that, if he told his wife, Julia, about something that had happened at the weekend, he would get better. As Julia is an atheist, Simon couldn't think what on earth he could tell her.

He had another dream, in which God told him that, if he told Julia he'd been filled with the Holy Spirit, he'd be cured! This seemed too embarrassing and ridiculous for words, and he almost chickened out, but eventually managed to say to Julia, 'I've got something to tell you. I feel as if I've been filled with the Holy Spirit.'

She thought he'd gone mad, but at that point his legs, which had become as skinny as matchsticks through lack of use, began to fill up like a hot-water bottle with warm fluid. He stood up and he walked. It was extraordinary.

When Simon walked into the doctor's surgery, the doctor couldn't believe his eyes. He wrote on Simon's medical notes: *Cured by religious experience.*

When we heard, we leapt into the car and drove down to Dorset to see him, bearing champagne and strawberries. It was quite a thing at the time. Simon did lots of talks and appearances, including on *Woman's Hour*, and was pictured in a newspaper holding his wheelchair aloft.

My wedding was a proper family day, too. My father gave me away, and he was so proud that it was a lovely occasion, although he refused to stay for the photographs because he wanted to go home and have a snooze. Routine called!

Donald Peyton-Jones, who had started it all off by lending me Silver and Magpie all those years before, came back for the service, along with his successor, Michael Courtney, who'd lent me my first stable.

It was all very jolly and comfortable. David and I had been together for so long, and were such good friends, it all felt very right. We were repeating the vows when David said, 'I will' too soon, and the vicar said, 'No, not yet!'

The horses were in attendance at the reception – William, Cuthbert and Star Appeal – looking over the gate and taking great interest. It was a sunny day, and we had all the wedding presents displayed, in the old-fashioned way, out in the yard. I can still picture Annie breaking off midway through proceedings to go and skip out to the stables, hitching her dress up over her wellies.

We had brilliant dancing later; during the Troggs' song 'Wild Thing', one of our friends, Miles Jennings, stripped off on the dance floor – much to the mortification of his girlfriend. I can remember another old friend, and long-time supporter of my eventing career, Nadine Orchard, standing on a chair to get a better look! The electricity blew at one point, but the band played on while cigarettes provided the only light.

The one blot on the horizon was that David was in trouble with the police. Two weeks before the wedding he'd been questioned, along with his father, Fred, about swapping the ear tags of cattle that were for sale to the Continent. It was around the time of the BSE crisis and was, therefore, a particularly sensitive issue, with local feelings running high. David had basically got on the wrong side of red tape and, while he was not the only farmer in the wrong, they had decided to make an example of him.

It was obviously a worrying time for David, and particularly horrid for his elderly father, and I had to try not to think about it. One of the great things about David is that he is very reassuring and always keeps calm, and he made sure that I was protected from knowing and worrying too much.

The day after the wedding, when we'd safely departed for our honeymoon in Corsica, Mum went off to buy the *Sidmouth Herald*, confidently expecting lovely coverage of her daughter's wedding. There was, indeed, a gorgeous picture on the front cover, but the headline was: *Mary's husband faces BSE cattle deception charges.* One of the captions read: *Mary marries her gaol bird!* And the article began: *A shadow hung over the wedding* ... The paper had known about the story but had deliberately held it back to coincide with our wedding. I couldn't believe it. The two journalists who wrote it usually covered my riding exploits and I knew them well, but I came to understand that they were only doing their job.

Local people were furious with the paper and very supportive of us. The next week there was a double-page spread of letters, condemning the paper's timing with headings like: 'Apologise!', 'So tasteless', 'Gutter press' and 'Sensational, shabby and disgusting'. The gist of the letters was that I had surely done enough to make the local area proud and what a way to repay me. Even Mum, who is one of the most forgiving people, wrote a short letter saying how dismayed she was that they'd devalued her daughter's wedding day.

David was arrested and charged when we got back from honeymoon. Like my mother, I'm not a worrier, and I took it quite calmly. Looking back, though, it was a horrid time for everyone. In the end, he was heavily fined that autumn, but it was such a relief when it was all over.

I had a particular reason for not wanting my new husband to be in gaol, because I was pregnant. We had decided that no time must be wasted in trying to have a baby at the start of

1996, so that I could prepare for the Atlanta Olympics that summer.

It was a major secret, and only David, Mum and Annie knew. Eventually, I told the team doctor, Michael Dooley, during team training for the Europeans. It was a real dilemma, but I knew I'd have to have a medical test with him before the championships and so, when I saw him, I blurted it out.

Michael was so supportive of me. He knew that in King William I had probably the safest cross-country horse in the world and he understood how desperate I was to ride at the championships. He advised me not to tell anyone else, because it would be too much of a burden for them. So I kept it a secret from Bridget Parker, the chairman of selectors, and Gilly and my team mates, knowing they would only worry and think they had to make concessions for me.

I would never, of course, have done anything to hurt my baby, but Michael reassured me that the most dangerous time for a baby is in the early stages of pregnancy. He said, 'Your baby is perfectly safe in there. If you have a bad fall, you would probably die before it did.'

And, ironically, I did actually have three falls that autumn. At Gatcombe, William jumped me off in a particularly extravagant leap; at Shamley Green, King Kong became over-excited and got in a tangle with some poles in the show jumping warm-up, and I fell off at the Trout Hatchery with him at Burghley. Poor Mum! I'm sure that at times the secret was almost too much for her and Annie to bear.

By the time Pratoni came round in October, I was five and a half months pregnant. I was extremely fit, but my clothes were definitely getting tighter and I surreptitiously let out the buttons of my team jacket and skirt before the first horse inspection.

At the event, I was talking to the British press, and Genevieve Murphy, who writes for the *Independent*, said: 'Oh, Mary, you do look slim!' I thought, *If only you knew*, and at that point I did feel guilty.

I shared a room with Lucy Jennings (now Henson), who was riding as an individual on Diamond Pedlar. She now can't believe that she never knew, but I took great care not to undress in front of her. I was amazed when I had a bath one night and the baby was visibly kicking.

I also struggled when walking the course. Pratoni, which is Italy's national equestrian centre and hosted the cross-country for the 1960 Rome Olympics, is very hilly – it is set in the middle of a beautiful mountainous national park south of Rome – and I couldn't keep up with the rest of the team, but no one seemed to notice.

I was, by now, praying to God that everything would be OK, and that William would look after us, but riding still felt the right thing to do. Although my baby was always in my thoughts, it didn't occur to me to be anything other than convinced that everything would be fine.

It was a happy championships. I still get teased about not realising who the line-up of women on the road outside the event were. Everyone else knew that they were prostitutes – it is one of the great traditions of Pratoni – but I thought they were waiting for a bus!

I was reunited with my World Games team mates Tina Gifford (now Cook) and Charlotte Bathe, and it was my first time on a team with William Fox-Pitt, who was to become a good friend.

The dressage at Pratoni is pleasantly low-key, which suited King William very well, and he produced one of his best tests for us to lie in second place behind the eventual individual winners, Ireland's Lucy Thompson on Ginny's former horse, Welton Romance.

William was the perfect gentleman around the cross-country, which includes the notorious scary slide, not to mention a couple of difficult water complexes, and we finished clear and inside the time.

Charlotte had a rare mistake for her, a run-out on The Cool Customer, but the rest of us went clear and the team was in the lead.

The show jumping was, of course, another nervous moment, but we had three fences in hand to retain team gold. When we got to the treble, which was rather close to the crowd, William ran through the bridle and lowered two fences, but he managed not to make any more mistakes. The team gold was secured and, thrillingly, we had won our first individual medal, a bronze.

As it was, unusually, an Open Europeans, non-European teams were eligible so that they would have a chance of qualifying for the Olympics. This doesn't happen any more, but it meant that the competition was as competitive as a world championships. We beat the New Zealanders into second – the 'real' European team silver medal went to France – but it has to be said that the Kiwis were riding a team of young and inexperienced horses!

There were terrific international celebrations, and I felt so pleased with my medal, with my wonderful, reliable horse, and with everyone who had continued to support me. It was a great result for Gilly, and for Bridget Parker, who had shown such faith in me, and I longed to tell everyone about my baby. However, I felt anything too public might detract from the medal celebrations.

In the end, I went up to Gilly in the bar and said, 'I've got something to tell you.'

'I know,' she said. 'You're pregnant!'

Then David and I went upstairs and found Bridget in her bedroom. She was a bit taken aback, but she managed to congratulate me. I explained that I thought, if I'd told her, she wouldn't let me ride. When I asked her what she'd have done, she admitted that I'd have only been an individual.

Later on, Gilly bumped into Jenny MacArthur, *The Times* equestrian correspondent, at the airport, and told her. Jenny thought that was an amazing scoop, and rushed to telephone her paper. My achievement – two medals while pregnant – was front-page news next day; Jenny had beaten all her colleagues to the news.

CHAPTER 12

Heartbreak in Atlanta

Many people thought that motherhood would mean the end of my career, and it spawned endless articles on the rights and wrongs of sport and taking risks while pregnant, as the careers of other mothers were discussed. People pointed out that Lucinda Green was 'never the same again' after having two children, but they were missing the point. She just didn't have such good horses again; it was nothing to do with her riding. Often, having children coincides with a natural winding down of the career, or just having young horses, and everyone goes through phases with not such talented horses to ride.

Where I had an advantage was that King William and my other top horse, Star Appeal (of whom more later), were both established at four-star level. I didn't have only young horses, which I can see might become unnerving, and I found riding perfectly comfortable – somehow I felt less pregnant on a horse.

To my face, everyone said, 'Well done, you're so brave,' but I'm sure a lot of them thought I was stupid. A journalist in the *Brighton Evening Standard* wrote: *I read with a mixture of horror and admiration the story of Mary King. I can't make up my mind if she was very brave or very stupid. But the truth is probably a bit of both.*

I rode the day before having Emily. She was due on 14 February, but about three weeks earlier I'd realised that I wasn't gaining weight, even though I was eating like mad. That did worry me a bit and I went to the doctor. He suggested another scan, and they found I had a full-grown but thin baby. To complicate matters, she was in extended breech position – bottom down and legs up in front of her face – and my placenta wasn't feeding her enough.

The doctor said I had to have a Caesarean, and that a date would be set the next week. I wasn't that keen because I thought that would mean I couldn't ride, but when I got home I started to feel really worried. Inside me was this baby getting thinner and thinner; I couldn't bear the thought of the baby starving inside me, and felt it should be born straight away.

Having a Caesarean is extraordinary, like having a baby by appointment. I even played tennis, as normal, the night before. Since 1992, David and I have religiously played tennis at the Exeter Golf and Country Club with the same six people: Richard and Zoë House, Paul and Penny Dart, and Will and Jackie Michelmore. Richard had been our best man and the Darts' daughter, Bea, was a bridesmaid.

We book two courts, from 7.30 to 9 p.m., and then take it in turns to cook. When we started, we were all unmarried, and now we have all had babies. We're a rather competitive bunch – each of the women tried to see how late into pregnancy we could play. I think I won!

I'd ridden William that morning, having left a message on the doctor's answerphone asking if I could have a Caesarean as soon as possible. Then I went to a lunch party with my mother, after which I received the call saying that I'd be having a baby next day!

The operation was to be at 9 a.m. on 26 January, and David was keen that I was on time as he had to go to market. I had a shower and put make-up on first – I didn't want to look completely bedraggled – and was very keen to watch the procedure, but the doctors were worried that I'd faint. However, they didn't realise that I could still see some of what was going on in the reflection on the chrome surrounding the lights above!

Out came this perfect, clean, but thin, baby girl. She weighed 4 lbs 6 oz, which is very light for a full-grown baby, and she looked rather like a skinned rabbit. I could hold her in one hand.

The name Emily had been on both our lists, and we gave her Maria as a second name, after David's mother. My father-in-law had come in with David. He was absolutely thrilled, although, probably thinking about his farm, his first words were: 'Shame it's not a boy!'

As soon as I'd been stapled up, David left for market. I was raring to go and couldn't wait to phone everyone. They kept me and my lovely little baby in hospital for six days. The nurses were brilliant, teaching me how to look after a baby, and I felt rather guilty, because outside the weather was freezing and here I was lolling around in a nice warm hospital with nothing to do other than to adore Emily. Annie, meanwhile, had the horses doing roadwork, and was battling with frozen taps, which meant having to carry water up the hill from my parents' house. She was, as always, very cheerful about it.

I seemed to adapt to having an extra little person to care for quite easily. Getting up every four hours to feed Emily didn't seem too much of a hardship – rather like getting up early for a horse trials! – and I was lucky not to suffer from any form of 'baby blues'.

Because Emily had arrived early, we were able to go on the Land Rover Rankings awards. The Rankings, which have sadly been discontinued, carried particularly good money then, from points earned at international events. If riders were doing well, they'd go to a lot of trouble to plan the last part of their season around it. I'd won in the first year, 1992, but, annoyingly, there was no prize-money at that time.

The rankings were organised by John Foden, a larger-than-life character from the motor racing world. Each year, he tried to outdo the previous year's party, and this time he commandeered a Brittany Ferries boat and we had an overnight party while sailing across the Channel to St Malo.

Emily slept through rough seas, a disco, and, on the way back, even a film, *Braveheart*. This fantastic film was quite violent, with people having their eyes gouged out and heads cut off, and the cinema emptied rapidly as most people succumbed to a combination of seasickness and squeamishness.

The surgeon who'd done the Caesarean had said, as he battled with my muscles, 'I can tell you're fit!' I healed quickly and within two weeks was back riding. My first event was Peper Harow, in the first weekend of March. I took King Solomon, and Mum had Emily in her pram.

Everyone warned me that I'd lose my nerve, but as I was going across country, I thought to myself, *No, this feels the same as usual*. I was aware that I was still riding forward, that I wasn't 'hooking' and, most importantly, that I still really wanted to do it.

Somewhat ironically, having a fall at Badminton played into my hands, as far as being selected for Atlanta was concerned. I was lying eleventh on King William, the best of the contenders for the British squad, when I managed, rather stupidly, to fall off my second ride, Star Appeal, at the very first fence.

He was the sort of horse who would fight if you checked him, so I'd let him go on and, foolishly, thought he would jump off a long stride. But he chipped in a stride and hit the fence and I fell off. I didn't think much of it at the time, but overnight my neck and back stiffened up, and the physiotherapist who was treating me insisted that I was x-rayed before riding again.

David drove me to Frenchay Hospital in Bristol. The doctors there suspected a cracked vertebra, and put me in a neck brace. In the meantime I was keeping in touch with the event, because I wanted to go back and show jump William, but all the while the clock was ticking as our start time grew closer.

It turned out that it was a false alarm, but Bridget Parker admitted that she'd rather I plead injured. She knew that if, as was only too likely, we whacked down lots of show jumps, she would be in an embarrassing position about listing us for the Olympics.

In the end, they named me with both horses. They asked William Fox-Pitt, who had missed Badminton with Cosmopolitan, and me, on Star Appeal, to do a final trial run at Bramham, where we were excused the roads and tracks.

Star Appeal was getting very strong at this stage, and ended up having a bad fall at an upright gate. Mike Tucker, one of the selectors, ran down to me and, as I got up, I pre-empted anything he was thinking of saying with: 'Don't worry, Mike! I don't want to ride this horse at the Olympics anyway!'

The incident almost put me off riding Star Appeal. I had pretty much decided that he was a man's horse, but later he came right in a way that was beyond my wildest dreams.

There was a lot of nervous talk about Atlanta as a venue for horses. The time of year – July – was about the worst it could be, there in America's steamy Deep South. The heat and humidity would be extreme and many people felt it was dangerous to take horses into those sort of energy-sapping conditions. This was the last thing we wanted for our horses, even if it was an Olympics, and it was a continual worry.

But, as a team, we had learned a lot from our experiences in The Hague, and a huge amount of research had been done at the Animal Health Trust into cooling horses. We attended several lectures, which I have to admit were quite technical and dry; I'm not sure that we completely grasped all that was being said, but it was reassuring.

It was probably the first time that any of us had really worked on our own fitness. I took up running – something I'd never bothered with before. We had to go into the heat chamber at Hartpury College, and to Bisham Abbey, the sports medicine centre, for a fitness test, where they tested the strength of different muscles, and our breathing and lung capacities. We rode exercise bikes, which were connected up to various computers and machines, and had tubes in our mouths hooked up to something else, so they could see how the body was coping with the exercise.

They could also tell how determined we were as characters, based on how long we pressed ourselves to keep going. As the doctor was a young and particularly good-looking Mediterranean, that made me pedal harder!

But the depressingly awful outcome was that, when they looked at the results, we were no fitter than the average man on the street. We had some smokers in our midst and this dragged our results down.

After the Olympic Village at Barcelona, which had been so exciting, Atlanta, by contrast, was very disappointing: a sprawling university campus with tiny bedrooms. I shared with Karen Dixon and there was barely room for our luggage, most of which lived outside in the corridor. The rowers had to move out because they couldn't fit in their beds.

We left fairly soon ourselves; the horses were at Pinetops, out in the country, and we lived in a motel in the local town, called, by coincidence, Thomson. We'd ride both early and late, so the horses could be prepared for the conditions ahead. Our only real problem was the flies. They were terrible and some of the horses had quite bad reactions.

It was certainly hot and humid, rather like being attacked by a wet hairdryer, but I have always liked the heat, so it didn't particularly bother me. We'd have spectacular rainstorms which would clear the air for a nano-second before it was back to being steamier than ever; one day there was a monsoon-like flood which ran through the stables.

The Germans were training nearby and, with Ian Stark in our midst, there were plenty of good parties. We went to the supermarket to buy some booze and invited the Germans. We played a daft game where you whirl round until you're dizzy, spinning a brush in the air, and then you had to try to run in a straight line and hit a tin. One of the Germans got so disorientated he keeled over into the bushes – one way of getting rid of the opposition!

Under Ian's direction, we'd all go running at 7 a.m. every morning. He was a good runner, who had done marathons. Leslie Law, too, turned out to be a good runner, and William Fox-Pitt was amazing, lolloping along for miles on his long legs.

Then we moved into the official horse park, and the first thing – of many – to go wrong was that Leslie's horse New Flavour went lame, literally just as the plane carrying one of his owners was taxiing down the runway.

It was terrible luck for Leslie. This was his first team opportunity and he'd worked so hard. His fourth place at Badminton in the spring, behind, yet again, all those New Zealanders, had been the best British result.

One of the toughest things about an Olympics is that without accreditation you're nothing. Leslie was immediately stripped of his, which meant he became a virtual non-person, cut off from the rest of us. Instead, Chris Hunnable and Mr Bootsie were shipped in to run as individuals.

For the first time at the Olympics, there were two separate competitions, for teams and for individuals, because of a controversial new ruling which said you couldn't win two medals for the same performance.

This was hard on some of the top riders who were needed by their nation to boost team chances, because it would preclude them from having a chance of an individual medal. It also meant that, if your team was wiped out, or was obviously not going to feature in the medals, the impetus to keep going was lost. This happened to Karen Dixon in our team; yet again, she was the most successful rider, in sixth place, but had nothing to show for her efforts, which made her pretty unhappy.

It was decided that the team would consist of Ian as trailblazer on Stanwick Ghost, William on Cosmopolitan, Gary Parsonage on Magic Rogue, who wasn't the best at dressage but was a very reliable jumper, and Karen on Too Smart.

I was initially surprised not to be in the team, and slightly disappointed to be left out of what I anticipated would be a medal situation, but I adjusted to it, not least because it meant that the team would not be reliant on our show jumping performance, which was a relief.

Things got off to a shaky start. There had already been bad feelings between Ginny – who had been appointed as 'jump trainer' to the team – and Ian and me, because we had gone off and had a jumping lesson with Lars Sederholm. This was not considered to be playing the team game and there was a feeling that if we did badly – and we did! – we had only ourselves to blame for not accepting training from her.

The team competition was a disaster, from a British point of view. Ian did a brilliant dressage test, which set the team up, but he had a fall at a water complex when Stanwick Ghost missed the step out and turned over. Nowadays, a bad fall like that would mean instant elimination, but back then you just kept going. Ian was incredibly professional to pull off a completion after that.

William Fox-Pitt had a fall on the flat when Cosmopolitan slipped on the wet grass and a stop. Even though Gary was clear and fast, the team was by this time so far behind that it was hard for Karen, who was last to go in the hottest part of the day, to feel motivated.

Yet again, the Antipodean riders steamed ahead. The Aussies won gold from the Americans and New Zealanders, and for Ian, Karen and me, it was a nasty feeling of déjà vu – Barcelona all over again.

The only good thing to come out of it, from my perspective, was that all the horses seemed to finish well and, after William's near disaster in The Hague, this gave me some confidence. The cross-country started so early in the morning that it was almost cold, and there were misting fans everywhere. All the research proved right on the button, and from a horse welfare point of view, the competition was a triumph.

Finally, it was our go. William did an amazing dressage test. He had an early draw, and felt soft and responsive, enabling me to ride him positively and elicit the very best of his impressive movement. The crowd went wild, Union Jacks flapped everywhere, and when I saw Annie, she was in floods of tears because she was so proud.

I received nines from all three judges for my riding and our overall score was 31, which was a terrific mark, possibly even a record for Olympic eventing. This gave me a commanding lead that I was already thinking would be handy for the show jumping phase.

When I came out of the arena, the late Dr Reiner Klimke, an Olympic gold medallist in pure dressage and one of the most revered figures in the sport, said to me, 'That was real dressage.' It is still one of my most treasured compliments and was a very special moment.

But the mark became irrelevant. Next day, William and I had the first cross-country mistake of our career. What a place to do it! And it was a pathetic mistake.

The course was twisty for William's long stride, with awkward cambers, but he was jumping smoothly. He also felt alert and keen, helped by the additional stop on Phase C and five minutes longer at the start of the cross-country.

Our undoing was three slightly angled log piles which were placed at the top of a steep, narrow track in the woods. We didn't get the best of lines at the previous fence, so when I came up the slope and turned towards the fences, I hadn't got William properly organised. We didn't jump the first log pile that well, and when we turned to the next, I'd lost my line. This meant we had to take the long route and, by the time we turned back to the third jump, William didn't know what he was supposed to be doing and couldn't jump it.

It was awful; such a stupid, elementary, costly error. I felt so useless. I'd let everyone down: the horse, Gilly, Lars, everyone in the British team, all our supporters both in Atlanta and at home and, not least, my baby, to whom I had longed to bring back a gold medal. I was so disheartened that I just drooped home. I had no incentive to kick on and, though I didn't exactly crawl, I didn't go that fast either.

I was well aware that people weren't going to be pleased with me and, indeed, I got heavily criticised, especially by Mike Tucker, for not giving it a better shot. But I knew the medal had gone and I just had no appetite.

We were now in seventh place. The next day was, if that were possible, even more humiliating. William was so nervous at the trot-up that he shook. He then hit eight show jumps, which was just ridiculous and still seems unbelievable, and we finished twelfth.

He had jumped the first fence in an encouragingly round shape, but then he saw a group of photographers, stuck his head up into the giraffe position, and bashed through the second fence. I tried everything, even supporting him with my hand in an effort to hold him off the fence, but his back hollowed and he hit the fences with his back legs. If I softened my hands, he ran at the fences and hit them with his front legs.

After all the lectures I'd had in the aftermath of Barcelona about not smiling idiotically after a disaster, I remembered to leave the ring looking sombre. It wasn't difficult. It had been two minutes of pure hell, but, in truth, I was beyond disappointment. In my heart of hearts, I had known this might happen.

Blyth Tait won the gold medal for New Zealand – on an eight-year-old horse, Ready Teddy. Comparisons were inevitable, and we got home to even more recriminations than after Barcelona. That I was criticised goes without saying, but Ian came in for stick for his fall and his poor show jumping round, as did Karen for going slowly across country. There was considerable examination of team management, as a result of which everyone, including Ginny, Charlie Lane, our chef d'equipe, and John Killingbeck, our vet, were replaced.

It was a second medal-less Olympics, as the show jumpers and dressage riders didn't do very well either, and there were many damning articles in the press. Mark Phillips was particularly harsh, and queried why Ian and I had bothered having lessons with Lars if that was the best we could do.

William, however, came home fresh as a daisy! I knew

I couldn't do a three-day event with him that autumn, but I phoned up Bridget and asked if I could ride him at the British Open Championships at Gatcombe. I didn't want to cause any more trouble for her, but he was so well that it seemed a waste. She said, 'Fine – as long as you win!'

I was aware that there would be huge criticism if I mucked this up as well, but I thought it would be worth a go. In Gatcombe's quiet dressage arenas, William led the dressage, and, with me beyond being nervous or hopeful, had only one show jump down. This dropped him to third, but he bounced back with a superb cross-country to win. I was also second on King Solomon.

Obviously this was some consolation, and I received rather better press, but I couldn't help wondering whether I would be so keen and motivated to tackle another Olympics in four years' time, or whether I'd ever have as good a horse.

CHAPTER 13

Other Stars Also Shine

King William was such a dominant presence – and I suppose he is the horse that most people associate me with – that he rather overshadowed the successes of King Kong and Star Appeal, the two other good four-star horses I had at the time, although the latter was to give me some of my best results.

I bought Star Appeal – 'Apple' – in 1990 as a five year-old. He came, like William, from Bernice Strong. He was bred by Michael McEvoy, from the good Irish eventing sire I'm A Star out of a hunter mare, and had arrived with Bernice from Ireland as a three-year-old. Bernice broke him in and produced him and, having followed William's career with me, phoned up to ask if I'd be interested in looking at Apple.

Though he was seven-eighths Thoroughbred, the predominant characteristic to come through was his Irish hunter blood, and he was certainly different from William, and not the most beautiful horse to look at in the stable. However, he became a much more impressive horse under saddle, when he really worked. I liked him; he was a strong, well-built 17 hh horse, with a big head, hocks and hips. He had a super attitude and moved freely, but I was a bit worried about his jumping. He didn't seem to fold his front legs as much as I would have liked.

However, when I rode him, he gave me an unexpectedly good feel over a fence. This was because he had energy and power and made an effort with his body, but I was still aware that, underneath, he was dangling his legs. I knew that I needed a horse that could help me in the show jumping phase, as that was my weakness. The worst thing for me, from both a practical and psychological point of view, would be another King William situation.

At the time, I was having jumping lessons with Kenneth Clawson, who later became the British team jumping trainer, and I asked if he'd mind calling in to see what he thought of Apple. He later phoned to say that he thought his jump was good enough and that he was worth buying. It turned out to be good advice.

Michael and Angela Pinder, who'd been my first owners, with Silverstone, paid for him and it was they who named him Star Appeal. They loved Thoroughbreds, having had Ferrari and Silverstone, and suddenly I was asking them to buy this heavier type of horse, but they were happy to be involved.

Apple was difficult on the flat, and I didn't push him because he was a big horse who didn't naturally carry himself, but his jumping was great from the start. Our first event was at Llanfechain in mid-Wales, one of the few events to feature lots of natural fences, like big hedges, on the cross-country. Apple gave me an amazing feel right from the start, just like William had. He was bold but sensible, as if he'd done it all his life.

On the flat, I worked him by doing lots of transitions to help him get his hindquarters more underneath his body and his front end up, all of which improved his balance and self-carriage. He won the Novice Futurity Championships at

Tetbury, which was pretty good going for a five-year-old, and he was second, behind King Kong ('Conker'), at Osberton, his first three-day event, a year later. By the time I rode him in his first advanced class at Milton Keynes in 1992, he was so smooth across country that I thought he'd be even better than William.

Unlike William, however, Apple was very laid back, calm but positive, and we nicknamed him Policeman Plod at home. He was lovely to hack out – marching on purposefully. I took him to a Burghley Young Event Horse qualifier at Bramham when he was five years old where, as soon as we arrived, he lay down in his stable and slept.

When it came to the in-hand part of that competition, I realised I hadn't got around to teaching him to trot up well. He plodded along like an old donkey and we got poor marks, for which his owner Angela Pinder was pretty cross, as she felt I hadn't prepared properly. We still came second, though, thanks to the jumping element, and I knew then that he was going to be a fantastic horse, a real four-star ride.

Also unlike King William, Apple was somewhat accident-prone. I took him to Bramham in 1992 where he developed a skin infection at the back of his fetlock. We lay eleventh after dressage, but the leg had become so sore and puffy that next day he wouldn't let me touch it. I withdrew him, and he ended up having the whole autumn off, because even when the infection recovered, a slight strain was evident.

He came out again in 1993, and had a stop at our first event, Ston Easton, which didn't please the Pinders, for they were competitive owners. However, our spring three-day event outing was rather more successful. I took him to Punchestown, where we quietly went up the order, from fourth after dressage to finish eventual second. After some of King William's less successful outings, where the spiral tended to be downward rather than upward, this was rather encouraging for me. Apple impressed the selectors, too; they listed him instead of William for the European Championships.

The rest of 1993 was rather a wash-out for Apple, though. At Montacute, as I was taking off his boots, I discovered a spot of blood in the hoof. Sure enough, a couple of days later, he was really lame. He'd got an infection which ran under his sole, with the result that he had to have a lot of his sole cut back and a special shoe made in which you could screw on a removable metal plate to protect the sensitive part. Boekelo, which had been Apple's autumn goal, was cancelled due to heavy rain, so he just did some one-day events.

That year, the Pinders delivered the bad news that they were going to pull out of owning event horses because their son, David, was going into racing. I was horrified when they told me that they needed to sell Apple. I'd worked so hard on his dressage, and I was convinced that we were going places.

Ironically, thanks to my efforts, Apple was now worth a fortune. After seeking advice, the Pinders suggested a price of £80,000. This was impossible for me, even with my Badminton winnings from the year before, which Gilly had let me keep. She is an incredibly generous owner and has always let me keep all the prize-money.

I took a deep breath and had a big discussion with Angela Pinder, explaining that I had put a lot of money and time into the horse myself and that, because of my sponsorships, they hadn't had to pay running costs. Eventually, the Pinders agreed to bring the price down and I made the big decision to buy Apple with David.

Initially, I was hugely relieved to have kept this horse in my stable. But it began to look like a very expensive mistake when, after a demoralising end to the previous season, Apple suffered a mishap at the start of 1994. He had been turned out after exercise, as usual, with King Kong (Conker), and the two of them were playing and doing little half-rears. Conker kicked out playfully and thumped Apple on the forearm, below the elbow. Apple limped away, but then seemed to be all right and there was no mark.

Next day, I was riding him out and he spooked at something in the hedge, after which he immediately moved off lame. My vet, John Fowler, was retired by then, but I still used him as my adviser, and he suggested Apple should be x-rayed. To my shock, this revealed a star fracture in the leg and a dangerously weak bone.

He was immobilised immediately, tied in pillar reins – one each side of the head collar, going out at right angles – as the important thing was that he didn't lie down because the pressure of getting up again could have snapped the leg. This seemed particularly hard, as no horse enjoys lying down more than Apple.

However, Apple was very patient, and would stand still, eating his hay. After about four weeks, though, he did start to behave oddly, and we had to give him a different box. He would try to sit, or kneel with his head up, but he never thought of pulling back.

Sue Dyson would regularly inspect the x-ray plates at the

Animal Health Trust and after about six weeks the injury had healed enough that I could untie him. The very day I got permission to do this, I arrived at the yard to find that he'd pulled back for the first time and had a blissful roll – thank goodness he hadn't tried it before.

He went a peculiar shape; he got a fat tummy and lost his topline, and looked very ugly. When I went to lead him out of the stable, he was pretty shaky and found it hard to walk, so we had to take it carefully.

We built up his fitness from leading him out for ten minutes at a time twice a day, to being ridden at walk for thirty to forty-five minutes. By June, he was back competing, feeling as good as ever, and I started aiming him for Burghley. This was a greatly satisfying weekend. Conker finished second, behind William Fox-Pitt on Chaka, and Apple, who had taken all the big fences in his stride, came in fourth behind Karen Dixon on Too Smart – a British top four.

Ferdi Eilberg, my dressage trainer, tells me that this was a real training highlight for him, as neither horse was good on the flat. And, after that other Burghley four years ago, where I'd moved down to second and fourth, here I show jumped clear on both horses to move up from third and sixth. It felt a real milestone.

This Burghley was Conker's purple patch. He was a super horse, but his career was dogged with misfortune, even more than Apple's. I'd bought him as a six-year-old from Clare Rushworth in Cornwall, having been tipped off about him by Hendrik Wiegersma's head girl, Caroline Creighton.

He had been show jumped by Clare. However, when I turned up to look at him, Clare was out, and her groom was clearly reluctant to show the horse to us because he was on holiday, all fat and fluffy.

Clare returned in the middle of this, and was furious that I was being shown a horse that wasn't in absolutely immaculate condition. But it was too late; I was already in love with him. He had a handsome head, long ears and dark brown eyes, and a cheeky disposition. He was a lovely glossy dark brown colour and, in my head, I'd already named him King Kong, which I'd been longing to do with a horse.

He was very green on the flat, but he had an impressive, balanced, tidy jump. His conformation wasn't great – he was narrow chested and his front leg conformation was not good. He failed the vet, which put me in a dilemma because I'd already made up my mind that I wanted him, but eventually I went with my first instincts. Gilly was as entranced by the horse's cheeky character as I was, and she kindly agreed to own him.

Because his jumping was so good, he upgraded quickly to advanced in his first season, and won his first two three-day events, at Osberton and Windsor.

I worked him hard before the dressage at Windsor and we lay third. He was superb across country and show jumped clear to win. However, in hindsight, the ground was very hard, as it often was at Windsor, and he'd felt a bit uncomfortable on the steeplechase phase. After the event, he had heat in his leg and examination by Sue Dyson at the Animal Health Trust revealed a serious tendon injury which put him out for a year.

I took him steadily around some one-day events at the end of 1993, always thinking carefully about the state of the ground before I ran him across country. In the spring of 1994, I took him to the Saumur three-day event. There, his dressage was too excitable for us to be in with a chance of a decent place, but he went well across country and, importantly, proved he had recovered and appeared to be up to the rigours of three-day eventing.

It was such a relief, as Conker was a horse I thought a lot of. Sue Dyson was particularly pleased, as she had predicted that he wouldn't do another major event.

The success at Burghley meant that in 1995, for the first time, I had three possible Badminton horses, and would have to choose two. I definitely wanted to take William there and, for Gilly's sake, I wanted Conker to have his chance to prove himself, especially as he'd been the better of the two at Burghley and had the best dressage. I reasoned that Apple had plenty of Badmintons ahead of him but that Conker perhaps still had something to prove.

Conker did a good test at Badminton, despite a cheeky buck and squeal, but across country he tripped out of the Lake and stopped, putting paid to any hope of a place. However, his tendons were still intact, and that in itself was really the big result.

Apple, meanwhile, had given me a wonderful wedding present by winning Punchestown, which his breeder, Michael McEvoy, was there to witness.

David used the event as an excuse for a stag weekend, and flew with a dozen of his friends to Dublin. They got in a rather bad way on Saturday night and arrived at Punchestown on Sunday morning looking very ill, unshaven and with croaky voices. They were thrilled that I was in the lead, but I think they found it hard to enjoy themselves.

Meanwhile, my hen night was a weekend at the High Bullen at South Molton with fourteen girlfriends. We spent the afternoon playing golf and tennis. Out on the golf course, I went to hit my first ball and found it was a trick exploding one. We had a great fun, girly night with rude presents and party games, like picking up the cornflake packet.

As a result of the Punchestown win, Apple was listed for the 1995 Open European Championships in Pratoni along with William. In August, he was second in the British Open at Gatcombe, behind William Fox-Pitt (on Chaka again). And so I set off for the final trial at Thirlestane Castle in Scotland with my three top horses. It was to turn into a dramatic weekend for horses and humans.

First Conker put in a stop, but I won with William and was second with Apple, who, with a shoe missing, stumbled badly out of the water. At the time, it just looked like a nasty gash. Next day, though, his leg was hot and a scan revealed a suspensory ligament strain. It was yet another setback for him.

At lunch we had been served some chicken that looked and smelled as if it might be on the turn. As I was pregnant by this time, I decided not to risk it, but Mum never wastes anything and so she had some. By the time of my dressage test on Apple, I couldn't find Mum. Someone said they'd seen her sitting on the bank by a loo, not looking at all well. In the distance, I could see some activity with the St John's Ambulance; Mum was lying on a stretcher in the back of the ambulance. She was taken off to Melrose Hospital, where she was diagnosed as having salmonella.

After the wonderful celebrations following my first and second place, I left the event to go and see Mum, who had been told to stay in hospital. But she pulled out the drip and discharged herself, saying that she'd had three days in bed and that was enough. She insisted on driving the lorry all the way from Scotland back home to Devon while I slept and recovered from all the excitement.

The selectors had been keen on Conker for Pratoni, but they'd gone off the idea when he refused at Thirlestane, leaving me free to take him to Burghley. But when he got there, he just didn't sparkle.

His dressage wasn't as good as the year before, and his jumping didn't feel so free on the steeplechase. I was a little uneasy, but put concerns to the back of my mind and set off across country.

It was soon apparent that he wasn't quite right; his jumping felt half-hearted and I considered pulling him up. Unfortunately, I didn't make up my mind quickly enough. As we approached the water at the Trout Hatchery, he began to 'prop' on the downhill slope. He didn't take off at the fence into the water, and I went over his head.

I led him back to the stables and, as soon as I took his bandages off, it was obvious that it had all gone very wrong. Conker's tendon was swelling in front of my eyes, and even his 'good' leg was showing signs of puffiness. In a funny way, I was relieved that there was an obvious reason for his recent lack of enthusiasm, as I didn't want to think that he wasn't enjoying the sport. But it was heartbreaking, knowing it meant the end of his competition career. After time off, he went hunting with Jonny Sumption, a friend who hunts with the Taunton Vale, who'd had a horse from me a few years before.

*

From having three potential championship horses, I was now down to two. Apple was longlisted for Atlanta, and I harboured thoughts of taking him there, because his dressage had improved, his cross-country was good and his show jumping, it goes without saying, was better than William's.

However, by the spring of 1996, Apple was loving the game rather too much. He was now eleven, a fully mature, strong horse, and he wouldn't listen to me when I tried to steady him. In fact, I was becoming quite scared of him.

I rather dreaded riding Apple again. While I was away at the Olympics, I'd discussed the problem with Chris Hunnable and Ian Stark, who both knew all about strong horses. Chris advised me to try his combination noseband, which lies slightly lower and helps to prevent them crossing their jaw, and Ian suggested a Dutch gag with a Waterford mouthpiece.

On my return from Atlanta, I took Apple to Hartpury where he felt unusually wound up, which was most unlike him, and I realised that perhaps he'd been as unnerved as I was. I made up my mind that I'd pull up if he got too strong, and spent a lot of time trying to relax him by riding him around at the start of the cross-country course, and being light with my hands so that he wouldn't try to fight me. He did get a bit stronger on the cross-country, but it was a definite improvement.

Two weeks later, I took him to Thirlestane, where, again, I spent time hacking him about and relaxing him. A hold-up at the cross-country start made him tense, but I kept telling myself to relax my hands, ride him forward and not hook. Fortunately, some of the technical fences on the course made him back off, and we had a great round which gave us the Scottish Open title.

This followed William's win at Gatcombe in 1996 and set me on course for another fantastic run of five successive international wins.

CHAPTER 14

Highs and Lows

Next in the 1996 calendar was Burghley. For me, Badminton is the cream, because it's the oldest and most prestigious event in the world; Burghley has always been secondary, a stepping stone on the way to the big one. But, in truth, that status has been changing over the years since I started competing there, partly thanks to the challenging courses set by Mark Phillips, and it's every bit as big a deal now.

The then director, Bill Henson, was ahead of his time in terms of presentation and innovation, and Burghley has always been one step ahead of the game when it comes to ground conditions. It is now many people's favourite event, and the organisation is always hugely friendly and considerate towards riders and owners.

I'd come close to victory quite a few times, having been second twice, fourth twice, and placed on Boris. When Ginny won it in 1988 on a young Murphy Himself, I'd gone up and congratulated her, as she was an absolute heroine of mine. She told me, 'This'll be you one day,' and it struck me that this might at last be the time.

I was also, though, quite firm in my mind that if Apple looked like returning to his bad old ways, I would pull him up. There comes a point when you have to admit defeat with a horse, and I knew that, as a mother, I couldn't ride a horse that was potentially dangerous.

I knew the steeplechase phase would be something of a litmus test for Apple, and, sure enough, he did get rather fast, finishing well inside the time. There was a long hold at the start of the cross-country, which may have worked in our favour, because he was relaxed and calm when we started off.

We had only one anxious moment, when he tripped slightly coming out of the sunken road, but I was pleasantly surprised at how manoeuvrable he was when I aimed him at the alternative route. He was a little strong towards the end of the course, but not alarmingly so.

We were in the lead; Bruce Davidson, with whom I'd shared the dressage lead, had a cross-country fall, and I just had Andrew Nicholson and Cartoon looming behind me. Andrew rode brilliantly, because Cartoon, though elegant, was not the most extravagant horse, but he did give me some breathing space with a show jump down. Apple also had one down, but we'd done enough to win.

It was thrilling, as I'd always hoped that Apple was a truly top horse; it's just that every time we seemed to be getting somewhere, he'd have an accident.

A week later, there were more celebrations when I won Blenheim on King Solomon. I couldn't believe how quickly my fortunes had revived after the disaster that was Atlanta.

Solly had missed Bramham through some sort of flu virus, but he was at the top of his game, with a second place behind

William at Gatcombe and a win at Thirlestane by the time Blenheim came around.

I took him to Ferdi Eilberg for a final tuning, and Ferdi said that, to get the best out of Solly, I must try and ride him with more courage. I tried to put this into practice at Blenheim, and was rewarded by a really super test. Solly's outline had matured, and his test was expressive and obedient. We went into the lead but, even more excitingly, I realised that I had another potential top horse on my hands.

Blenheim had its sticky moments, though. As I had only the one horse to ride, I decided I could manage to look after him myself for the first two days. I tied Solly up to the lorry on a long rope and, thinking I was near enough to keep an eye on him, went next door to Gilly's 'passion wagon' for a coffee.

Suddenly, there was a terrible commotion. To my horror, Solly had put his foot over the rope and pulled back, giving himself a horrible rope burn. He was slightly unlevel at the start of Phase A, and the stewards were clearly keeping an eye on us. Fortunately, it settled after lots of icing, and he trotted up perfectly sound on the Sunday morning, but I was so cross with myself for nearly scuppering my chances through such carelessness, and felt a complete idiot for doing something that I'd have ticked off one of the grooms for doing.

Blenheim ran an experiment that year, and had the cross-country in reverse order of merit. With more than a hundred competitors, this made for a long and nerve-racking wait for me.

Our round didn't get off to the smoothest start. Solly started to back off the first fence and, with me driving him on, he ended up making an awkward cat-jump. This shook us both up, and we progressed rather shakily, not helped by the fact that the crowd, by now excited at the climax of the day, was running from fence to fence behind us.

I had to take a couple of long routes, which meant that our precious lead was being eaten up with time penalties, but when I took a risk at the last combination and asked him to go the direct route, he flew.

The show jumping phase was particularly exciting, because I was neck and neck with Andrew Nicholson on Dawdle, who was definitely the better jumper. Andrew went clear but, very unusually for him, he had a time fault. This gave me just the leeway I needed to have a fence down and still win.

I didn't realise that I could have a fence, though, until the crowd started cheering and I slowly grasped the fact that I'd won. It was totally unexpected, and even Mike Tucker, who was commentating, seemed to be struggling with the maths.

A huge contingent had come up from Devon to support me, and the party in the lorry park went on for hours. We didn't get back home until midnight.

After all the excitement, David and I decided to go to Morocco for a holiday. Emily, our well-travelled daughter, was going to come with us but, amid everything else, I didn't think about getting her a passport. It just never occurred to me. We got to the check-in desk at the airport, and they said, 'Oh no, you're not taking the baby.' So it was another case of my mother coming to the rescue, and we set off a day later, with no baby!

My successes in 1996 – after the disappointment of Atlanta – put me in second place behind Blyth Tait in the Land Rover World Rankings. This time, the party was in Reims, France, with a visit to the Taittinger Champagne caves. We all travelled over by boat and, again, John Foden had laid on a stunning dinner.

His wife, Pattie Biden (organiser of 'Little Gatcombe'), had been quite ambitious with the flower arrangements. They comprised tall glass vases, a bit like spaghetti jars, with goldfish swimming around. Unfortunately, the flowers at the top of the vase cut off the fishes' oxygen and, very soon into dinner, the fish started to look distinctly floppy. Mayhem ensued, as everyone started chucking out the flowers, scooping out the goldfish and running into the kitchen, where they soon revived in saucepans of cold water.

Solly carried on his good work by winning Saumur in the spring of 1997, despite being chased by a dog on the cross-country. The course went through the main arena, where there was an awkward fence with several angles. It had caused a lot of trouble and, as it was nearly at the end of the course, I was mindful of not blowing it. Suddenly, through my concentration, there was this annoying yapping at our heels. Solly was very good to keep his line.

I had travelled out with Matt Ryan, whose weekend hadn't gone nearly as well as mine, always a hazard that balances the fun of travelling with someone. While Annie made her way home with Solly, I stayed out of Matt's way by travelling with Gilly. She had prepared a huge trifle and I was so hungry that I ate the lot. Gilly couldn't believe that I didn't throw up on the ferry.

Solly had sealed my second five-in-a-row of international wins. It was nearly six. Apple and I finished second at Badminton to American rider David O'Connor on Custom Made.

I was so pleased with the horse that I didn't really mind not winning; I felt the result had sealed his reputation as one of the best horses in the world at the time, and I was really proud of him.

Even more importantly, I had produced another horse suitable for team selection, and was about to embark on what felt like a second career in the British team.

In late August, we were in team training for the 1997 Open European Championships, which were to be held at Burghley in September, when we heard the news about Princess Diana. We all sat around the radio at breakfast, listening to the news, unable to believe our ears.

Back at home, Mum was busy with several foster children and didn't catch the news. Apparently, Dad had heard the headlines while he was still in bed and, as he was walking off for his 8 a.m. 'constitutional', he mumbled to her, 'By the way, Diana's died.'

I was a great admirer of Diana's, and felt shocked, unsettled and empty. A week later, Blenheim, where I was riding King William, was a very strange competition. As the funeral was to be held on the Saturday, it was decided, after much to-ing and fro-ing between officials, that it would be inappropriate to run the cross-country that day, so it took place on the Sunday instead and we show jumped, in an empty arena and a rather weird atmosphere, on Monday morning.

It was to be a tragic weekend at Blenheim that year. On the Sunday, Sam Moore, an Irish rider, died in a fall. His horse chested a brush 'owl hole'-type fence and turned over. It seemed unbelievable that this should happen in the midst of an already traumatic weekend.

*

Not long after this extraordinary period, it was time to head off for Burghley and the Europeans. I was in the pathfinder role again, with new member Chris Bartle on Word Perfect, William Fox-Pitt on his Atlanta horse, Cosmopolitan, and Ian on a classy New Zealand Thoroughbred called Arakai.

We had a bit of a family drama on the Friday. When Emily, who was by now eighteen months, was standing in the lorry doorway, where we thought she was safely out of the way of any horses or vehicles, when a gust of wind slammed the door, trapping her thumbs. Mum had a terrible job to free her, as her little fingers were causing the door to jam. Seeing her screaming with fright and pain, I felt awful. The team competition and my own concerns forgotten, I ran to the doctor, who took one look at Emily's poor little flattened thumbs and sent us to the hospital. She had actually broken her thumbs, but there was nothing they could do except give her bandages and painkillers.

Fortunately I had done my dressage by this stage and the British team was in the lead. Apple then went brilliantly across country, which helped keep up the momentum, as this time the Kiwis were mounted on their best horses and were breathing down our necks.

The course was supposed to be 'three-and-a-half' star, but it caused a lot of problems and both David O'Connor and a Canadian rider ended up in hospital. Chris Bartle was very demoralised about falling 'out the side door' at a coffin fence, but both William and Ian were clear to keep us ahead.

In some ways, the final horse inspection was the most dramatic part of the whole competition, and proved quite controversial. Cosmopolitan wasn't seriously lame, but he didn't look terribly sound either, and our gold medal hinged on him. Bettina Hoy, who was lying second individually for Germany, was in a similar position with her grey horse, Watermill Stream, and both horses were sent to the holding box.

William kept an amazingly cool head during what was a pretty tense few minutes, but when he led up Cosmo for the second time, a somewhat partisan British crowd started clapping, and Cosmo shot forward, all thoughts of lameness far from his head. We were extremely lucky.

Bettina survived too, and ultimately won the European title – Mark Todd took the Open title on Broadcast News – but Philip Dutton's horse was failed by the vets and this put out the Australian team, who were understandably annoyed. It just shows that a trot-up can go either way.

Britain won the gold, quite comfortably, from New Zealand. They'd lost a good score when Andrew Nicholson had to pull out Dawdle. However, it seemed that there was no escape from the show jumping nightmare for me – I had two fences down, which put paid to my individual medal hope. Ian also had fences down on Arakai and, yet again, he and I came in for stick.

Yet again, though, I was to be cheered up after a championship. I took King Solomon to Achselschwang in Germany where an Audi A6 would be awarded to the winner. This was the first time a car prize had been on offer for eventers and it caused quite a stir. I was very excited about it until the show jumper John Whitaker nonchalantly told me that he'd won ten of them!

I also had another distraction, for I was by now twelve weeks pregnant. I hadn't told anyone, apart from David, Mum and Annie, as I felt that I wasn't far enough on for it to be any sort of an issue with the selectors. I wouldn't be nearly as big as I'd been when riding at Pratoni on William two years earlier, and no one had spotted it then.

During the journey, however, I started bleeding. I was obviously concerned about this, but also felt quite fatalistic about it. I couldn't see my doctor, because by now I was abroad, so there seemed nothing for it but to somehow carry on as if nothing was wrong.

Theo and Barbara Steinle, who ran the event, are extremely hospitable people who lay on marvellous hospitality for overseas riders. However, you do need to be in form. We all went to a beer festival and fair. Ian Stark was egging me on to go on the thrilling fairground rides, something he knows that I normally love, and he was somewhat mystified when I made out that I didn't like them.

I was in the lead after cross-country and went, with David, Mum and little Emily, to the event party to celebrate. Again, in normal circumstances, it would have been a great party, but by now I was seriously uncomfortable, and nearly doubled up with stomach pain.

I took myself quietly off to the loo where, after a while, it was quite clear that I'd miscarried. I went back to find David, who was rather enjoying himself, and said, 'I've just had a miscarriage.' At first he didn't take it in, then he realised that I needed to be swept away.

Next day, I felt pretty sore, but trotted the horse up in front of everyone as though nothing had happened. It was a lovely sunny day and, as I'd be last to show jump, David and I went off for a quiet day together. Achselschwang is in Bavaria; it's beautiful countryside and we went off to look at the lakes.

We hired a pedalo boat, and I lay quietly in the back of it as we floated around the lake. It was completely surreal. Here I was in the lead at a three-day event and I'd just had a miscarriage. It was weird and I really didn't know how I felt.

Even more strange, a few hours later I was the proud owner of an Audi A6 (albeit a left-hand drive one which I later sold back to the dealership) and performing a lap of honour in it. The New Zealanders won the informal team competitions, and were given bicycles, on which they chased me around the arena. It so happened that there had been a few events recently where Andrew Nicholson had finished second to me, and he wrote in his *Eventing* magazine diary: *Achselschwang was typical of my year; Mary drove off in an Audi and I rode off on a bike!*

All I could think, though, was 'Gosh, there can't have been too many women who've won a three-day event and lost a baby all in the same weekend.'

CHAPTER 15

Breeding an Empire

I never had anything to do with mares until I clapped eyes on The Kings Mistress (Lily). I had always stuck to competing geldings, probably influenced, in part, by Sheila Willcox, who was never keen on mares either. Then when I got my own place, I felt that having mares on such a small yard was asking for trouble because there can be friction when it comes to turning the horses out in the field, often because the geldings get possessive. There's enough that can go wrong in my sport as it is without having added complication.

So when John Poole and his wife Jane tried to persuade me to look at a four-year-old mare they'd bred, which they thought would be perfect for me, I had no problem refusing. I had wanted a 16.1 hh bay gelding and they were offering me a 16.3 hh mare! Oh, no! Eventually, though, I was passing their yard in Warwickshire and agreed just to have a look.

It was the winter of 1995 and I was six months pregnant with Emily at the time, so John popped Lily over a few fences for me. I had to admit to being impressed. She was gorgeous and elegant, with a superb, natural loose action and a huge jump. She was also very well-bred, being a full sister to the show jumping stallion No Complaints, by Louella Inschallah, sire of several good sports horses.

I persuaded Gill Robinson to take a half-share in her and, after Emily arrived, I started riding Lily in the spring of 1996. She was bold and big-striding and rather towed me along, but it was clear that she had the right attitude and lots of promise. We had a handful of quite successful novice runs and then, later in the summer, we won a novice section at Lulworth on the remarkable score of 10, which was probably some sort of record at the time. Everyone admired her and it seemed that I had a world-beater on my hands. Unfortunately, that was to be Lily's last event.

That winter, we found her in the field with a severed tendon. It was a horrible shock, and I thought we'd have to have her put down, but as she was so well behaved the vet said there was a chance that an operation would work. She spent months in a plaster cast, and it was touch and go as to whether she would be anything other than badly lame as a result. In the end, although her leg looked ugly, she was only slightly unlevel.

I knew I'd never compete her again, but the breeding potential was obvious. However, breeding was completely uncharted territory for me – like most event riders, I've only ever been interested in riding the finished product.

And while I might be interested in knowing how a horse is bred if I've got one along similar lines, or by the same sire, it's not the first consideration when I choose a horse. Conformation, movement and, above all, aptitude, come first. This will horrify dedicated and knowledgeable breeders, but having seen the astonishing differences between the horses I have bred I am sceptical when it comes to the importance of bloodlines. It is no accident that some of the most successful breeders have opted for the most talented riders to showcase their horses.

Bridget Parker, who has bred successful event horses for years, all prefixed 'Cornish', was my mentor in the project. We chose Sarah Bullen's eventing stallion Rock King as Lily's first 'husband'. He was a Thoroughbred, and a magnificent stamp of horse, and I wanted some real quality to balance out the little bit of 'foreign' in Lily, as her sire is part warmblood. Despite the popularity of warmbloods for their qualities of good movement and jump, I still believe the Thoroughbred is the best horse for eventing, for its toughness, speed and stamina, and this has been borne out by the successes at top level of Thoroughbreds such as the four-star winners Moonfleet, Master Monarch, Ringwood Cockatoo plus dual European champion Galan de Sauvagere.

All my foals – except one – have been born at stud, because I don't have the facilities or the expertise to supervise this, especially given that foaling time often coincides with the busiest part of the season, in May. I don't feel I'm missing out – I'm just relieved that it's all being taken care of by experts. My real satisfaction comes in handling them at home and breaking them in. I feel this is the point at which I come into my own, and I do the backing at the end of each eventing season, usually when it's just me working in the yard. Being on my own with them makes me feel that I'm establishing a really special bond with my young horses.

Lily's first foal was Kings Fancy (Nancy), a beautiful, strapping, dark brown filly who looked just like her father, with a white snip on her nose. She is now eleven. The following year, Kings Gem (Gemma) was born, also by Rock King. Oddly, she looks completely different in every way. Instead Gemma is a bright little chestnut who takes after her 'uncle', the show jumping stallion No Complaints.

The sisters went on to have foals themselves, in the same year. When Gemma was two, I got her in from the field because she had an abscess in her foot. She seemed very flirty and 'up for it' so, after puzzling about this, I rang Edward Bleekman at Whorridge Farm Stud and asked if it was possible to breed from such a young filly. He said it was worth a go, and so I took her to Mayhill, Mark Todd's former advanced stallion, who was standing nearby at the Bleekman's.

I put Nancy in foal as well, to Primitive Rising. They both went to stay with Paula Lee, at Nutwell Court, which is where King Boris and King Solomon went for their retirements, and I asked her to foal them for me. Nancy produced a colt, Kings Rock, and Gemma had King Albert. Both are now nine: Rocky is owned by Gill Jonas and Albert is owned by Patsy Mason.

Lily's third foal, Kings Temptress, was by Primitive Rising, and one of my previous owners, Derek Baden, agreed to buy her so that I could keep her. Her birth was somewhat dramatic because somehow we got the wrong due date. I hadn't noticed the telltale signs of Lily waxing up, which means a mare is about to give birth, and she was still at home with me.

I'd gone to an event but when Annie went to check Lily she discovered that she'd had the foal all by herself. We were so lucky, because it was a stormy night and she was still wearing a New Zealand rug, which had a fillet strap under her tail. This could have got horribly tangled up with the foal's arrival, but luckily they had both survived.

Next, Lily produced a lovely colt foal, Kings Command. He

is a full brother to Tess, but completely different. She is smaller and neat and relaxed; he is a big loose-moving seven-year-old whom I sold to Charlotte Martin in 2008.

Lily went to Ireland for a fifth foaling, but she absorbed this one, so I tried again with another visit to Mayhill, but luck wasn't with me for Lily's fifth and final foal. He was a beautiful grey that we called King Silas. However, he looked rather strange and grew very quickly, getting astonishingly tall.

Then, when he was weaned, he started going lame in the field. I suspected wobbler syndrome, and looked it up in my *Haynes Veterinary Manual*. One symptom is wobblers heel, which means horses over-reach (tread on their front heels), even though they're unshod, because they can't control their back legs. Another is that if you stand behind the horse and pull their tail, they'll collapse sideways.

Next day, I went up and tested for these things. To my horror, I looked down at Silas's heels and all four bulbs on the heels were bleeding. Then I did the pulling tail exercise and, sure enough, he started to collapse. The veterinary advice was that the prognosis wasn't good, so I took the decision to have him put down. I felt sad, but realistic.

After Silas, Bridget Parker suggested putting Lily to Kuwait Beach, a successful Thoroughbred stallion whose progeny included Ingrid Klimke's successful horse Sleep Late. The pregnancy started to go wrong, however, as Lily was suffering from lymphangitis. It was manageable, but unpleasant, as her legs were oozing and it wouldn't go away.

I worried about it, because I was due to go on holiday and didn't want to leave Mum dealing with it. I feared that we would probably have to have Lily put down, but the plan was to have the foal and then think what to do when the foal was weaned.

Poor Mum was busy looking after the children, and had gone up to check the horses with them when she found Lily had slipped into a small drainage ditch. Her stiff hind legs meant she couldn't get herself out, and the struggle caused her to kick out some flints which had lacerated her front legs.

It was pouring with rain and Mum knew she couldn't do anything, so she ran to call the fire engine and then went to borrow some straw from the nearby Donkey Sanctuary. Annie came and helped, and the firemen and vet managed to get Lily out of the ditch, by which time Freddie and Emily were sopping wet and shivering with cold.

Lily was clearly not well, and, as I'd said to Mum not to hesitate to have her put down if something went wrong, she instructed the vet to put her out of her misery. I found out when I made my daily phone call home and Emily, who was then seven, answered. She told me in a matter-of-fact way: 'Lily's dead.'

Tess had a baby as a youngster, too: King Casper, who is five now. He is by a little stallion called Med Night Mahout, a little eventing stallion owned by Tessa Spencer. She's a good friend and was one of my travelling companions in the old days, and had asked me to compete him for her. We got as far as intermediate level, at which point I felt that we'd gone far enough, and Tessa kindly offered me a free service. This seemed like a good opportunity to see if I could get a foal out of Tessa, who was a three-year-old, and it was a more economic solution than paying a stud fee.

I also had it in mind that I'd like to breed something for Emily to ride as a teenager, and Med Night Mahout was a nice type, only 15.2 hh and by the good eventing sire Jumbo, who is part Irish Draught.

King Casper grew to 16 hh and is ideal for Emily. She broke him in herself and he moves and jumps well. Emily has now started to event him. He is a good mover, is naturally brave, with a good enough jumping technique, so I hope she will have plenty of fun with him over the next few years.

CHAPTER 16

King Solomon

By the spring of 1998, I had, in theory, the world at my feet, with two top horses to choose from for the World Equestrian Games in Rome in October, where the British team would be defending our gold medal won at The Hague.

Star Appeal was a Burghley winner, a Badminton runner-up and European team gold medallist. King Solomon had won a remarkable three consecutive three-star three-day events. I and my horses were right up there, what could possibly go wrong?

I'd had Solly for five years by this stage. I'd heard of him in 1993 through a friend, Lisa Rowlands, who was working for Mary-Rose Weston near Cirencester. Mary-Rose was pregnant and, as Solly was young and cheeky, she'd decided to sell him.

I watched him in the Burghley Young Event Horse qualifier at Gatcombe. Although he was naughty, I liked the look of him. He was by Old Lucky, and was quality-looking, more of a Thoroughbred type than any of my previous horses. Through the much-publicised championships successes of the lighter-bodied New Zealand and Australian Thoroughbreds, I was beginning to grasp that this was the type of horse I needed to look for: one that was tough and agile and better able to cope with difficult conditions at championships.

The Swiss rider and trainer Tomi Gretener had been to see Solly and really wanted him, and he had first refusal, but I phoned Tomi and pleaded with him to let me have the horse because I was desperate to buy him.

Solly had a habit of lulling his rider into a false sense of security. You'd be thinking what a nice, quiet horse he was, and he'd suddenly spin around and do a huge fly-buck. He didn't manage to unseat me, though, and was obviously rather shocked when I told him off. He stopped doing it after that, although the threat was always there. He knew when a rider was apprehensive and he would take advantage; for that reason, Annie never enjoyed riding him.

Solly was a very different type to Apple and William. He was smaller, at 16.1 hh, and an attractive, well-proportioned, quality horse. He had a big jumping bottom, which was a bit croup high, but he was a smart little horse.

Also unlike Apple and William, he could be spooky at his cross-country fences and was more sensitive. He was never a naturally brave cross-country horse, and was wary of ditches and water. Although he became consistent, he never felt totally confident across country and I had to take longer than I had done with the other two to produce him up to the top level.

However, he had three good paces and a nice athletic jump. As a six-year-old, he won the Frizzell British Novice Championships at Somerleyton, beating Lucinda Murray on Azupa Gazelle, and he was second in good company at Le Lion d'Angers in France.

We went across country there in pouring rain and finished on an equal score with Andrew Hoy on Darien Powers, the horse with whom he went on to win two Olympic gold medals.

Darien Powers was two years older than Solly and had gone faster across country, so he won.

In 1995 Solly and I won the two-star at Compiègne, beating Andrew Nicholson on Dawdle, after which he had some leg trouble and was off for nearly a year.

Solly had his problems. He went through a stage early on when I was concerned that he would become a head-shaker. I'd seen the difficulties Bettina Hoy had with her top horse Watermill Stream at certain times of the year, and Solly was starting to twitch in an ominously similar way.

However, I learned that a fly veil hanging on his noseband would help alleviate it while he was warming up for dressage. Thunder bugs buzzing around his nostrils on a sultry day would always make him twitch a bit, but, fortunately, he seemed to grow out of it.

He also started gurgling and making horrible, alarming noises while going across country. I took him to Geoff Lane at the Langford veterinary hospital at Bristol University, and a soft palate was diagnosed. This was just before Le Lion, so Jeff suggested that, before he operated on our return, I could try the temporary measure of alleviating the problem by syringing 20 ml of glycerine down Solly's throat to help prevent the dryness just before he was put under stress.

I did this immediately before the steeplechase at Le Lion, and it worked a treat; Solly made no noise at all. I squirted another bit in before the cross-country, which probably looked a bit suspicious, although I had told the stewards what I was doing. After that, I did it every time before cross-country. The odd time I forgot, he would make a hideous noise, but the glycerine was so successful that he didn't have to be operated on.

To help work his lungs, I used to trot Solly up lots of hills which, in our part of Devon, go up to 600 ft. The perceived wisdom in those days was that trotting on the road hardened the horse's legs, but I don't do that so much any more, as it is now thought to cause long-term damage. I hope that nowadays I ride better too, in a more measured way across country, which is kinder on the horse's legs.

Sadly, by the spring of 1998, Solly was in the wars again. However, Apple was the first of the two to go lame. I took both horses to Aldon in March and, on checking their legs next day, discovered to my horror that Apple was lame – although, strangely, his legs felt fine – and Solly was sound but had heat in a tendon.

After delivering the bad news to Giles Rowsell, who had taken over from Bridget Parker as chairman of selectors, I took both horses up to Sue Dyson at the Animal Health Trust to be scanned.

By coincidence, they both had lesions to the superficial digital flexor tendon, but what was strange was that in each case the injured leg was externally so different.

The World Games was obviously a write-off now, but then it would have been anyway; I was four weeks pregnant and due to give birth in November.

Embarrassingly, I had just signed a sponsorship contract with the insurers Hiscox, and now I had the awkward job of explaining to them that the exciting horses they'd taken on were lame and the rider was pregnant and out of the British team that year. Amazingly, Hiscox proved very tolerant.

I decided that I would stop competing after Bramham in June, by which time I'd be four months pregnant. I took William there, and not only forgot my dressage test but then had a daft run-out. The papers had a field day with my senior moments, saying 'of course' when they later realised that I was expecting.

By this stage, and in contrast to my pregnancy with Emily, I was feeling rather big and uncomfortable, and was pleased to stop riding. I'd also started to 'spot' during Bramham, and was careful to lie down quietly in the back of the lorry on the way home, but this time all was well.

I had a strangely restful and relaxed summer, probably the laziest time I've ever had. Instead of riding, I got a lot done in the yard; Ascot Timber Buildings, who were a sponsor, changed my stable windows and I did the plastering around the frames.

I was invited to judge the ridden Welsh Cobs at the Royal Welsh Show in June. I still hadn't really told anyone I was pregnant and stood with horror in the middle of the ring as cob after cob came in, showing off the breed's typical high moving trot. They all looked the same. I hadn't a clue how to sort them out into an order and the thought of riding them all was rather daunting!

Fortunately, my steward was very knowledgeable. She reminded me that a lot of Welsh cobs can't gallop properly, and that should be an important factor in my consideration. On that basis, I was able to sort them out a bit. I rode quite a few of them and the crowd was brilliant, really getting behind me and cheering as I galloped past them each time.

It was hard work, though, and, naturally, I ended up putting the favourite in second place and someone else first. The runner-up was not pleased with me, but I had based my decision on the ride, and it was a ridden class.

I also opened a country fair at Southleigh, plus a local hospital fête, and I gave a lecture-demo at Addington with Robert Lemieux and Daisy Dick.

Solly and Apple, meanwhile, were undergoing a new treatment, involving a number of injections into the tendon, and both were put on a strict regime of controlled walking exercise.

Annie had finally left me in order to work at the Donkey Sanctuary. She had been with me for eleven years and needed a change. I understood her decision because it meant she would learn new skills, have more civilised hours and become computer literate, but I was very sad and she was very torn and sat down agonising over a long list of pros and cons.

I'd given the girls time off – my head girl, Becky Buley, had left anyway, to work for Andrew Nicholson and then Mark Todd – and so I was riding and mucking out the horses myself.

While I got fatter and fatter, the horses got naughtier and naughtier. I realised the situation was getting dangerous, and it made me invest in a horse-walker.

At the end of August, tragedy struck. I got a phone call to say that my great friend and former travelling companion Katie Meacham had been killed. She was working at the time for the racehorse trainer Henrietta Knight, and had been so happy there. It was a terrible shock.

It turned out that she'd been checking out a flat tyre on the slip road and, as she was looking down, a car came around the corner and hit her. At the funeral, the Irish event rider Sally Corscadden, who had called her young daughter Katie after her friend, was sitting on the other side of the aisle. She cried so much that it set me off; the pair of us came out of the church awash with tears. Gwen, Katie's mother, was so strong . . . what a huge loss for her, especially as they were wonderfully close to each other. Katie was one of my dearest friends and I knew I'd miss her.

In October, the British team won bronze at the World Games. It had been a nightmare season for lame horses, and neither Chris Bartle, who had won Badminton in 1998, nor Ian, William or Tina had horses available. Only Karen Dixon and Gary Parsonage survived from our Atlanta squad and, with Nigel Taylor and Polly Phillipps, they made up lots of ground in the jumping phases to win the bronze medal behind New Zealand and France.

At 11 a.m. on 10 November, our baby son, Freddie, arrived. He was on time, but that was because I'd elected for another Caesarean, being wise to the fact that this involved lovely soothing drugs and no pushing or screaming. Freddie was 6 lbs 4 oz, a good healthy little baby, and David's father was thrilled with his grandson.

Freddie seemed a much simpler baby than Emily – until he got a cold in January and couldn't breathe through his nose. This meant that he couldn't feed, because he wasn't able to breathe and feed at the same time. I took him to the doctor, who told me that his bronchial tubes were closed.

The poor little thing had to go to hospital to have a tube up his nostrils. The doctors warned me not to listen because he would scream. He had to spend three days in hospital, so I stayed with him. The only good thing about it was that it gave me a chance to catch up with my paperwork, which helped take my mind off Freddie, but I found it a very unnerving experience, seeing my baby so helpless.

*

When I was first married, the half-hour 'commute' to my yard came as a shock. Now, with two tiny children, the strain began to kick in. Again, my wonderful mother came to the rescue. She gave up fostering children and helping with the Guides, and instead devoted herself to her grandchildren, while I restricted myself to five or six horses and just rode in the mornings.

I had to be incredibly organised with my packing each day. When I set off in the morning, I'd prop Freddie up in the front of the car in his chair with a bottle. Ten minutes later, I'd stop to burp him, and then we'd drive on. Everything had to be done on the go, even plugging in my breast pump while I was driving, which, of course, you shouldn't do.

Fortunately, Dad didn't mind staying at home on his own while Mum accompanied me to events. She would drive while I spent time with the children in the back, and then she'd mind them while I was riding.

Mum would leave Dad casseroles that he could put in the Raeburn. While his lunch was cooking, he'd go to the pub for a pint, and after lunch he'd have a sleep. In the evening, he'd make his own bacon and eggs, although he wouldn't worry too much about washing up. If Mum was away, she paid a local farmer's wife to look after him.

Dad enjoyed his grandchildren, within reason, and as they got older they soon learned how far they could go with him. He wasn't the most reliable baby-sitter, though; once, when Freddie was two and a half, we found him sitting calmly on the wall, an unlit cigarette in his mouth!

CHAPTER 17

Tragedy Strikes

The year 1999 was a turbulent and tragic one for the sport, but for one reason and another I wasn't much more than a hapless bystander.

In April, I took King William to Saumur, in the hope of picking up some prize-money, but we had one of our rare mishaps, mainly because I took a bit of a risk.

There was a jump out of a pagoda which was followed by upright rails on a distance of either a short four strides or an open three strides. As I was on William, and he was bold and big-striding, I decided to go on a forward three strides. But we didn't jump out of the house very smoothly and, instead of my reacting to that and holding him for the four strides, I tried to commit him to going forward.

He couldn't do it, and took a real rotational fall over the rails, which was pretty frightening. Fortunately I was thrown clear, but I knew instantly that I'd broken some bones. As I was grovelling around in the dirt, David Green, who is always good in a crisis, rushed on to the scene. I couldn't put my foot to the floor and David was insistent that I got my boot off before the foot swelled. He ran off to get some scissors and cut the boot.

I went to a local hospital, where they told me I'd broken my wrist and my talus, which, rather like the horse's navicular bone, is a low ankle bone. Fortunately, as part of Britain's elite squad of riders, I had BUPA cover, so was able to fly back to England in a little aeroplane.

My wrist and ankle were put in casts at Frenchay Hospital. The doctors were concerned that the blood supply to the talus would cut off and I'd have to have my ankle fused. I said, 'Well, if it's got to be fused, it must be in a riding position: heel down, toes up!' I had several MRI scans to check the healing process, but the surgeon had obviously done a great job because it healed very well.

Because the broken wrist and ankle were on the same side of my body, I had to spend four weeks in a wheelchair. David was busy on the farm, so – as if she didn't have enough to do – Mum now had to look after the children full time. They rather liked me being immobile and a captive audience. Emily enjoyed looking after me, making my food and getting my full attention as I'd watch her trampolining.

Freddie had to stay with Mummy, because I couldn't lift him. He adored her, and would gaze lovingly at her, while I tried in vain to attract his attention and remind him that I was the mother.

With no competing, we took the opportunity to go on a family holiday to Greece with my parents. Freddie spent a lot of time either hung in a bouncer from a tree or having long walks in Mum's rucksack. Dad hadn't swum for years, and was determined to do so. Everything was all or nothing with him and, to my horror, he dived in at the deep end. I was worried that the cold would give him a fit or a heart attack; as it was, he floundered back to the edge. It was the last swim of his life.

At the airport on the way home, David wheeled me into one lift while Mum was sorting out the children. Dad got impatient with her, so squeezed in our lift – and that was the last we saw of the rest of the family for forty-five minutes. Mum's lift got stuck but, fortunately, she had an attendant with her, not to mention bottles and nappies. It's a good job she's so calm!

Due to my injury, I missed the fiftieth anniversary of Badminton, which was won by Ian Stark on the eight-year-old Jaybee. The anniversary was – literally – a damp squib, with terrible rain and mud, and major rows over a temporary new scoring system and also how the course had been roped.

But a week later, it all paled into insignificance when Peta Beckett was killed in a fall at Savernake. I had got to know her on a previous trip to Achselschwang. She was a lovely girl, a former model, and great fun, and the whole thing was made more shocking because she left behind two small children, which resonated with me.

Later on, there was a fund-raising ball for the family. I donated my dressage saddle for auction, and it fetched a reasonable amount of money.

A few weeks later, a friendly and charming young Australian rider, Robert Slade, who had become quite a friend of Gilly's, died from a fall at Wilton.

By this stage, I was out of my wheelchair and hobbling, so I was able to go to his funeral, which was on a beautiful sunny day at Kingston Lisle church near his owners, Jane and David Tolley. The worst part of it was seeing the devastated faces of his poor parents. Only weeks before, they'd flown over for his first Badminton and been so proud of him when he completed.

Gilly gave an address, as did Robert's fellow Australian Clayton Fredericks, and everyone was completely choked by the time we came out of the church.

In addition to these tragedies, there had been a sting in the tail to Britain's world bronze medal. Polly Phillipps's horse, Coral Cove, had failed a dope test, which meant the team would not only lose the medal but would not be qualified for the Sydney Olympics in 2000.

All of this had been concealed from British Eventing officials and members over the winter, and when it came into the public domain all hell broke loose, with everyone blaming everyone else for how the forbidden substance got into the horse's system.

At the front of the firing line were Andy Bathe, the team vet, who had to step down, along with Giles Rowsell, and Polly herself. Polly took the brunt of people's wrath because she had not been suspended and was out there competing still, albeit under hideous pressure.

I had begun competing again, at Montacute, in July, and so came in for the dreadful climax to this saga.

It happened up at Thirlestane, in the Scottish Open Championships, which, like Gatcombe, has the cross-country run in reverse order of merit. There were only a few of us left to run across country when Polly set off. We heard she'd had a fall, and then it all went quiet.

Not realising at first what had happened, those of us milling around at the start of the cross-country felt rather impatient; we were all in with a chance of winning and wanted to get going. But the hold-up continued and then the news came over the loudspeaker that the event was being abandoned due to Polly's death.

Mum saw it. Apparently, it was terrible. Coral Cove, going at speed, took off miles too soon over a spread fence and turned over, landing on Polly. She was killed instantly, and someone then had the awful job of ringing her husband, Vere, who was at a show somewhere else.

It was absolutely shocking. Everyone was completely silenced by it, and I can remember the look on her poor groom's face as they packed up the lorry. It was a desperately sad end to a drama that had consumed the sport all summer.

Two weeks later, another rider was dead. Simon Long, making his Burghley debut, lost his life when his horse Spring-leaze Macaroo tipped over a rail coming out of the sunken road and landed on him. He was a rider who competed for fun and loved his hunting and team-chasing.

The course caused a lot of trouble for riders that day: a couple were taken to hospital and Blyth Tait broke his leg at the same sunken road where Simon died.

By this time, Apple and I were a much more comfortable partnership, though our chance of winning Burghley had evaporated when he tripped coming out of the Trout Hatchery and we went splat. For Solly, however, it had been a four-star run; he went very well and finished fifth. I was pleased with him, for he'd done well to master such a serious course, with three difficult waters in a row plus the sunken road, which was a horrible fence.

I'd had my doubts that Solly really was a four-star horse. Across country, I had to be constantly behind him, urging him to jump the fences and giving him encouragement, something I wasn't really used to after being towed around by Apple and

William, who, provided you steered, would just keep powering on.

In contrast, if you just sat there on Solly, there was always the chance he'd stop, and so I had to be confident and brave myself. I always felt that the only reason he got as far as he did was through trust. Our relationship was different to anything I'd experienced with my other top horses, because I felt I was contributing more to it, and that was very satisfying.

It was just as well that Solly was beginning to come into his own, because in the autumn of 1999 William pulled himself up on the cross-country at Blenheim – something he'd never done before and a sure sign that he'd had enough. During his career he'd won loads of one-day events, at which he excelled, becoming the first horse to win more than 2,000 horse trials points. The decision to take him down a level had proved massively successful in 1997, when he came sixth at Punchestown, third at Blenheim and won the international one-day event at Chantilly in France. Mark Todd was riding a new horse, Stunning, that day, and they had a fall which resulted in Mark getting a stud hole to the head. As he was in the lead on his second horse, I had to confess that I hoped he might stand down from that ride but, being Toddy, he just wound a bandage around his head and carried on. However, he did have a stop, and William and I won.

William was given to Annie in his retirement, which was appropriate as she adored him and had been one of the most constant, reassuring presences in his life. He was the soundest horse I have ever had, so it was ironic that a couple of years into his retirement he sustained a cut in the field which became infected and led to his having to be put down. It was a very sad and ordinary ending for such an extraordinary horse.

CHAPTER 18

Sydney Olympics

After celebrating the Millennium at a ball thrown by Paula Lee's parents, followed by a few days' skiing, my thoughts turned to the 2000 Olympics and a new chance to win a medal. I was confident that, provided the spring went well, I'd be guaranteed a place at Sydney, as I'd been listed with both horses.

My chance was quickly halved, though, when Solly had heat in his leg before Badminton.

Everything therefore hinged on Apple. We were fifth after the dressage but, as mishaps befell some of the leading riders, Apple and I found ourselves in the lead at the end of cross-country. We finished inside the time and just overtook the long-time leaders, Leslie Law and Shear H2o. However, we didn't have a fence in hand for the final phase.

It was a slightly fraught Badminton. We were staying, as usual, with Sarah Gerald, who had been a chalet girl with me in Zermatt, but Emily had chickenpox. She was really suffering and on the Saturday night she was at her worst, itching like mad.

I had been up all night, trying to comfort her and feed her Calpol, but even if I hadn't, I doubt I could have slept. I was really worried about show jumping clear. I couldn't bear the thought of losing another major prize in the show jumping arena.

King Kong on his way to winning Windsor three-day event, 1991. (*Peter Ayres*)

Unauthorised water skiing during the 1991 European Championships
at Punchestown.

William was the most stunning-looking horse.

New star arrives. King William loves to show off and he and I are in perfect step at the Badminton trot-up, 1991.

We did it! The dream now realised thanks to King William, Badminton, 1992.

Before it went wrong - the ill-fated British Olympic team after the trot-up at the Barcelona Olympics, 1992: Richard Walker, me, Ian Stark (with daughter Stephanie) and Karen Dixon.

David makes a great cushion for Karen and me during a quiet moment at the Barcelona Olympics.

Golden Girls. Left to right: Karen Dixon, me (on King William), Tina Gifford, Charlotte Bathe winning Team Gold in the Hague, World Championships, 1994.

Showing off my world gold medal with King William's owner Gilly Robinson, my staunchest supporter.

My brother Simon's miracle moment, 1993. (*Evening Echo*)

My parents,
Jill and Michael
Thomson, on my
wedding day in
June 1995.

Above: A very
happy day —
I become Mrs
David King.

On Star Appeal, my new team horse for 1997, at Badminton with William Fox-Pitt, my team mate and friend, on Cosmopolitan.

Press conference at Badminton with my daughter Emily, aged one. Eventual winner David O'Connor (middle) and Ian Stark interviewed by Julian Seaman.

Winning moment! Star Appeal clears the last fence at Badminton, 2000.

Sydney Olympics, 2000 – the squad: Yogi Breisner, Jeanette Brakewell, Tina Gifford, Pippa Funnell, Leslie Law, Karen Dixon, me and Ian Stark.

However hard we tried, Star Appeal and I couldn't make any headway on the medals at the 2000 Olympics in Sydney. (*Kit Houghton*)

Mum was watching anxiously in the stands when four-year-old Emily, oblivious to the tension of the moment, insisted on spending a penny. Mum had to take her round the back of the stand, so she missed seeing my round.

To my great relief, poor Leslie had a fence down but, in the end, we didn't need the leeway. Apple rose to the occasion brilliantly. He jumped beautifully, only tapping the last part of the treble, which stayed up. I waited for the crowd noise to tell me what had happened, and the wall of noise made it quite clear that I'd won the first Badminton of the twenty-first century.

Unusually for me, I was quite tearful – I am not a 'weeper' when I win things – and it was the first time I'd seen Mum cry, too. I felt overwhelmed by the fact that, in the eight years since my victory here on King William, I'd got married, had two children – I was the first mother to win Badminton – and proved something to all the people who doubted I'd come back.

Leslie remained in second place, his best Badminton result, and Rodney Powell was third on Flintstone. It was a British one-two-three and, as Leslie pointed out to the press, this time no one could criticise our show jumping performances. Sydney, here we come!

Olympic preparations got under way in earnest when the horses went into quarantine in Eddy Stibbe's yard at Waresley Park in Bedfordshire. Eddy is Dutch and rides for the Dutch Antilles. He lives for the sport, being incredibly generous to fellow riders and playing a high-profile part on their behalf. Although he was nearly fifty-two at the time, he was still planning to compete at Sydney.

My then head girl, Becky Ball, stayed with Apple, while

I commuted between Waresley Park and home. I knew I had five weeks away in Australia coming up, and didn't want to miss being with the children beforehand. I was also worried about Mum. She was having a hard time with Dad, who had become very ill – one night she was up nine times in all – and she had become run down as a result.

Although Waresley Park had wonderful facilities, I was amazed by how quickly I got bored with hacking around 100 flat acres. After all the Devon hills and space, I felt quite enclosed.

We had a new British team regime by now. Mandy Stibbe, Eddy's ex-wife, had become chairman of selectors and both she and our new Lottery-funded performance manager, Yogi Breisner, were popular with the riders.

Yogi, who is Swedish and had trained with Lars Sederholm at Waterstock, had only a short time to get to know us before Sydney, and he much took the attitude that we were responsible adults who knew our horses and what we were doing, which was refreshing.

We left for Sydney on 24 August. At first, we stayed in the Olympic Village, but it was some way from the equestrian site at Horsley Park, on the west side of the city, and so we moved out to Panthers Hotel for the competition which was nearer.

Despite the detailed quarantine restrictions – we were forever disinfecting and changing our clothes – we had plenty of fun. The weather and food were fantastic and the Australians couldn't have been more welcoming. Team spirit, however, flagged slightly behind the scenes. The day after we arrived, while out on a hack, Flintstone spooked, shot up a bank and then slipped. Rodney fell off and broke his ankle. It should have been his first Olympics, a just reward for many disappointments, and we felt desperately sorry for him. He was, though, very good about it all, and was soon resignedly cracking jokes and being the life and soul of the party.

After this, Tina Gifford, who was reserve with The Gangster, a horse on whom she'd won team gold at the 1999 Europeans, thought she might get her chance to run. Instead, to her dismay, it was decided that Ian Stark should be allowed to ride in both the team and individual competitions.

We understood that this was Ian's last championship after sixteen years in the British team and at the top of the tree, and that after all he'd done for the sport he deserved his chances, but it did alter the atmosphere in the camp. Ian was emotional about it being the end of his career and, unusually for him, kept himself to himself, spending more time with his owners than us. For me, this was a shame, as we'd been team mates for a long time and some of my best memories involved spending time with Ian.

As in Atlanta, there were two competitions, team and individual. Apple was fifteen by now and getting slightly creaky, so I quite understood that the younger horses would go in the team, while we would run in the individual contest. In fact, I was happy about this because, having won Badminton, I felt quietly hopeful about my individual medal chances.

Leslie was chosen for the team on Shear H20 with the other three members of the reigning European gold medal team, whose triumph at Luhmühlen in 1999 had qualified Britain for Sydney: Jeanette Brakewell as pathfinder on Over to You, Pippa Funnell, the individual gold medallist on Supreme Rock, and Ian as anchorman on Jaybee.

The team competition was a real thrill, because Jeanette, Leslie and Pippa went clear across country – Ian did his best to avoid a rather dramatic water fall, but succumbed – and they won silver, thus ending Britain's humiliating Olympic medal drought. Deservedly, they received a great deal of praise for their spirited riding, even though they were initially disappointed at not being able to overhaul the Aussies in the show jumping.

But it was strange for me, watching them all do their bit from the sidelines and knowing I'd be doing it in a few days' time. Apple was very confused; he could hear all the loudspeakers and wondered why he wasn't doing anything himself.

Normally, he was never one to get excited in a dressage test – he didn't really get lit up at any time. I could always rely on him to be accurate and secure, and that was how he gained his extra marks, through his calmness. He worked in beautifully before his test, and when I went in, I thought, *This is it, the next few minutes are the most important of your life.*

We halted, saluted and tracked right, all as planned. The next movement was a medium trot across the diagonal . . . and Apple suddenly went into canter. He broke four times into canter going across the arena, when he should have been trotting.

The rest of the test was ragged and flat and there didn't seem to be any way of rescuing it. We finished in a hopeless thirteenth place. I felt heartbroken because I knew I'd blown any chance of a medal.

The cross-country courses, designed by Mike Etherington-Smith, were beautifully built, big, solid and decent tests, with serious waters. The team competition rode well and the optimum time was achievable. Because they had been built, quite rightly, to cater for all nations, the individuals course was unlikely to play into the hands of an experienced cross-country horse like Apple; my fellow individuals, Ian on Arakai and

Karen Dixon on Too Smart, were in the same boat.

I had a fantastic ride, clear inside the time, and with just one show jump down, we pulled up to eventual seventh place. It was so frustrating. I was despondent that I'd had the chance to go to three Olympics – three more than most riders ever get to and still couldn't get it right. It didn't seem possible that I had any hope of still being at top level by the time Athens came around in four years' time.

In my gloom and disappointment, I was so looking forward to going home. I'd been sending Emily and Freddie regular postcards, and now I was desperate to see them. As soon as the competition was over, David and I flew straight back to England.

Another urgent reason for getting home was to see my parents. My father, who was seventy-two, had been in and out of hospital all year. A bad bout of flu in February had weakened his heart.

By November, he was in hospital and in a very bad way. One night, I found him crawling up the ward, so after that we made sure that either Mum or I remained with him every night, taking it in turns to sleep on a lilo on the hospital floor.

It was during my shift that he died, on 18 November. Mum had just gone home and had taken her first mouthful of lunch when I had to ring her to say he'd died. His final week had been terrible; they'd taken him off his medication, and we knew it was only a matter of time.

It was desperately sad, the end of a life that had promised so much and gone so badly wrong. But, for Mum, it marked the end of a forty-three-year struggle. Without her, I could never have had my career, and now I hoped she might have more freedom to really enjoy it.

CHAPTER 19

A Test of Nerve

The King family had a rough time of it in 2001. The year got off
to a bad start with Britain's farming industry – and, indeed, the
business of horse trials – paralysed by foot-and-mouth disease.
Then in May I had a fall which nearly ended my career. In fact,
I was lucky that it didn't end my life.

The foot-and-mouth outbreak was worrying for us because
David's cattle-dealing business came to a standstill, as did life
generally. The farm was, thankfully, just outside an infected
area, with the main road outside acting as a barrier, but the
county of Devon was badly affected. Everywhere there was the
dreadful smell of burning pyres of cattle carcases. Our animals
survived, which was obviously a great relief, except that there
was no compensation for months without any business.

David's father died not long after mine, and we were almost
thankful that he didn't have to see the disasters going on for
our farming neighbours because he would have been so upset.
It was a tough time for David. But, as always, he kept calm and,
if he was worried, he didn't show it.

I had been harbouring a plan to take King Solomon to Kentucky in April for the four-star event there, as the spring horse
trials season in Britain and Europe was a washout. Hacking out

was obviously restricted, but I would drive him over to trainer Stuart Pike's racehorse gallops to keep him fit.

A few British-based riders did go out to the States, but they had to be brave and go straight into a four-star without a one-day prep run. My idea was to try and get to the States earlier, so I could do a one-day event, but in the end quarantine restrictions put paid to that idea. As a result, months went by before I was able to compete again.

Towards the end of May, by which time a staggered start to the British season was in view, I was riding a sharp young horse called King George, who was rather good at bucking. I'd taken him to a nearby field for a canter and, as he felt fresh, I thought I'd get his back down by trotting him briskly around the field. I then pushed him on into canter, and he was being very good when a pheasant suddenly flew up out of the hedge. George shot sideways in fright, and I was thrown off balance, making me rather crooked and loose in the saddle. Startled by my shift in weight, he could feel that I wasn't sitting square and, before I could regain my stability, he began bucking violently, like a bronco, with the intention of getting me off.

He succeeded. I fell off head first, with the top of my head meeting the ground first so that my head whiplashed forward. George then galloped off, tail in the air and stirrups flying, back to the yard, while I lay very still and took stock of my predicament.

My immediate concern was that I had pins and needles shooting up my hands and arms, and I knew I'd done some damage, though I could at least move my legs. I tried to get up, but, alarmingly, I couldn't lift my head off the ground.

After a bit of wriggling around, I rolled on to my side and

pushed myself up, supporting my head in my hands. I had a pain between my shoulder blades, which made me think I might have chipped a vertebra.

I walked gingerly back to the yard, where I found George just standing there, wondering what to do. I tried to take his bridle off, but my arms wouldn't go up high enough to undo the throatlash.

When I phoned Annie at the Donkey Sanctuary she immediately whizzed down, untacked George and took me to Exeter Hospital. I was extremely uncomfortable by now. Every bump in the road hurt, and I sat tensely on the edge of the seat as I didn't seem to be able to sit back.

At the hospital, they immediately immobilised me, but after looking at the x-ray they said I had no fracture, just a whiplash injury at the back of the neck. They gave me a soft neck collar to wear and told me to come back in a week's time to see the consultant.

I felt sore and tight, but the discomfort did ease and I started riding again. I had to – I was endorsed by Strongid-P, a Pfizer worming product, and they had arranged a photo-shoot. I explained to them that I was very stiff, but we carried on and Annie took the horse down to the river for me, where they did shots of me riding in and out of the water. By this stage, my neck actually felt reasonably good, so much so that I almost didn't bother to go back to Exeter for the check-up.

I was late for my appointment, so I ran recklessly into the hospital from the car park, only to be brought up very short. The consultant looked at my x-rays, turned to me and said, 'This is a good broken neck. Your C5 vertebra is fractured; in fact, it's in half. I hope you haven't been riding!' I admitted

I had, because I'd been told there was no fracture.

He said the initial diagnosis had been a mistake, and that my head was very insecure and resting on strained ligaments. Of course, my head *had* felt loose, but I'd told myself not to be silly, and that I was imagining it.

The consultant sent me away in a beastly stiff collar and told me to stay quiet for the next two weeks. Towards the end of the fortnight, I could feel a bit of a lump at the back of my throat, which made me uneasy. I wondered if I was imagining that, too, but the prominent bone at the back of my neck was definitely becoming more prominent and felt as if it was sticking out. In addition, my tongue was painful and swollen because I'd bitten it in the fall, and a bit of that was hanging off. Eating was uncomfortable and I couldn't really chew solid food.

When I went back to hospital for the follow-up appointment, Mr Chan, the surgeon, pinned up my x-rays on the wall, shaking his head as he did so. I could tell by his body language that things weren't good. It was horrible seeing that the bone was coming out of the front of the line of vertebrae so that my whole neck seemed to be collapsing forward. This was so shocking that I came out in a clammy cold sweat. The blood seeped away from my head and I could feel myself fainting, so I sat down hastily.

Mr Chan said he wanted to operate on me straight away and that I was to stay in hospital overnight for an operation the following morning. He planned to take some bone off my hip to fuse the neck vertebra, and warned me that this would be painful.

I felt terribly shocked and shaky as I phoned David to tell

him what was happening. I couldn't bring myself to ask about my riding career, but I was wondering to myself if this was the end. It was a bleak few hours.

When I came round from the operation, my first thought was that my hip wasn't sore after all, which I was soon told was because, when they opened me up, they discovered that the vertebra was so shattered that they couldn't graft it back together.

Instead, they took the vertebra out, removed the discs above and below it, and broke it up even more. They put it in a wire mesh cylinder and then slotted it back in, plating it to the vertebrae above and below. In time, they said, the bone would produce more bone and it would fuse together naturally.

Eventually, I asked, 'What about my riding career?'

Mr Chan said, 'How many times have you fallen off?'

'Hundreds,' I replied.

'And how many times have you hurt your neck?' he asked.

To which I was able to reply truthfully: 'Only this time . . . so once.'

'So then, the risk is minimal,' he said. 'But if you do have a fall, there will be a little more pressure on the joints above and below the plated area.'

He went on to explain that it would be my nerves that would decide if I was able to continue competing, and that the decision about that was in my head, not my body. He advised that, if I was really that keen to continue riding, I wasn't to get on a horse for eight weeks – and not to fall off for ten!

I felt so elated and relieved that I actually did as I was told, though this was partly helped by the fact that, due to foot-and-mouth, there were few events on anyway. My first outing was

Wilton in July, where I showed Andrew Nicholson my scar – a very neat job, cleverly placed in a crease in my neck. Andrew said, 'Well, that'll save you wearing a necklace!'

Fortunately, the accident didn't dent my confidence, though it did make me think. I suppose it is always in my subconscious. Even now, when I fall off, if I have time as I sail through the air, I think to myself, *My neck, my neck!* And it's the first thing I check.

I owe a lot to Mr Chan, who is a world-renowned surgeon. Much later, I was teaching on the Isle of Man when I met a man who had a trapped nerve in his neck, which was restricting his life. I phoned Mr Chan there and then, and fixed the man up with an appointment. He went and had an operation, and it has changed his life.

There were very few events that summer but Burghley did run, thanks to the Herculean efforts of organiser Bill Henson to secure funding from supporters of the sport.

I took Solly and Apple. Solly went clear across country but, unbelievably, I managed to fall off Apple at Capability's Cutting. We were going well and confidently when he left a leg on the first part of the fence and threw me forward. I fell off, and Apple galloped over me. He couldn't avoid me and trod on the outside of my thigh, his studs giving me a real V-shaped cut and digging out a lump of flesh.

So there I was in hospital yet again, this time having eight stitches. Poor Mum was torn in two, because Freddie, aged three, had chosen the moment of my fall to get stuck in a tree. She was busy watching me and hadn't noticed that Freddie, who was never terribly interested in the horses, had managed to get quite high up this tree next to the ten-minute box, from which he had to be rescued.

I was oblivious to this particular incident, but I did sometimes make mistakes when distracted by the children. I would sometimes hear them crying in the background and then find it hard to concentrate on my dressage test or walking the course.

For the most part, however, they were extraordinarily well behaved. Mum always managed to keep them occupied, but they were good at entertaining themselves, too. For a long time, Emily's preoccupation was with creating a jumping course made out of whips and buckets. She would run around jumping this for hours – just like I did as a child.

I decided to show jump the next day at Burghley – the wound was on the outside of the thigh, so it wouldn't be affected by the saddle. This caused a bit of a fuss with officials, but I was determined to jump Solly as we were well placed.

There were two jumping rounds at Burghley that year, because it had been decided that this would provide useful practice for the new competition format that had just been announced for the Athens Olympics in 2004.

Unfortunately, this didn't really work in my favour. I jumped clear in the first round, and under normal circumstances would have been second. Sadly, I had two fences down at the second attempt, and ended up in fourth place behind Blyth Tait on Ready Teddy.

At least Britain won the informal team competition – myself, Pippa Funnell on Cornerman, William Fox-Pitt, who was then riding Simon Long's former horse Springleaze Macaroo, and Vere Phillipps, who was successfully eventing his late wife Polly's horse, Coral Cove.

*

The next weekend was Blenheim, to which I took a nice young horse called King Richard (Ricky). He went clear across country, and I set off back for Devon, on a somewhat mad outing, to go to a friend's fortieth birthday party that Saturday night. Keith Authers, David's right-hand man on the farm, kindly drove me back up to Blenheim at 4 a.m., but after all that Ricky failed the trot-up because he had a painful bleed under the sole of his hoof.

He was a nice horse, with a great character – his party piece was to show his teeth when you said 'Smile' – but his career later ended sadly. I rode him at Burghley in 2004 where there was an upright gate with an arch over it and he caught his stifle, as did a few other horses apparently, and chipped a bone.

A year later, he was still unlevel, with a suspected pelvis injury, and I steeled myself to have to put him down. But when I went to a dressage lesson with Carl Hester and told him what I was fearing, he suggested that he would take Ricky as a nanny for some young horses.

After he'd been with Carl for a year, I got a phone call: Ricky appeared to be sound, and would it be all right for a friend of Carl's to hunt him. I agreed, with the proviso that I would have him back if he appeared to stand up to work. The friend reported that he wasn't level on a ten-metre circle, but he was a wonderful hunter. I was just thrilled that it had all worked out so well.

The year ended as badly as it had begun, with yet another drama. It was 23 December 2001, and the children were really excited about Christmas. Although we could have moved into the farmhouse after David's father died, it was right beside the main road and we decided it would be easier to stay put. I have to admit that our bungalow was pretty basic; because I'd always secretly hoped to move, I'd never done much to it.

The bungalow had a huge attic, where I kept loads of stuff. The baby kit was up there – just in case I wanted another one! – along with all my Olympic memorabilia. And during the winter my good competition tack was stored up there, because there was no security in my yard.

I'd always been conscious that the recessed lights in the kitchen ceiling would get very hot, but that was yet another domestic detail that I did nothing about and, as I went to bed that night – around midnight, after wrapping the last of the Christmas presents – I noticed a particularly hot smell, as if I'd left the oven on, but I checked and it was off.

David was already asleep as I clambered in beside him. Two hours later, I awoke to hear what I thought was a loud hailstorm. I lay there listening for a moment, until I suddenly realised that the noise was a crackling fire. I leapt out of bed, my brain struggling with the frightening realisation that we were sur-rounded by smoke.

David was in a deep sleep, as were the children – Freddie's room was next door to us and Emily's room was up by the kitchen, where flames were licking through the ceiling. They were all in a complete turmoil as I shouted, 'Grab the children!' I now understand how people die in their beds from smoke inhalation; even though you're in terrible danger, a soporific feeling comes over you and you're tempted just to lie there.

As we all ran out of the house, wearing nothing but night clothes and coats, the kitchen ceiling came crashing down. It was a freezing, crisp night, but we'd managed to pick up the car keys and a mobile phone, so we sat in the car at the bottom of the lane with the engine running for warmth and phoned the fire brigade. I was desperate to go back in and grab my handbag and briefcase, but David wouldn't let me. Instead, we just sat in the car and helplessly watched our house burn. It was quite surreal.

I'm not the sort of person who does 'distraught', and once I knew we were safe, it all seemed really quite exciting and interesting. The children absolutely loved it – they were waiting for 'Fireman Sam' to turn up! When the fire engine did arrive, it got stuck and the firemen had to run up the drive with their equipment.

By now, it was 4.30 a.m. and too early to phone friends. The firemen helped us collect a few extra clothes and we went to the local Travel Lodge, where we booked in and, amazingly, slept soundly. Next morning, though, our throats felt tight, which was a sobering reminder of our lucky escape.

We found our house in a very sorry state. The remains of my tack – bits of charred leather and saddle trees – were spread all over the garden. The attic was, by now, completely cindered, and there was a huge amount of smoke damage to curtains and clothes. Unfortunately, the scruffy kitchen units weren't badly damaged enough to warrant an insurance claim.

The main concern, though, was Father Christmas. How would he find us? David's brother-in-law and sister, Geoff and Carina Persey, who live in a lovely big house near Cullompton, invited us to stay and the children left a note for Father Christmas saying, *We're now at . . . and please bring our presents there!* Miraculously he did – fortunately, I had put the presents in a separate place and they escaped being burned.

We stayed with Geoff and Carina for two weeks, then spent the next year renting various cottages – one of which was great for me, being just down the road from the yard in Harpford. We had to move out of one house on the day before Burghley. I was frantically scrubbing it, because it belonged to friends and I wanted to leave it spotless, but I remember David had another day there and I was worried that he'd make a mess!

Buying new tack was a bit of a nightmare, but Cliff Barnsby, my saddlery sponsor, was a great help. We managed to salvage a few items of clothing that weren't too smoky, surviving for the rest of the year on one bag each – which just goes to show that it can be done if you have to.

The final house, before moving back into the bungalow, was David's father's farmhouse. It was strange living there, because it was permanently lit up from the roundabout and the birds sang all through the night.

In the meantime, we took the opportunity of upgrading the bungalow, applying for a loft conversion, opening up some of the rooms and putting in double glazing. It was quite exciting, as it had been rather a plain farm bungalow before. At least the fire galvanised us into doing something about it.

CHAPTER 20

Olympic Success

As we shakily entered 2002, Solly was my main hope on the competition front. With two good Burghley results behind him, I hoped that would be good enough to get me back into the British team for the 2002 World Equestrian Games in Jerez, Spain.

Apple had been retired, aged sixteen, after our Burghley mishap and had followed William by going to Annie. She was married by this time, to Jonty Corbin, and it meant that they had two horses to ride out together.

My grand plan for Solly, however, didn't quite come off. When the vets examined him in the ten-minute box at Badminton, he showed a fibrillating heart. I was so shocked, because he had felt fine to me as we trotted around the roads and tracks, but clearly we couldn't continue and go across country after a result like that.

A fibrillating heart does not have to mean a horse's career is over, but obviously the incident made Solly less attractive to the selectors. They made us non-travelling reserves for Jerez, where the team won bronze and Jeanette Brakewell a deserved individual silver. I missed out, but at least this left me free to take him to Burghley again, where we finished third.

I had a fall on my other ride at Burghley. Ryan, a big chunky brave horse owned by Nick Engert, had previously been ridden by Graham Law and was a new ride for me. I had space for another four-star horse, so, when I was offered him, I thought he might be an interesting horse to have and wanted to see what I could do with him.

Ryan was powerful and a super show jumper, but a little numb in the mouth. Our round at Burghley was going quite well, but then he landed steeply in the Trout Hatchery and couldn't help crumpling forward.

The following spring I got Ryan qualified for Badminton 2003, which I was excited about. I took him for his final run at Weston Park, by which stage he was looking much more streamlined. In fact, he looked superb and so fit that I was thrilled with his progress.

He felt like a machine as we set off across country, but then, as we approached the seventh fence – a plain, steeplechase-type obstacle – I suddenly felt him slow up about five strides out, which was not like him at all. He jumped the fence and landed, but very slowly and laboriously, with an oddly rolling gait.

I thought, *Oh no, he's pulled a muscle behind*, and pulled him up to walk. He still felt all right, so I didn't think to get off but simply loosened his girth and started walking resignedly back to the lorry.

Suddenly, he staggered and, as I leapt off, he went down on to his knees. I thought, *Help, he's going to die*. It was horrible; he looked at me and whinnied. It was heartbreaking, because I felt so helpless. He tried to sit up, but then lay down flat, panting, and eventually he shuddered horribly and was dead.

It was surreal. There I was, in the middle of the cross-country course, with a horse who looked beautiful – fit, shiny and freshly clipped – but dead. Then everything happened very quickly: people rushed over to help and get the tack off, and the horse ambulance arrived to take him away.

I went back to the alone in absolute dread. The Engerts adored this horse, but they were away in Thailand. At least it meant they didn't see him die, but I would have to ring them to break the news.

I spoke to their daughter, who was shattered. I felt awful, having to tell them that kind of news on their holiday. The family was really knocked back and, for me, it was a horrible experience and one I hoped I'd never go through again.

And so, yet again, Solly was my sole top horse, even though I knew in my heart of hearts that he wasn't really a Badminton horse. He was a super horse, but he was careful and cautious by nature. If you got in front of the movement with him across country, he could stop. This meant that I had to always be sitting behind him, and sometimes my hands were on the buckle end of the reins, which I know looked a little hairy. Nevertheless, I felt I should give him a chance to prove himself.

As we were going around the roads and tracks, I was still feeling quite indecisive about running across country. It was wet and, for once, thoughts about my responsibilities towards my two little children kicked in, and I wondered if I was really being wise. However, Solly surprised me by coping well and rising to the occasion. We finished fourth, which was very pleasing and certainly more than I'd expected.

Despite Solly's undoubted four-star consistency, we were only made reserves for the 2003 European Championships at

Punchestown. I was disappointed, but aware that Solly's style of going across country didn't always engender confidence in watchers.

So I entered him for Burghley, yet again, and when it didn't look as if I'd get the nod for Punchestown, I started in the dressage phase. We only scored 51, which was nothing like the best we could have done, and I felt rather demotivated about the whole scenario.

I was late in the day to go across country, and spent a lot of time sitting in the competitors' tent, trying to rev myself up and be competitive. I noticed that Tina Cook (née Gifford), who had been selected for Punchestown with Captain Christy, had had a fall, but she got up and I didn't think anything of it.

When I heard a call over the tannoy for Lucinda Green, chairman of selectors, my mind began to tick slowly. Next thing, there was a tap on my shoulder, and I was informed that Tina had, in fact, been concussed and would have to stand down from Punchestown. Would I come instead?

Immediately, I asked if I would be in the team or an individual. I was told that I'd only be an individual, so I did have to wrestle with the decision as time ticked nearer to my cross-country start time. I wasn't too thrilled about being only an individual, but, on the other hand, I wasn't exactly going to win Burghley either with that dressage mark.

Eventually, I decided to try my luck at Punchestown; it was worth the gamble. As always, Gilly was very good to go along with my decision, as she was never all that keen on the added formality of championships, where owners can be sidelined.

The squad was to stable at Blenheim the next weekend, and set sail for Ireland early on Monday morning, and the plan was that I'd travel with William Fox-Pitt in his lorry.

However, nothing is straightforward in this sport. Tina managed to get the decision about being stood down reversed, thanks to a note from another doctor. This put the selectors in an embarrassing position, because they'd asked me to withdraw from Burghley. It was all a bit of a stalemate, with neither of us keen to give way. The situation resolved itself when poor Polly Stockton's horse Tangleman went lame at the last minute, meaning that both Tina and I could go, as individuals.

On Monday morning, William and I loaded up, with Solly in the space in the lorry between William's horse, Moon Man, and all our equipment. Solly can be a bit odd about travelling, so William was driving extra carefully.

Suddenly, there was a crashing noise. Solly had stuck out a hind leg, in order to stand square and balance, and had pushed out the loose rubber of the partition. His foot had gone down through the foot pad of William's quad bike, which was in the next partition. Any sudden movement, and he could slice a tendon – or even break his leg.

William was brilliant and calmly took charge, eventually managing to undo the levers of the partitions, although we phoned the fire brigade for extra help and paged Jenny Hall, the team vet. It was a relief when we were finally able to move the partition so that Solly could lift his leg out safely at a vertical angle.

Solly was a bit sore; he'd rubbed the hair off his leg and had a sore patch on his pastern. Jenny Hall treated his leg and was happy about us progressing on the journey. We rearranged the lorry and carried on, but it was a horrible journey for me (and I expect for Solly, too) as I was wondering whether we'd get all that way and then be unable to run. However, Solly came out of the lorry amazingly well.

It turned out to be an exciting competition, with course designer Tommy Brennan again producing some dramatic fences, including a precipitous slide down between waterfalls. There were several water fences, and plenty of dramas, including one for the British team when Jeanette had a surprise fall with Over to You. They are normally such a faultless pair, so the team had to work that bit harder for their gold medal, and Leslie did a brilliant job as pathfinder – the only rider all day to finish inside the optimum time.

Solly and I finished fifth, and I found the whole experience rather dispiriting. I felt a bit left out of the celebrations – not that I really was – and yet I was the third best Brit behind Pippa and Leslie and, had I been in the team, would have contributed. I know I was the oldest – by a distance – but it was even more deflating when I saw myself described in the press as a 'veteran'!

The following year, 2004, was an Olympic year, and the selectors gave me a bye for Badminton. I was rather pleased about this, partly because I felt Solly deserved the recognition and also because there was no doubt that the course there would have been a stretch for Solly.

Innocently, I assumed this meant that I was a certainty for Athens – my fourth Olympics! But when the shortlist was released, I found, to my shock and horror, that I was only a reserve again. Three of us had been named as reserves, with no hierarchy between us, so I wasn't even first reserve.

I realised that at no point had I actually been told that I was on the team, but I had assumed that the consistency of our results would have been enough. Yogi Breisner was clearly embarrassed when he had to talk to me about it, as he had said before Badminton that it would make no difference to my position whether I ran at Badminton or in the World Cup qualifier at Chatsworth a week later, and I had taken that to mean that we were going to be chosen for the team.

I spent an anxious summer, trying to be philosophical, telling myself that it wasn't the be-all and end-all of everything, but of course I desperately wanted another Olympic chance, and it niggled away at me.

As team training went on, I was at least promoted to first reserve. This is an unenviable position, as you can't help but hope you'll get a run, but you know if it comes it will be at someone else's expense. Nevertheless, I tried to remain pragmatic and reasoned that if I didn't go, we could head back for another shot at Burghley.

When we arrived in Athens, Solly and I were immediately segregated into the reserve stables. This was a new and unwelcome Olympic experience. The reserve stables were near the airport. It was scruffy, with rats scuttling around the stables and planes zooming noisily overhead, and the hacking was limited, though there was a huge outdoor school.

The other riders went off to the Olympic Village, while I stayed in the Team GB lodge with the team officials. That at least wasn't such a bad experience. I was given a nice hire car so I could take my groom, Andrea Kerlin, out – she was staying in dressage rider Emma Hindle's lorry – and the team would come over and socialise in the evenings. The lodge was the place where they could meet up with their families, and it was fun;

everyone was very friendly, and I began to feel the tension of my situation evaporate.

I lived in this limbo-like state for about a week, as the competition got closer and closer. Each day I worked Solly, who felt fine, and I started to relax. Will Connell, our chef de mission, had kindly managed to get me tickets for the competition and I felt I was now here for the beer and might as well enjoy my Greek holiday.

Two days before the Olympics began, I was driving back to the lodge when my mobile went off. It was Yogi: 'Mary, we need you.'

Sarah Cutteridge's (now Cohen) mare, The Wexford Lady, had gone lame. It was terribly unfair; she is a great rider and team player. This should have been her first Olympics but, instead, it would be my fourth, which must have been very hard for her.

My emotions were mixed at this point. I wasn't at all psyched up to the idea of competing in an Olympics and not even sure if I really wanted to do it any more. The other part of me, though, felt so lucky and excited.

It was panic stations on the admin front, as the first horse inspection was to take place the following day. Andrea and I had to get accredited, and Solly and The Wexford Lady had to swap places. This was an awful moment, as Sarah's groom was so devastated, and Andrea and I had to hide our excitement.

It had become Team GB policy not to let athletes who were performing early go to the opening ceremony but, as I'd been before, I didn't mind, and we watched it on television at the lodge. Then, the competition was upon us.

*

The Olympic eventing format had changed yet again ahead of Athens. It was now one competition, with five riders in a team; everyone was competing for both team and individual medals, but the top twenty-five had to show jump a second time to decide the individual medals. This format satisfied the diktat that the second medal would be for a separate performance.

The team consisted of the by-now regular quartet of Pippa Funnell, Jeanette Brakewell, Leslie Law and William Fox-Pitt, plus me. I was third to go for the team, by which time a strong wind had whipped up. It made the heat bearable, but was not conducive to good dressage tests.

Solly was, however, very good and quiet. He made a few little mistakes but, generally, I was quite pleased. I was less than pleased with the mark, however. It was in the early 50s and, as he'd previously scored in the early 40s and even late 30s, I was disappointed and felt the judges had been hard on him.

Thanks to the others, though, most notably Pippa and William, we were just in gold medal position, ahead of the French and Germans.

The cross-country – built by Albino Garbari, the Italian who did Pratoni – was fascinating, and completely different from anything we'd seen. It was on a strip of beautiful green grass, which seemed to spring out of the dusty, rocky surroundings. The going was so good that we walked it barefoot, the grass feeling luxurious underneath our feet.

Basically, the course went straight up and down this strip, with a U-turn at the top. Although a lot of riders thought it lacked technicality and scale for an Olympics, there was still a lot to jump in a small space.

I always worried about water with Solly, as he tended to be slow jumping into it, and the first water complex, at fence 6, was a real eyeful. You went up a bank, over a log, down a slope, over a rolltop into the water, and then over two angled boats in the water.

There was a lot to jump there and we debated as to whether I should take the direct route or go round. As I waited my turn to go across country, I was relying on instructions from Yogi. We were also in unknown territory because this was the first 'short format' Olympics – no roads and tracks or steeplechase – and no one had really learned how much warming up we needed to do. There were galloping strips provided, but not a massive amount of room.

Jeanette was first to go. She was worried about a narrow fence in the shape of a Greek urn, where she felt Over to You might get away from her and leave a leg. She was right to be worried – it caused falls for Andrew Hoy and Andrew Nicholson – but taking the long route cost her time penalties.

Leslie also went clear but, again, with time penalties, and he had a lucky escape when Shear L'Eau scrambled over the boats.

Then it was my turn, and Yogi told me I had to go all the direct routes, because he didn't want any more time penalties on the team score, particularly as other riders were achieving the time.

Despite the pressure, I had a lovely ride on Solly and finished four seconds inside the time. I felt an overwhelming sense of relief, which is unlike anything you might feel following a performance which is just for yourself, like Badminton.

The responsibility of a team place is massive; you're desperate not to let your team mates down and, at an Olympics especially, your performance feels much more important to you. It's about the whole of the British Olympic team, the government money which has funded you, and the millions of people watching on television at home, and it can weigh so heavily that you almost wish you weren't there. I was also desperate to prove that the selectors had made the right decision in including me on the team – I didn't want anyone to think that my reserve status was justified.

Despite five clear rounds, our lead began to slither away. Pippa's Primmore's Pride, a magnificent, long-legged galloping horse who had won Kentucky and Burghley, was not at all suited to this winding, narrow track. The proximity of the crowds made the horse pull even more – I had considerable sympathy, remembering my awful experience in Barcelona – and Pippa had no option but to slow the horse and get time penalties, or else she could have had a fall.

William, our ever-cool anchorman, did a brilliant job to keep us in the running, Mary Guinness's wonderful little horse Tamarillo, who had won Badminton that spring, skipping around as if it was a pony club course.

The team had slipped to third place by this stage, which didn't entirely impress the mainstream newspaper journalists who had travelled out from the centre of Athens to, hopefully, see Britain win a gold medal, but William, ever the articulate diplomat, gave some great interviews saying that we were still fighting and that, with our good show jumping record, we could still win the gold.

Half an hour later, that possibility became even more remote when Tamarillo went lame, and x-rays revealed a chipped stifle.

He was our best score and, without him, we would be pushed to get a medal at all.

For William, it was unspeakably awful. His only previous Olympic experience had been our dreadful week in Atlanta, and he was as eager as anyone to atone for previous disasters. On a personal level, he was clearly in a position to win the gold medal and no one deserved it more. He is the best rider in the world and he adores Tamarillo.

I was on the beach with David and Emily when we heard the news. The short format cross-country had been so short that the phase was done and dusted by lunchtime. Normally, Olympic cross-country day is an epic, draining occasion; this felt rather shallow by contrast. One minute we were Olympic athletes, the next holiday-makers. It was very odd.

That evening the team slumped. We felt really dull. Yet again, as a nation, we'd blown the Olympics, and much gloomy introspection took place. We could win European gold medals like falling off a log, so why couldn't we do it on the world stage?

Yogi was great at rallying us. He pointed out that we weren't that far off the medals, and that there were two rounds of show jumping, which could change everything. How right he was.

After several lean years, the Germans were in the lead, having gone brilliantly across country. They had celebrated noisily on site at the event, toasting Chris Bartle, their team manager. We felt very envious.

Even though they lost Ingrid Klimke's horse at the horse inspection – it was lame, having slipped on a bend at the top of the course – they were still strong without her. The French were in second, with Nicolas Touzaint, the reigning European Champion, at the head of the individual table, and the Americans had gone well, too.

Solly was sixteen by now and, although as a young, spooky horse he'd been a careful jumper, he'd become more casual as he got older. I had to try and increase the power in him to get him off the ground and keep him making a good shape over the fences, but he still had two fences down, including the last, a set of planks. I was so disappointed; I expected four faults, but had hoped for no more. However, the course caused a lot of trouble and we were by no means alone in making errors, and I still had the third best score of the team.

When Pippa and Leslie jumped clear and the USA's Kim Severson had a fence down, we secured the bronze medal. I was watching in the stands with Ken Clawson, desperately trying to keep up with the scoring. When I realised that I'd at last won an Olympic medal, and genuinely contributed to it, it was very exciting.

Bronze certainly wasn't the colour medal we'd gone to Athens for, but, in the circumstances, the relief was overwhelming. To me, it seemed like the best thing in the world, although Alice Fox-Pitt – who had worked out that William could have won gold – was, not surprisingly, very down.

Little did we know, an extraordinary drama was unfolding . . .

Bettina Hoy was the penultimate rider in the arena in the team round. I didn't notice her mistake, but the show jumper Nick Skelton, who was standing next to me, cottoned on immediately and muttered, 'My God, she's gone through the start twice.' A real murmur went up, because all the German show jumping team realised as well, but nothing happened about it, mainly because a volunteer 'button pusher' spotted Bettina's mistake and, thinking they were doing the right thing, restarted the clock. Germany were therefore announced as the gold medallists, ahead of France and Britain.

But enough people with an interest in seeing the anomaly rectified made a noise, and so the Olympic officials issued a shock announcement that Bettina had, in fact, incurred 14 penalties – 4 for a fence down and 10 for time – due to her circle at the start. The Germans were thus demoted to fourth; the French would take the gold and Britain the silver! But before anyone could say anything, or even think about celebrating, an inquiry was announced. It was all terribly dramatic.

Only three riders per nation were allowed to jump in the second round and, although Jeanette had finished below me, Yogi asked whether I would mind if she jumped instead of me, as Over to You was a more consistent horse than Solly. I didn't mind in the slightest; I knew I had no hope of an individual medal, and was feeling thrilled with my team medal, whatever colour that might turn out to be.

I skipped off to the international supporters' tent. All the Brits cheered as I came in, someone handed me a drink and I got stuck into the business of serious partying. Then the mobile rang; Yogi again.

The rules weren't clear and it turned out that I *did* have to jump: only the top-placed three riders were eligible and you couldn't pick and choose. I was rather thrown; I'd had a couple of glasses of wine, the horse had gone back to the stables and been untacked, and I hadn't a clue about the new course.

By this stage, the competition was within minutes of starting and I couldn't walk the course properly. I started to run around it, but was asked to leave, so I had to run around the edge of the arena, hopping and jumping to look over people's heads, as there wasn't a single gap where I could stand and watch.

I felt like laughing. I'd never been so unprepared at a championships – not that it really mattered in this case. However, I didn't want to make a pig's ear out of it and get eliminated. We got through it, but it wasn't my finest hour – the fences had been raised and we had three down.

Good old Leslie, though, jumped a double clear, one of only two riders to do so. It was a tremendous feat of horsemanship on a horse that arguably wasn't the world's most confident jumper, and it was exhilarating to watch as he rose up the order towards the medals.

No one knew whether Bettina would jump in her demoted eighth place or in second. In the end, she appeared as second to last to go, looking grimly determined. When Nicolas Touzaint demolished the course, the gold medal was hers, with Leslie in silver. The mumbling began almost immediately, though, and I think poor Bettina knew she was doomed.

The medal ceremony was very special, even though we were back in bronze position, the team silver seemingly no more than a fleeting glimpse. The atmosphere was a bit strange as, obviously, some people were highly dissatisfied with the proceedings – not least the French, who at one stage thought they were gold medallists. The press conference was an awkward affair; we were all pretty bemused, except for William who, again, was the model of articulacy, despite his own disappointment, and said that we were delighted with the bronze and not expecting anything to change.

As far as I was concerned, the situation was closed and

I returned to England with a bronze medal. It was, therefore, an astonishing moment when, three days later, we heard that the Court of Arbitration for Sport, which met in Athens, had found in favour of the French, British and American teams. They upheld Bettina's mistake, which meant that Germany would lose double gold and that Britain, at last, had a gold medallist in Leslie Law — thirty-six years after Richard Meade at Munich! To add to our haul, Pippa Funnell now had the individual bronze, behind Kim Severson.

In no time at all the bronze medals were whisked away. I was competing at a horse trials in Brockenhurst when I had to hand it over. Six weeks later, we received our rightful silver medals from the Princess Royal at Buckingham Palace, in front of all the other British Olympians.

It was the culmination of a British athletes' bus parade, in which Leslie was honoured, at last, with the National Anthem. Although it might have been better if we'd received the medals at the right moment, in Greece, this was in some respects even more special, as it was in front of all the other athletes. Our achievements in Athens meant that eventing had accounted for 10 per cent of Britain's total medal haul, an amazing statistic which put our sport right at the forefront of the news, even if it took a controversy to achieve it.

For me, though, whatever the rights and wrongs of a hot and dramatic night in Athens, which continued to be debated fiercely for many months, it felt like a major milestone. Olympic success had eluded me for so long that it just seemed fantastic to get a medal of any colour.

CHAPTER 21

Cavvy and Caffrey

Two weeks after Athens, I found myself a spectator at one of
the saddest days in the sport. Though I didn't have a ride at
Burghley, I had driven up to see sponsors, and so spent cross-
country day watching the closed-circuit television in the riders'
tent. The atmosphere was tense because, even before the competition started, riders had been requesting that the steeplechase
phase be reduced in deference to the sticky ground. The weather
was hot and humid, and the ground felt dead and holding
underfoot, but, controversially, the officials refused to make
the changes riders requested, despite being asked daily, and, as
a result, the feeling on cross-country day was almost one of
hysteria among riders.

The cross-country course was a long one, with some tough
fences towards the end, and this, too, had been questioned. As
the day unfolded, it turned out that riders were right. The
taxing steeplechase phase was taking its toll and horses were
finishing the endurance phases tired, in some cases disastrously
so. There were quite a few falls, and several horses clearly
weren't enjoying themselves.

As I watched, I was half wishing I was competing and half
thankful I wasn't. I don't know how I would have reacted if I'd

been riding. Probably I'd have stood back and waited to see how things unfolded. I've never been one of the most prominent riders politically – I'm not a great one for standing up at meetings and complaining; when there's been a controversy, I'm afraid that I've always rather let others take the lead. Because he's so articulate, William Fox-Pitt often gets dropped in it when riders want a point made, and he and the rider representative Eric Smiley really took the brunt on this occasion.

When I saw Caroline Pratt fall, near the end of the day, I knew instantly that she had been killed. Her horse, Primitive Streak, had been going well, but he caught his shoulder on a fence in the last water complex, rotated over it and landed on Caroline. We all gasped when we saw that terrible, fatal splash. The cameras cut out, but we all knew instinctively what had happened and an awful, tragic chill settled over everyone present.

Feelings ran high in the stables that night and an emergency meeting was called between riders and officials. As a result of that day, rules have been put in place to ensure that, in the case of another such controversy, there is a fall-back committee which must be heeded by officials.

Caroline's funeral in Cheshire was terrible. Not only was she a lovely girl, but she was also an excellent rider. The fact that such an accident could happen to a professional rider left everyone shaken.

I didn't know her that well, but I liked her very much and I felt particularly sad that, after years of her slogging away, she'd finally landed some great backers in the form of Dick and Frances Kinsey, and some good horses to ride, none more so than the first horse she'd piloted around Burghley that fateful day: Call Again Cavalier.

*

I'd been following the progress of Call Again Cavalier for years, because he'd been produced in the West Country by Vicky Brake, and I thought he was a terrific little horse. Vicky was put on a provisional longlist for the Athens Olympics with him at the end of 2003, but she knew he was a valuable horse that she couldn't afford to keep, so she'd put him on the market at the start of 2004. Yogi Breisner had phoned me up to see if I'd be interested, as this was a horse the selectors wanted to see remain in British ownership, but I didn't have an owner with that sort of money.

After Burghley I wondered who would get the ride on Call Again Cavalier. I'm sure most riders were, like me, thinking what a lovely horse he would be to have. I was aware that I was now weak at the top level, with Solly having come to the end of his career, and I did consider writing to the owners, saying will you consider me, but I felt I couldn't do that. Caroline's death had been such a shocking tragedy that things needed to settle down, and I felt the owners should make up their own minds what to do.

A few months later, I was up at the yard and my mobile phone rang. It was Yogi, saying would I consider taking on Call Again Cavalier! I couldn't believe it. I was overjoyed, and when I put the phone down, I was so excited that I jumped around like a child. I was about to go away with David for our annual break, this time to Goa, and I almost didn't want to go because I couldn't wait to get the horse in my yard. I was also looking forward to meeting the owners, Sue and Eddie Davies and Janette Chinn.

Eddie is a very successful businessman, the owner of Bolton

Wanderers Football Club, and he and Sue live on the Isle of Man. They are competitive, but true sporting people, and, as I was to find, riding for them would be a terrific experience.

Sue's daughter, Janette Chinn, was also a part owner of Cavvy, and while I was away on holiday, I got in touch and arranged to meet her in Cheshire the day after I got back.

I spoke to a few people about the horse first, including Vicky, who warned me not to over-bit him. Janette said there were two things I should know: first, that 'Cavvy' didn't seem a big mover and that his extended trot was fairly non-existent; and, secondly, that he wasn't particularly fast. Both Vicky and Caroline had given him a beautiful ride across country, but I noticed that both had incurred quite a few time penalties on him.

However, when Cavvy arrived at my yard in January, he immediately exceeded expectations. He had plenty of trot movement hiding. He didn't really work properly through his body, but after some experimentation, I discovered that he had a beautiful extended trot.

He also had plenty of speed. He was capable of galloping really fast, but the problem was that, when you set him off in top gear, he had a tendency to run at the fences through the bridle. This made it difficult to be accurate as a rider and would result in him sometimes standing too far off the fence, or else getting alarmingly close.

At my first competition with him, at Tweseldown, I just couldn't stop. We were so out of control that it wasn't fun at all; it felt dangerous. A few weeks later, we went to Belton, where the owners came to view for the first time their horse with his new rider. As we set off, I felt all eyes were on me, but it was going reasonably well, until he started fighting me on the approach to a narrow fence. He ran forward and caught a leg on it, dislodging me in the process.

Cavvy then merrily galloped off into the distance and, feeling a complete idiot, I ran after him. Someone caught him and came running towards me leading him; to my huge embarrassment, it turned out that someone was Vicky Brake. I can't imagine she was too impressed. I felt I had really let the side down, and my new owners were visibly disappointed.

Yogi consoled me by saying, 'Don't worry, it's the best thing that could have happened. He needed to hit a fence to steady up, and you needed to learn more about him.'

We went to Badminton, amid considerable expectation, but, again, I didn't have enough control and actually felt quite scared. It had been about ten years since the alarming days of Star Appeal, and I'd grown accustomed to King Solomon, a horse that had to be encouraged across country rather than charging off.

We somehow got around most of the course unscathed, but when we came to a double of offset logs near the end, I lost my steering. I was struggling for control, Cavvy was blithely running on, and we missed the fence and ran out. This was frustrating, but I was aware that it could have been a worse result and just hoped the Davieses would manage to be patient with me. Next day, Cavvy did a clear show jumping round, so I knew that I had a good horse, but it was obvious that I had to sort out the bitting arrangement.

I tried different nosebands, mindful that I had been warned not to over-bit him, but ended up using an American gag with a cherry roller mouthpiece; once he was wearing that, I could just leave him alone. When I did pick up the rein and ask for control, Cavvy would give it to me because he respected this bit.

*

Despite our Badminton mistake, the selectors were interested in us as a combination for the 2005 European Championships at Blenheim, although our lack of form meant we would compete as individuals and not in the team. My immediate reaction was that I'd rather go to Burghley and have a chance of winning some decent prize-money. I was fairly sure that we didn't have much chance of an individual medal at Blenheim, and Sue, Eddie and Janette were happy with this.

Burghley was notable in 2005 because it was to be the last time long format – roads and tracks and steeplechase – would be part of cross-country day. The change had been triggered by the necessity to simplify the Olympic eventing competition, but it had led to a huge amount of debate for and against, with many diehard eventing people feeling this was the beginning of the end of the cross-country being an influential part of the competition, and modernisers arguing that the extra phases were obsolete.

Personally, I didn't mind at all about losing the steeplechase. It was my least favourite part of the competition, one I always found nerve-racking, as I always worried about having a fall. I also felt, like many people, that horses might last longer if they didn't have to do so much extra mileage.

Unfortunately, my last steeplechase ride turned out to be memorable for all the wrong reasons. I've never been a great one for wheeling and measuring the steeplechase and working out where the minute markers are. I'm afraid I usually ask someone else who knows, and I also rely on myself just sensing how the time is going. On this occasion, though, I got to the halfway mark and suddenly realised I was way too slow. It was too late to make up the time, and, with a sinking feeling, I heard that I'd earned a stupid four time penalties, which was a ridiculous error to make.

I felt absolutely suicidal. The feeling of idiocy bugged me the whole way round Phase C. I was so embarrassed and dreaded getting back to the ten-minute box and seeing everyone. Eddie and Sue Davies were very good about it, but by this stage they must have been wondering if I was ever going to deliver the goods.

Cavvy was clear across country and, again, clear in the show jumping, and we finished fourth. William Fox-Pitt won on Ballincoola and I pored over the final results sheet with dread, fearing that I'd find out that I could have won had it not been for the steeplechase penalties. Fortunately I wouldn't have been better than third.

Burghley 2005 signalled the end of an era in the sport with the loss of the endurance phases which had made cross-country day such an intense test and earned event riders and horses respect for their toughness. On a personal level, though, I was happy about it. Horses like King William, Karen Dixon's Get Smart and New Zealander Vicky Latta's Chief, who went on and on competing at four-star events without suffering any lameness, were exceptional and certainly not the norm.

The mileage involved in long format had been tough on many horses and, with them becoming more and more precious in value, there was a limit to how often you could compete in such events. The new, short format would mean that horses could have more high-profile outings, which meant better value for owners and more fun for the public.

My main worry was whether the cross-country phase would

be still kept long and hard and properly influential. I felt quite strongly about that, all the more so because, in the beginning, this wasn't the case. Course-designers were nervous, most notably at the Athens Olympics, which was too easy and short. It seemed so shallow: that big day, gone in a flash. Now, I've got used to the idea, and have to admit that it's a relief not to have so much to think about.

Two weeks after Burghley, I heard that William Fox-Pitt had had a heavy fall at Gatcombe horse trials. He'd been knocked out, which meant that he wasn't allowed to compete at Kreuth, in Germany, the following week, and to my excitement, he asked me if I'd deputise for him on a horse called Birthday Night. I was thrilled. Chance rides don't really happen to me – it was people like Mark Todd who used to get asked to take over rides at short notice, and I felt particularly honoured that someone like William thought I was good enough to take on one of his horses. I think he thought we were similar in our cross-country styles in that we both tend to let the horse gallop on and neither of us is that demanding of a horse in front of the fence, leaving the horse alone to do his job.

Birthday Night's owners, Sir Michael Turner and Jane Walter, came out to Germany and were very friendly, making me feel that I was under no pressure. I'd only ridden the horse for a few days at home and found him quite difficult on the flat. He was safe and genuine across country, but not a natural careful jumper in the show jumping phase.

In Kreuth, I managed to squeeze a reasonable dressage test out of Birthday Night, and, though it rained and rained, he went clear and inside the time across country. However, I knew show jumping was his Achilles heel, and I wasn't too optimistic. But it was decided the show jumping phase would take place inside because the arenas were flooding, and this worked in my favour because it lit the horse up. The arena seating went up very high and the whole atmosphere was electric. Birthday Night became sharp and alert, and his whole body suddenly came alive. He jumped a clear round – I think that was probably sheer luck – and we came second, which was lovely. I was so relieved that I hadn't disgraced myself on someone else's horse.

I was also competing a horse called Apache Sauce (Caffrey) at Kreuth, who finished seventh. He was a bright chestnut, white faced, nine year-old that I'd had for a couple of years. Originally he'd been ridden by Chris Johnson, a well-known trainer in Devon, but Chris felt he'd gone as far as he wanted with Caffrey – who was a difficult young horse, quite scatty and a real redhead, and he wanted to stop eventing himself – and so he told Gill Jonas, his co-owner, that he wanted to sell his half.

When Chris had asked if I'd be interested, I went to take a look and quite fell for Caffrey straight away, even though he was very badly behaved and had a tendency to charge at fences with his head in the air. But I liked his slightly Roman nose, and characterful demeanour, and I was also thinking that he might be a suitable horse for the Engert family to own, as I'd been looking for a horse for them since Ryan died.

I agreed to have Caffrey back at my yard to assess him. I could tell there was a lot of work to be done and I wanted to see if it was worthwhile. I was worried for the Engerts that it might not work out, but in the meantime, Gill Jonas decided to take the plunge and own him entirely herself.

Caffrey was the sort of horse that every so often I'd think we had reached the limit of his capabilities, but he would somehow keep going and produce something that made me decide it was worth persevering. At first, he was very difficult in the dressage, being easily distracted and upset. He was also an awkward show jumper; he would stick his head in the air and we had some disastrous rounds in the early days.

But he was an amazing cross-country horse, so quick-thinking, tough, sound and with a real will to jump whatever was ahead of him. We had a hilarious moment early on, at Tweseldown, when I fell off him. It was at fence 8, where there was a step down and a couple of strides to a house. Instead of taking the two strides, he took off on one and sprawled over the house. Then, having got rid of me, he belted off back to the lorry park, on the way jumping fences 7 and 6 backwards. The lorry park was incredibly full, but he worked his way through it until he found our lorry, and trotted up the ramp, much to the astonishment of a groom who was plaiting another horse. I realised then that he had a brain and there was something special about him.

CHAPTER 22

Best of British

The end of 2005 saw the first proof of real success with my modest breeding programme. Kings Fancy (Nancy) – Kings Mistress's first foal in 1998 – finished eighth at Le Lion d'Angers, a prestigious two-star competition for seven-year-old horses. It's a real showcase for youngsters and the emphasis is very much on breeding.

Few riders breed their own horses, and so the result was that much more special and, to my amazement, won me the British Breeders' prize for the best British-bred young event horse. I received the trophy at their annual dinner and couldn't really believe I was there; this kind of prize usually goes to a big-time breeder like Sam Barr or Vin Jones, and for a rider to be up there is almost unheard of.

In the spring of 2006, Nancy's career, and mine, very nearly ended in a ditch. It was her first advanced competition, at Withington. Nancy was a little green on the approach to the rails and ditch complex, and, to make matters worse, pulled off a shoe on take-off. She flipped over, landing with her body and three legs in the ditch and with one hind leg sticking out. Because she couldn't get any purchase with this one free leg to push out, she was stuck.

Officials told me to keep clear, as she might kick me, but I could see what needed to happen. I knelt on the ground and pushed with all my strength to get the spare hind leg in the ditch so that she had some grip. After that, she was able to push herself out. In hindsight, it was a disconcerting accident; if I had landed underneath her in the ditch, the consequences could have been serious but, in this sport, it's no good dwelling on what might have gone wrong or you'd go nowhere.

Nancy recovered well from this drama and finished second at Punchestown two-star. But then she went lame a couple of months later. There was nothing to show externally, but she was persistently unsound, so I paid another visit to Sue Dyson in Newmarket. Sue found that Nancy had a carpal bone in her knee that was becoming sclerotic – in other words, changing in consistency – and the prognosis was very poor.

Sue always tends to paint the bleakest picture, which in a way is a good thing, because you know it can't get any worse! She predicted Nancy wouldn't event again and, indeed, when the mare went lame again the following winter, I was quite philosophical, took her shoes off and decided to start thinking about breeding from her in the spring.

However, horses will always surprise you. Nancy had been out at grass with some young horses in the valley. After dropping the children at school, I'd go to feed them and Nancy would come galloping down to greet me, slipping and slithering quite healthily, so I decided I'd get her shod again and have another go. Amazingly, she hasn't been lame since.

Another chance ride came my way in the spring of 2006. The selectors had asked me not to take Cavvy to Badminton as, having finally produced the goods at Burghley, we were in contention for a team place at the World Equestrian Games in Aachen, Germany, that August, and they wanted me to save him.

My initial reaction was obviously relief and delight that I was back in the running for the team, but also disappointment that I wouldn't be riding at Badminton. It is still my absolute favourite event, it's the ultimate competition and the one that means most to me, and I hate to miss it, almost more than anything else. So I joked to Yogi, 'You'll have to find me another ride for Badminton, then!'

I didn't think any more about this, however, and was on a family outing on Mothering Sunday to the Bedford Hotel in Sidmouth when the phone rang just as I was walking in. It was Yogi, asking: 'Do you want a ride at Badminton?' to which I replied 'Yes!' without even asking what the horse was.

Terry Boon, a successful rider based in Leicestershire, had broken his leg the previous year and, while it had healed, he felt it wasn't strong enough for him to ride two horses at Badminton, and he wanted to concentrate on one of them, Foreign Exchange, on which he had won Bramham the previous year. His other ride, Cashel Bay, was therefore going spare.

Yogi put me in touch with Cashel Bay's owner, Sue Wilkinson, and I agreed to try the horse at Belton and take it from there. Cashel Bay was another strong bay horse, but I felt I'd ridden enough of that type to be able to cope. Knowing I rode very differently from Terry, who is much more precise than me, I hoped that it might work.

My word, the horse was strong! I came down the centre line

in the dressage and nearly carried on straight out of the arena. I just couldn't stop him and, in fact, I never succeeded with him on the flat in the way that Terry had done. However, I liked what I found across country; the horse was powerful and strong, but I tried to leave him alone and it seemed to work.

The dressage was another matter, though, and I struggled. I was having help at the time from Carl Hester, Olympic dressage rider, and his partner Spencer Wilton, and they too found the horse difficult and admitted defeat. Sue Wilkinson was so disappointed, and she was such a lovely owner, that I thought surely there must be something I could do. Ferdi Eilberg, my long-time trainer, was busy as performance manager to the British dressage team, and it was difficult to get a lesson, but I flung myself on his mercy.

Ferdi was brilliant. He got on the horse, something he rarely did, and said, 'I see what you mean!' He went and got out an elevator double bridle with a long shank, and we did the curb chain up tight. It had an immediate effect; Cashel Bay respected the bridle and worked far more nicely, which was a huge relief, as I had visions of being carted straight out of the arena at Badminton.

We scored 56 in the dressage, which wasn't horrendous, but it was a year when quite a few riders were going clear across country inside the time and I knew I wasn't going to pull up a huge amount in the rankings.

Cashel Bay was very genuine across country, and we finished eighteenth overall. I felt it had been an interesting experience. Though I wasn't prepared to commit myself totally to Cashel Bay, I agreed to ride him at Burghley. On the way, we were third in a CIC three-star (international one-day event) at Hartpury and we finished tenth at Burghley, which felt like a major improvement. Sue was over the moon.

Caffrey, meanwhile, went to Punchestown in Ireland. The weather was horrendous. It rained and rained, so much that the stables flooded and, on Sunday, prize-giving had to be held indoors. The going on the cross-country was bottomless, and it completely turned the dressage order upside down.

I'd sent Caffrey to Lizzie Murray, an international dressage rider, because I'd seen the good effect she'd had on William Fox-Pitt's Ballincoola, who was also a bit of a hothead. I'd been having trouble with Caffrey's flying changes, because he tended to explode, but embarrassingly, he was a changed horse when he came back from Lizzie's!

We lay third after dressage, but were still miles behind William Fox-Pitt on Idalgo. Unfortunately, Caffrey hated the cross-country footing and felt as if he was floundering. We came to the water, where he stopped, which took me by surprise. When he stopped a second time, I retired.

This was very disappointing, but I was enjoying some compensation with my young home-bred horses. Kings Fancy (Nancy) was second in the two-star at Punchestown and Kings Gem (Gemma) was third in a two-star competition, her first, at Tweseldown.

Meanwhile, at the other end of the scale, Cavvy's preparation for the World Games was going remarkably smoothly. We had a final outing at Gatcombe, where we led the British Open with a great dressage mark – 20 – and show jumped clear, but withdrew before the cross-country. It was obviously tempting to run, in the circumstances, but it would have been awful if something had gone wrong before the championships.

I travelled out to Aachen with William Fox-Pitt, somewhat mindful of our last trip together three years earlier, when we'd had the episode with Solly and the quad bike en route to Punchestown, but this time the journey passed without incident.

We arrived in Aachen to find that the British team had been allocated stables in a long corridor and Cavvy was at the end without much ventilation. Opposite were the vaulting horses – there are seven different disciplines at a World Games: eventing, show jumping, endurance, carriage-driving, reining and vaulting – and one had an ominously snotty nose. However, there was nothing we could do about it.

Aachen, a pretty old spa town near the Belgian and Dutch borders, is home to one of the most famous annual jumping and dressage shows. I hadn't been before, and was bowled over by the huge and beautiful main arena, the excellent surfaces to all arenas, and the way it was all maintained so well all week. It was a condensed site, but very well organised; very Germanic, in fact.

David and Emily came out to join me, and we stayed, as a team, at a hotel in the town. One of the big things for me at a championship is the camaraderie. I love being part of a team and all of us eating and spending time together in the evenings.

We were full of high hopes, because we were, on paper, a very strong team, despite having lost Pippa Funnell and her 2005 Badminton winner Primmore's Pride with lameness that summer. I was picked as pathfinder this time, and Daisy Dick, who'd had some good Badminton results on her brilliant cross-country horse Springalong, would be second for the team. Zara

Phillips, reigning European champion, was to be third on Toytown, who had some great four-star form. And William was the anchorman on Tamarillo, who had bounced back amazingly from his Athens injury to be second at Badminton and win the European silver medal behind Toytown in 2005.

We also had two new arrivals as individuals: Sharon Hunt on Tankers Town and Oli Townend with Flint Curtis. Both had done well at Badminton, and they were great fun to have along.

There was a bit of teasing about the fact that I'm old enough to be both Zara's and Oli's mother. This was my first team experience with Zara, and I was very impressed. She fits in so well and is friendly to everyone, not just people connected with the team; she was particularly kind to Emily, who thought she was wonderful. I don't know how Zara copes with the pressure and the attention, but she just carries on as if the press aren't there. She seems oblivious to all the people looking at her when she's warming up, or trying to walk the course, and all the clicking cameras.

She had a particularly difficult start to the week at Aachen when, on Sunday night, we heard the dreadful news that Sherelle Duke, an Irish event rider, had been killed in a fall at Brockenhurst. She was one of Zara's best friends and I don't really know how she picked herself up to go and do what she did that week.

My championships got off to a pretty disappointing start. Cavvy and I scored 51 in the dressage – a far cry from our mark of 20 a couple of weeks beforehand. It is true that Cavvy felt quite lit up, but not enough to warrant that bad a score. I was horrified, and so frustrated, especially when I discovered huge discrepancies in the marking. Two of the three judges were 26 marks apart, and I felt hard done by – I was so sure that I had cracked this phase, and expected a score in the 40s at least.

But there was nothing to be done about it except concentrate on the rest of the competition. I wasn't the only one to be disappointed in the dressage. Springalong was very badly behaved and gave Daisy a terrible ride, and Oli found Flint Curtis's poor test a difficult pill to swallow on his first squad appearance when he was out to prove himself.

Zara, however, calmly rescued our flagging team fortunes with a lovely test on Toytown, scoring 38, and William did a great job to score 45 on Tamarillo, who would have quite liked to be naughty too. Amazingly, we were in second place as a team, but all four of the Germans had done well and they were miles ahead of us, with the Australians and French close on our tails, so we were in a nervous position.

The cross-country, designed by Rudiger Schwarz, wasn't huge, but it was a typically Germanic, accuracy-testing course with several places at which one could make a mistake. I wasn't too worried, though, because I felt that Cavvy and I had gelled by this stage, and I set out confidently.

I soon realised, though, that my confidence was misplaced. As early as the three-minute marker, I found that we were behind on time, despite the fact that I'd been riding forward to the fences. Cavvy felt lacklustre; I was used to him being brave and free, and now I was having to press him. He felt 'leggy', which was worrying and, at the far end of the course, I had that horrible sinking feeling that he was running out of steam. I had to give him a smack – something I hated doing and hardly ever resorted to – but there was no response, which was odd because he hated being hit. He felt dull to my leg and as if he was floundering.

Near the end of the course was a water complex, which Yogi had instructed me to approach direct if I was behind the clock. I was quite confident that Cavvy would jump it, and we seemed to have the right line, but he ran out at an angled boat.

A few seconds later, we were at the finish. We had so nearly made it. I felt absolutely crushed. The feeling of having let the side down was overwhelming, but, even though I felt there must be something not right with the horse, I didn't want to make excuses.

When I hear people say, 'Oh, the horse had a virus,' to make up for a poor performance, I always think 'Oh yeah?' In fact, a subsequent blood test did reveal Cavvy to be below par, but I kept quiet about it, swallowed it down and hoped to have the chance to prove myself later on.

Daisy made up for me with a storming round, and Zara survived a few hairy moments to go into joint lead with Bettina Hoy. Sharon and Oli also went clear, ending up in individual ninth and eleventh places, so they had a competition to remember, but William wound up in the same boat as me when Tamarillo ran out at a narrow brush arrowhead which was situated at the bottom of a bank. William was as mortified as I had been, but Yogi did a great job in galvanising team spirit. He pointed out that the medal was by no means lost, and there was plenty of time for other riders to make mistakes. We found this hard to believe but, astonishingly, he was right.

The reigning world champion, Jean Teulère, and Australia's anchorman, Andrew Hoy, both faulted in the same place as William, and there were errors for Sweden's Linda Algotsson,

New Zealand's Andrew Nicholson and Germany's Ingrid Klimke. Suddenly we had bounced back to team silver medal position and I have to admit that everyone else's blunders made me feel a lot better.

Cavvy show jumped clear the next day, as did Daisy, and we held on to the silver medal. Zara kept her head remarkably, despite confusion over whether the bell had rung, and won the gold, which was thrilling. She was, as ever, so modest about it, and was overwhelmed with emotion thinking about her friend, Sherelle.

Rosemary Barlow organised champagne in the stables and, that night, there was a party in the town centre for all the medallists. We went up on to a stage in front of what seemed like thousands of people, and it was a terrific atmosphere. The Germans really know how to celebrate in style and it was a great win for them on home ground, their first world title, a deserved recompense for what had happened to them in Athens, and a great tribute to their team trainer, Chris Bartle.

As Yogi later put it, it was the right result for the sport. Germany deserved their moment, and Zara's gold medal, which helped her to win the BBC Sports Personality title, was an obvious fillip for eventing.

But I couldn't help but be full of mixed emotions. Like everyone, I was thrilled and excited with Zara's gold medal, but I was bitterly disappointed that we hadn't won the team gold, and I was deeply depressed that that was partly down to my own less than brilliant performance. William was suffering from the same sentiments, and we were both a little subdued on our midnight journey home to England.

*

Next, I gathered myself for Burghley, but without any great confidence. I felt it was quite a big step up for Caffrey. Perhaps fortuitously, he knocked himself halfway through his dressage test and went lame for a couple of strides, before recovering. He had hit the place on his front leg where he had an old splint, and next morning, although he was sound, the leg had come up in a huge swelling, so Gill Jonas and I thought it best to withdraw him.

My next outing turned out to be a damp squib, too. I took Nancy to Blenheim, but we had an early stop in the sunken road. I was a bit wary of that type of fence after our frightening Withington experience and, knowing she was a fast horse, I decided to take the alternative route. This still didn't work, though, as she leapt too bravely into the sunken road, missed her jerk coming out and just couldn't jump the rail, stopping at it. We were high up after the dressage, so I was instantly depressed by this. I have a tendency to go cold if something goes amiss early on the cross-country phase and, not wanting anything else to go wrong, decided to call it a day.

The next outing was to Boekelo in Holland, with Caffrey, and I travelled there with Pippa Funnell. The weather was terrible, with pouring rain and a howling gale. There was a parasol behind the dressage judges' boxes which had flippy bits and started spinning like a top. Caffrey caught sight of it and refused to go anywhere near it.

However, we pulled up to eleventh place – best of the British riders – thanks to an excellent double clear, but the event was mainly notable because Yogi acted as my groom! He took it very seriously, cleaning my tack and putting in the studs and, actually, I think he enjoyed the mixture of roles.

My head girl, Andrea Kerlin, had decided to leave after four years. She was very torn because she was loving the job and we got on very well, but she felt she needed to progress with her life and have some further education. Andrea was a great character, with a strong Irish accent and all sorts of entertaining little expressions. We met when she came to me for work experience and then pleaded to stay on. She was full of energy, always dancing and singing, and the year resounded to her favourite R & B music. She was also quite fiery when she first arrived, and I'd like to think that we – especially Mum, who is so placid – helped her to settle in life.

Andrea's replacement was Hannah Menaldino, who started working for me, with Bernie Shonk, another ex-work experience student, at the start of 2007. At first, I found it quite tricky as, both being 'new grooms', I had to remember to tell them everything, but it worked out well. Hannah stayed with me for a year then went on to do a master's degree, as she wanted to lecture and have time to event her own horse; she also rode out racehorses for Richard Barber as a fill in.

The final event of my 2006 season was a return trip to Le Lion d'Angers in France, with another of my home-bred productions, Gemma. I was a little worried, because the event is such a showcase for young horses and I thought she'd be outclassed in the dressage. I was also a little embarrassed by her appearance; I'd been reluctant to clip her as her winter coat was coming, so she did look rather fluffy.

However, it rained and rained and got muddier and muddier, and all these beautiful horses around us were slipping and sliding in the muddy dressage arena and losing their action.

Gemma's neat round action meant that she did a really good test; she completely ignored the mud and was totally correct.

She loves the jumping phases, so she zapped around clear and in the time, and ended up third. This was good enough to win me my second breeder's award, which seemed an amazing achievement.

Yogi and I had chatted after Boekelo, and I'd said that, now that I had three four-star rides, with Cavvy, Cashel Bay and Caffrey, it would be fun to take one to the four-star event at Kentucky in the States in the spring of 2007.

This was to be Caffrey's big moment, and I only hoped that he would justify the Lottery funding which would be spent on sending him out there and not disgrace himself.

It was a great experience. Kentucky is quite different to the English four-stars at Badminton and Burghley. It's set in Kentucky's Blue Grass country, which is the centre of the Thoroughbred breeding world. Everywhere is white rails and endless tempting grassland. The event was immaculately presented, with no expense spared.

We had a great time. Gill Jonas came out to watch her horse – it was a big trip for her, as she doesn't often travel, and she loved the experience. Polly Stockton came with Tangleman, who had been second the year before – sadly, they had a run-out – and it was to be Ian Stark's final four-star run. There were big celebrations when he went clear on the Duchess of Devonshire's Full Circle. It was also the year that Karen O'Connor was riding the little Theodore O'Connor; he was only about 14.2 hh but was amazing to watch across country.

The course, designed by Mike Etherington-Smith, was big and open; it was a superb galloping course and the weather was great. Caffrey gave me a super ride but, sadly, he had two show jumps down the next day, which was disappointing. I had been quite confident about the show jumping because he had so improved and warmed up beautifully, but halfway around the course he suddenly did a peculiar twitch, I think because he had bitten his tongue, and it all went wrong. He became so sensitive that I couldn't touch his mouth with the reins to steady him, which felt horrible. We finished ninth, but we could have been fourth, so it was all somewhat deflating.

Most of my spring was taken up with thinking about Badminton. I knew that after the Aachen debacle my grasp on a team place at the 2007 European Championships in Pratoni del Vivaro, Italy, was somewhat shaky and felt I had to pull something out of the hat. I also had the worry of Mum, most unusually, being ill. She had a cold, which she couldn't shake off and, being Mum, didn't go to the doctor soon enough. The cold got worse and became pneumonia, and she ended up with a painful chest. But, of course, it was almost impossible to make her sit still – in fact, the only time was when she was behind the steering wheel of the lorry. One of her diary entries simply reads: *Mowed lawn, vacuumed, pneumonia!*

I was full of excitement about Badminton. Cashel Bay was capable of a good placing and Cavvy's preparation had gone to plan with a fourth place at Belton, the main pre-Badminton spring event.

But I hadn't been at Badminton very long before rumblings about the poor state of the cross-country going were circulating. At the competitors' briefing on Wednesday morning, the director Hugh Thomas and technical delegate Mike Etherington-

Smith warned that the going was hard, but said they had plans to get it right for Saturday's cross-country and that they were hoping for some rain. I'm not sure what weather forecast Badminton was tuned in to, however, because no one else could see any hope of rain.

William, very cleverly, withdrew Ballincoola immediately after the briefing and quietly went home. There's no doubt that some officials were annoyed by this, and it didn't help with the negative press reports, but he could see that the weekend was going to be a fiasco and knew that he would be the one who would end up having to front rider complaints.

I just hoped for the best and that the organisers would fulfil their promises, but when I walked the course, I knew I was expecting a miracle. The ground was horrific. Everywhere, there were cracks and splits, and bits where animals had left deep prints that had become solid. The arena and warm-up areas were rock hard, too, and it was so disappointing, knowing that it was too late for any real improvement to be made.

Throughout the two dressage days, the sole topic of conversation among riders was: 'Are you running?' Everyone was being asked their opinion on the ground, and everyone had a different take. Some people were outspokenly angry, some were more diplomatic, and some of the foreign riders rather unhelpfully said it was no worse than the ground they competed on at home. However, many of the visiting overseas riders were just bewildered at finding this chaos on their first visit to the most famous event in the world. I think all the British participants were just thoroughly embarrassed.

On Friday, the topsoil delivery arrived, and the course-building team and Mike Etherington-Smith worked incredibly hard all hours of the night to put it on the track. I had to do a talk for *Your Horse* magazine, and I told them how sad I felt that I wasn't going to be running across country next day.

I did get up early to have a look at what had been done, but it wasn't enough to make me run. There were places where, if you were lucky, it was an inch thick, but in other places it was like powder and would make no difference to a galloping horse. A quarter of the field pulled out, most of them British, leaving the foreigners — many of whom felt that, having travelled so far, they had no option — to scoop most of the placings.

For once, my feelings got the better of me in public and I forgot about being diplomatic. Clare Balding interviewed me for the BBC and, among other things, I think I said that ground like this was cruel to the horses. Afterwards, Patrick Beresford, the former team chef d'equipe, said to me, 'Well done for standing up, but you made one major mistake. By saying it was cruel to run horses on this ground, you insinuated that all the riders who did so were cruel.'

Perhaps I should have been more tactful, but it just burst out of me. Of all the events in the world, Badminton is the one that matters most to me and to see it in this state was just shocking. And, no matter what anyone says, you know some horses will have been affected for life as a result of galloping and jumping on ground like that.

The following weekend Cavvy was hastily re-routed to the World Cup qualifier at Chatsworth. There, in a somewhat ironic contrast, the heavens opened, but I felt I could hardly withdraw because it was too muddy!

Cavvy pulled out all the stops and did a super test; he went clear across country and show jumped clear to give me my first international win with him. By the time we went in the arena, it was raining so hard I could hardly see the fences. No one could say I'd had easy conditions, which made it a particularly satisfying win.

Cavvy came out of the competition in really good shape and I felt good about showing people what we could do. The fortunate thing for me was that none of the leading British riders had competed at Badminton in the end, so my non-appearance hadn't cost me a team place, and instead my Chatsworth win had sealed it for me.

The next outing was a consolidatory two-star run for Gemma. I decided to take her to the new event at Houghton Hall, run by Alec Lochore. I have to admit that my decision was largely based on finance, as I didn't want to pay for a foreign trip for a horse that I owned myself. The event received a massive amount of entries in its first year, and Gemma having not done a particularly remarkable dressage, we finished lower down the placings despite finishing on our dressage score.

Cashel Bay, meanwhile, was re-routed to Luhmühlen, Germany, so that he would get his four-star run, but I had been struggling with him in the spring and was beginning to wonder if I had gone as far as I could with him.

We hitched a lift to Germany in another lorry and, in hindsight, that lorry was too small. I am a great one for stopping every so often and letting horses stretch their legs and pick grass, but this non-stop journey across Europe didn't suit Cashel Bay, and by the time we got to the event he was travel sick and couldn't run, which was a complete waste of time and effort on everyone's part.

Our next outing was Barbury Castle, where Cavvy was third and Caffrey ninth. Cashel Bay, though, did a terrible dressage test, which made me feel I was back to square one with him. He was horribly rude in the show jumping, too, having three fences down, and I realised I wasn't really enjoying riding him much. I felt we needed to make a decision about the horse's future and began preparing Sue for the fact that our partnership would have to end.

It was a very wet summer. A couple of weeks after Barbury, Aston-le-Walls, a good advanced event run by Nigel Taylor in Northamptonshire, was dramatically washed out by a huge thunderstorm which caused massive flooding across Gloucestershire. We were on our way home down the M5 when we got trapped due to the flooding. The four-hour journey took twenty hours.

It was quite an adventure. We let the side ramp down on the lorry so the horses had plenty of air and fortunately we had a good supply of food and hay for them. There was nothing for it but to sit it out, and at least we were in a lorry and could cook supper, watch the television and use the loo. In the end we felt we had to draw the curtains so the other poor stranded travellers couldn't see us having a jolly time. The only annoying thing was that every so often the traffic would shift, and we'd have to get out and put the ramp up again.

Things turned serious, though, at about 4 a.m., when Caffrey suddenly started shaking uncontrollably. His temperature was above normal and he was clearly becoming poorly. I phoned up the team vet, Jenny Hall, who said I should try and get off the motorway as soon as possible and she'd get a vet to meet me at the next junction. I got police permission to drive down the hard shoulder, where I met one of Jenny's colleagues, who treated him. Fortunately, by this time, the traffic was moving, so we continued to Devon. There, we discovered that Cashel Bay was shaking in the same way, in his stable. It turned out to be a small viral infection in the yard, but fortunately none of the other horses got it.

I was having a good run with Cavvy, but I decided that we still needed another reasonably high-profile outing under our belt before the Europeans. I always enjoy competing in the British Open at Gatcombe, another event that's special to me, and so we headed there to see if we could win the title we'd been in line for the previous year when we pulled out before Aachen.

Again, Cavvy led throughout the first two phases, so with the cross-country in reverse order of merit, I had another long, sick-making wait before it was our turn. Fortunately, I also had Caffrey to ride, which gave me confidence, as he zoomed round for ninth place. Gill Jonas was a bit upset that I'd racked up nine time penalties, but the time is always tight at Gatcombe and I explained to her that I'd gone as fast as I safely could on him.

I had a lovely round on Cavvy. There were some big corners at the far end of the course which caught out a few riders and he was very good there.

It was such a thrill to win my fifth national title. It's a great competition to win, one that everyone covets.

But although my summer was going well from a competitive point of view, under the surface I was struggling with a crisis close to home.

CHAPTER 23

Family Matters

In June 2007, Mum was diagnosed with breast cancer. Ironically, she had been reading a medical report about how few women paid attention to breast checks when she noticed that she had a lump herself. Her immediate reaction to the diagnosis was typically calm, to the point of flippancy – 'Well, I don't need my breast any more.' I was very concerned, hearing the dreaded word 'cancer' and wondering if this was the beginning of the end. But Mum didn't let any of us get maudlin about it; she was amazingly upbeat.

She had an operation on 10 August, and according to her diary entry, was completing a Sudoko puzzle later that afternoon. Twelve days later, we went to Urchinwood Horse Trials near Bristol with four horses, two grooms and four children. Mum had been told she mustn't drive the horsebox for at least a month, so there she was cooking eggs and bacon for eight of us while I drove the horsebox on the M5 hardly using a muscle. Next journey she drove while I cooked. Freddie's reaction was, 'Oh, so you're not going to die yet, then!'

She underwent a course of radiotherapy in Exeter hospital, and sailed through that without even feeling tired. Every afternoon, she'd put on tidy clothes after gardening, drive to hospital, and then take the opportunity to visit friends on the way home. At the end of the course, David and I were away on holiday, and Mummy had the children to stay and ten horses to feed.

Her prognosis is good and, now, I can't really take in the fact that all this happened, but I am aware of how lucky we have been. My mother's resilience never fails to amaze me, and this alarming interlude only emphasised how much I owe her. The reality is that I simply couldn't have this career without her.

That August a new horse arrived in the yard. Sue and Eddie Davies had kindly said they would like to buy me a second string behind Cavvy, but it had to be potentially top class. There was only one horse on the circuit that I had always admired: Imperial Cavalier, a beautiful horse produced, like Cavvy, by Vicky Brake.

He was competing at Punchestown in 2006 while I was there with Nancy and Caffrey, and I told Sue, who happened to be out there with Janette, to come and have a look, as I thought the horse was really special. However, Vicky didn't really want to sell him and, in the end, he didn't go particularly well at Punchestown, so the issue went away – temporarily.

When I'd mentioned to Yogi that I was interested in Imperial Cavalier, he just said, 'Are you sure?' But I was convinced the horse had what it takes and so I phoned Vicky for another try. She was adamant she didn't want to sell, but she did say she'd let me have first refusal. I had a few more tries, and asked again, more seriously, after Blenheim 2006 when Vicky had gone clear across country on him, but by this stage I was reduced to making feeble jokes like, 'How's my horse, then, Vicky?' In reality, I'd given up hope.

Unbelievably, it transpired that behind the scenes, Sue and Eddie Davies had made Vicky an offer which she'd accepted, and they'd sent Jenny Hall to vet the horse. The first I knew of it was when Sue phoned me up and said, 'Do you know where Vicky Brake lives? You wouldn't pick up a horse for me on the way back from Gatcombe, would you?'

I still didn't twig. When I told her my lorry was full and I couldn't do it, she finally burst out: 'We've bought Imperial Cavalier and we'd like you to have him!'

I went up the day after Gatcombe to collect him.

It was the most wonderful surprise. I couldn't believe my luck and was so thrilled and grateful that Sue and Eddie had trusted my instinct, even though I was asking them to buy a horse whose results hadn't been that special. It did mean, however, that I'd be under pressure to justify myself and, remembering the shaky early days with Cavvy, it made me very determined to repay their loyalty.

In the meantime, I took Cashel Bay to Burghley for a last fling. It was not a success. He flew down the drop at the Leaf Pit and took off straight past the next fence. I perhaps had too long a rein, which he took advantage of, just galloping off. I retired him and that was when I finally said to Sue, 'I'm so sorry, I've had enough.'

The parting was, fortunately, made easier as J-P Sheffield had taken over from Terry Boon in her yard, and Sue agreed it would be an opportunity for J-P to have a four-star horse to ride, and for her to have him at her own yard.

I then took Nancy to Boekelo where she was a bit hot in the dressage but did a superb cross-country round, clear show jumping and finished twelfth. Gemma, a year behind, went to Blenheim, did a somewhat unremarkable dressage but pulled up with her good jumping to sixteenth.

Straight after Blenheim, the team flew out to Italy for the European Championships. Mum came up to Blenheim to collect the lorry and I went on to stay with Nick Turner, who was laid up after a nasty fall at Burghley, before meeting everyone at Stansted Airport.

David took Cavvy to Bournemouth Airport. He was fascinated by the process, as the plane looked so rickety. There was a delay because there was no fuel in it, which had to be pumped in the old-fashioned way. But obviously looks were deceiving; I'm relieved to report that the horses arrived in fine form in Italy.

I was very much the senior person on this squad, apart from Rodney Powell, who was riding as an individual, and there were more cracks about how I could be everyone's mother. There is now a system where we are 'buddied up' in pairs to make sure no one is left out, and I was asked to look after Georgie Davies, whose good Luhmühlen performance meant she got one of the individual slots. To my surprise, she said she was totally overwhelmed at sitting next to me on the plane, and it took me back to my early days when I was equally in awe of the likes of Ginny Elliot.

The rest of the team consisted of Daisy Dick, who would be pathfinder on Springalong, Oli Townend on Flint Curtis, and Zara on Toytown, who was defending her European title. There was a lot of talk about how Britain was going for a seventh successive gold, but we felt that we had a tough task against the French and Germans.

The week got off to a fun start. A tradition had begun whereby each nation had to produce a cabaret at the opening party. It seemed that the British effort at Blenheim two years previously had been rather lame, and Rodney Powell, determined that we wouldn't make fools of ourselves again, had taken a hand in our performance.

Alex Franklin, his head girl, was despatched to find us costumes and Tracie Robinson, our dressage trainer, was designated choreographer, and we practised at Blenheim. Our song was the Eurovision Song Contest entry by Scooch, and Alex had found us brilliant costumes on the internet. They were tight-fitting turquoise air hostess suits, with zip-up jackets, and caps. We got a prize but, really, I think we were good enough to win.

It was a great night. Here we were at a serious event and everyone was letting their hair down. It was a great way to get all the teams together and in the right spirit. The only team who probably regretted it was Sweden – Sara Algotsson, a useful member of the team, tripped up on a bit of rough ground that night and injured her ankle so she couldn't ride.

Twelve years after my last trip to Pratoni, with King William, it looked much the same, a relaxed, rural event in a beautiful setting. The weather was gorgeous and Cavvy felt great. The atmosphere was really good; because we didn't have our lorries, a smart Winnebago had been hired for us to use as a base. It was very luxurious and even had washing machines, and we created a little British camp in the area around it.

We stayed at a lovely hotel, which was a bit of a drive

away but overlooked a lake and had the most amazing view. David flew out with Emily, Freddie and Mum, and the children were thrilled to miss a day of school. Freddie had a good time that weekend as his best eventing friend, Alex Corscadden, was there, and they played football all week in the warm weather. Although Freddie always keeps his ear to the commentary and knows exactly what is going on in the competition, it looks as though football will remain his first love. He represents Devon in junior teams and plays for Sidmouth, our local club.

In this, he has a great deal in common with his father. Breakfasts in the King household tend to be a bit of a double act. Emily and I will be gossiping about our horses, and Freddie and David will be talking football – Freddie fires questions at David about what's going on in the papers, who's replacing whom, and so on, and in the evenings they often practise together outside. More often than not, while I'm doing my emails in the evening, David will be watching football. He is a Manchester United supporter and gets passionate while watching them play – I find it hilarious watching him when they score a goal.

Pratoni was a fun championships for us as a family, because it wasn't officious and everyone was able to mix with each other, without there being any barriers or places you couldn't get into.

David and I enjoyed catching up with our friends the Corscaddens. Alex's mother, Sally, was riding on the Irish team. She used to ride for Britain and she and I had been friends for years. I always felt I'd been a bit of a matchmaker with her and her husband Brendan; we'd travelled to Punchestown together in 1989, and she and Brendan had fallen for each other. After that, I'd encouraged her to come out with me to Stockholm because

I knew he'd be there, and their relationship blossomed from there.

The British team got off to a useful start in Pratoni with good tests on the first day by Daisy and Oli. The standard of dressage was high, partly because we were riding a three-star test – European Championships are always at three-star level – and for the more established horses, it seemed quite easy, having been used to more intense four-star dressage tests.

Cavvy's test was lovely; he scored 36, his best ever mark. Zara did even better, and the team was in second place behind the Germans.

When we first walked the cross-country course, which had been designed by Giuseppe della Chiesa, I couldn't help but think how easy it was. Everyone was going on about the hills, which I thought were perfectly all right, and I predicted that loads of people would go clear inside the time. I had got it completely wrong, though, and it turned out to be a very cleverly designed course.

There was a dramatic slide fence down to a double of skinny fences, and that caused a lot of trouble. Daisy, as first to go, made it look easy, but then everyone started running out at it, including Oli and the first two Germans, Ingrid Klimke and Peter Thomsen. It turned out later that Daisy and Georgie were the only two riders to jump it clear all day.

This was the one fence I was nervous about, and I was desperate not to let anyone down this time, so when Yogi said, 'I'd prefer you not to go the straight way there,' I thought, *Thank goodness*. Cavvy felt really fit and well; he'd been galloping strongly all year, and I was fairly confident that I could make up the time elsewhere.

I was feeling really positive when I set out. Zara had done a good clear and, with the trouble that was occurring for other nations, we were in a strong position. I knew that taking the long route at the slide would be time-consuming, so I had to take the most economic routes I could everywhere else, knifing around the corners. Cavvy felt as though he was loving it.

The only blunder we made was at the last fence. We were on a lovely open stride. I felt, though, that he was going too freely and so grabbed hold of him; making him have to screw over it, and I thought, *Oh no, no, Mary, hang on!* But all was well.

The team was now in a very strong lead, which meant, barring something awful happening, we couldn't lose. I had pulled up from seventh to fourth and, with Cavvy's show jumping record, had an obvious chance of going up into the individual medals.

Zara was in second place behind Nicolas Touzaint, who was the only rider to achieve the optimum time, but the French team was some distance behind us, having suffered all sorts of mishaps. The Germans were, astonishingly, out of it, and, one year after their triumph in Aachen, were downcast. Hinrich Romeike's wonderful grey horse, Marius, was injured and not able to show jump, and Frank Ostholt had pulled up Air Jordan. Their only hope was Bettina Hoy, who was riding as an individual, and she salvaged some glory, finishing in bronze medal position on Ringwood Cockatoo.

The show jumping course proved influential. Cavvy was again wonderfully reliable and jumped clear in fourth place, which was eventually to give me the individual silver medal behind Nicolas. Zara, however, had a nightmare. Toytown stopped at a double; they had become unbalanced and Zara was clever not to fall off. It was just one of those things; perhaps he had seen something which distracted him.

As she came out of the ring crying, we all rushed to shield Zara from the photographers who came crowding in. Although she was quick to pull herself together, I felt for her in her moment of devastation and later at the press conference, where journalists were keen to question her. I pointed out that she was far more successful than I'd been at that stage – it took me until I was thirty to get on a team, and then I fell off.

There was no time to celebrate, as we had to rush and catch a flight to Stansted. I had decided that I would just sleep in my car at the airport while waiting for David's flight to arrive – I was much too tight to pay for a hotel! – before driving home to Devon, but at Stansted I was talking to one of the British supporters, Judy Gardener, who said, 'We can't have our silver medallist sleeping in a car!' She insisted on taking me home to her house for the night and her husband Robert drove me back to my car in the morning.

A lot of the press attention from Pratoni understandably centred on Zara's mishap rather than my silver medal, but I was still thrilled. The whole competition had been so satisfying, chiefly because Britain had triumphed on the cross-country and because we had fit horses, which is what the sport should be about. Having achieved bronze and silver individual European medals, I couldn't help but wonder: Surely it was only a matter of time before I got a gold to complete the collection?

On my return from Pratoni, my immediate task was to get to know Imperial Cavalier. The plan was to take him to his first four-star, at Pau in France, a month afterwards, and our partnership needed to gel if I was to show his owners that their faith in my judgement was not misplaced.

Imperial Cavalier (Archie) is a big horse. When he arrived, he was beautifully calm and relaxed but, to my mind, living in rather a dream world. Like Cavvy, he had been beautifully produced by Vicky, but he needed to learn to stretch and use his body. The first time I cantered up the hill I use for my fast work, which one of my young horses would go up easily, he ran out of power halfway. This was somewhat alarming for what was meant to be a four-star horse.

He was effortless over a fence, but he could be a bit careless. I took him to a fun invitation class at Blenheim, a mixture of small cross-country fences and larger show jumps, and, to my alarm, he was quite ordinary. He knocked down a few fences and I worried that my judgement was all wrong and he wasn't that special after all. Then we did the South of England horse trials, which he won ... having felt rather surprised at being asked to go fast cross-country.

I didn't know how Archie would cope at Pau, and decided that I would just have to play it by ear. Dressage was still quite difficult; he'd only started learning his flying changes with Vicky the year before, so they weren't very established. However, his test wasn't too bad, and I felt it was worth trying to crack on a bit across country.

Archie felt a bit naïve in the cross-country, but he was so willing and naturally brave. At one complex, there were steps out of water with a big arrowhead brush at the top. He had run out of power at the top of the bank and just trotted at the brush, but he was genuine and kept going.

To my horror, though, when I went to look at my stopwatch,

it registered nought, because I hadn't set it. There was nothing for it but to kick on. We finished just inside the optimum time, but it was more by good luck than good judgement.

Next day, Archie show jumped clear. This was really the best bit of all, because I had begun to worry that I'd chosen a horse that would have a tendency to have fences down. I finished second, by just 0.2 pen, to Nicolas Touzaint (this time riding Hidalgo d'Ile) – again! My overwhelming feeling was relief. In particular I was relieved on behalf of the Davies family that Archie was proving to be a potential world-class horse.

We came home from Pau with an extra horse in the lorry, entirely thanks to Emily. It was her half-term and, aged eleven, she was grooming for me. She was conscientious, not allowing me to get out of bed in the morning as she insisted on turning Archie out herself, stitching in all his plaits. Emily has always liked to do things for herself – she has clipped her ponies herself since she was six – and I tend to let her get on with it as it's good for her.

Pau has a young horse sale, which fascinated Emily. She had never seen horses loose-jumping before, and she spent hours hanging out around the arena, watching riders like Andrew Nicholson trying the young horses.

Then she came back and said, 'You must come and see lot 30.' This was a lovely young grey horse of about 16.1 hh, short-backed, quiet and a good mover. I was impressed that Emily had shown such a good eye and picked out the horse that was most suitable for her, but the answer to the question as to whether I'd buy it for her was a firm no.

Clearly not taking me seriously, she then asked if she could go and ride the horse, which I thought wouldn't do any harm.

She didn't seem to be fazed by the fact that a lot of people were watching, and loved the experience. Andrew Nicholson also got on the horse, and Emily started getting anxious that he would buy it, but I continued to ignore her pestering.

Then I spotted her doing a text on my phone. She showed it to me, and it was to one of my owners, saying, 'I've seen a horse which would be a really good junior horse, Granny will pay half, would you pay the other half?' Mum was going to give all the grandchildren a lump sum of money each, but I was horrified at Emily contacting my owner, as I didn't want them to feel obliged. Emily's approach worked, though, with the owner agreeing to buy the entire horse but with the caveat that she wouldn't fund the running costs.

The next thing I knew, we had a strange grey horse in the lorry! I firmly told Emily that I was not paying to run this horse. Undaunted, she sat down and wrote to the clothes company Joules, who were already branding her little trailer and clothing, offering to register the horse as King Joules with British Eventing in return for them paying the running costs. She sent them a picture as well, saying, 'He's very attractive.' Fortunately, this approach seemed to amuse them and they agreed to pay for the majority of his running costs.

Emily is determined that she will be more successful than I am, and she is extraordinarily driven about getting up early in the morning to ride, or riding after school, while still managing to do all her school work.

I try not to interfere with her riding, or to nag, but if she does ask for my advice or help, I very happily help. Just as I was at that age, jumping is the thing, and she can be impatient, but her interest in flatwork is growing all the time.

*

The year was completed with a third consecutive young horse breeder's award, after Kings Temptress (Tess), who won three consecutive intermediate sections on the national circuit, followed her sisters by being placed (fourth) at Le Lion d'Angers.

It had been one of my best ever years in the sport, but 2007 ended with one dreadfully sad episode. My friend Sarah Dick-Read, whom I'd been close to since my chalet-girl days and who was Emily's godmother, died. She had been fighting ovarian cancer for eight years and had been incredibly brave; her glossy black hair all fell out as a result of the chemotherapy, she'd had to face up to the fact that she would not be able to have children and had been big enough to send her boyfriend away.

Soon after her fortieth birthday, Sarah's cancer had come back in her brain. She died in a hospice in Taunton, where I had been to visit her. She was such a lovely, kind person and it was a tragedy.

CHAPTER 24

Hong Kong Here We Come

I started 2008 on a real high: I'd got a choice of two good horses to take to my fifth Olympics, and not many riders have been in that fortunate position. I couldn't believe my luck. Five consecutive Olympics would equal Ian Stark's record – although he has won rather more medals than me! I'm not one to sit around analysing statistics, but when you consider how few people can go each time, it's not a bad record!

I knew that if the British team could just maintain the momentum of the European Championships the year before, with the return of a strong competitor like William Fox-Pitt to boost us, a gold medal could be a reality. What a thrill that would be for the sport in Britain.

The other big excitement was the progress being made on our new house. I had finally got around to obtaining planning permission to convert part of the old flint farm in the yard into a house. It would be a stunning position, with a view of the sea from the top windows, but it all took a bit of discussion, because it would mean David having to commute to work instead of me, and it was a while before he was really convinced he wanted to do that. But I got my own way in the end! The prospect of not driving for half an hour every morning to get to the horses, something I'd done for thirteen years, was blissful.

We had been thinking about it for many years, but it had seemed too big a plan. Then one of my owners, Nick Engert, who knows a lot about planning, persuaded me to get the ball rolling.

I took both Cavvy and Archie to team training and, knowing Cavvy was my preferred horse for Hong Kong, because he was more experienced and lighter-bodied and thus more able to cope with the expected humidity of Hong Kong, the selectors gave him a bye for Badminton.

When I took Cavvy up to the World Cup qualifier at Burnham Market in Norfolk, which was a competitive class, he felt terrific. We led after dressage and finished eventual third, having picked up eight time penalties across country.

There was then a discussion as to what to do next. I didn't want to run him competitively at Belton two weeks later, the next big spring event, but, mindful of what happened in the run-up to Athens, nor did I want to ruin my chances of getting in the team by not doing enough. The selectors advised me to give him a quiet time before building up to the Olympics.

Meanwhile, Archie was heading for his first Badminton. His dressage was improving steadily, although his flying changes still weren't spot on. He'd been quite strong at Burnham, though he had two show jumps down which was a little disappointing, but he jumped well over the big course at Belton, finishing second behind Ruth Edge on Mr Dumbledore.

At Badminton, riders were overwhelmed by what Hugh Thomas and his team had achieved in twelve months. It seemed they had really listened to rider criticism and had made all sorts of improvements to the whole event. Everything had been smartened up and the whole atmosphere was noticeably more helpful and friendly, while the work done on re-seeding and preserving the cross-country track, which was beautifully presented this time, was fantastic. Badminton was back to being the cream of the cream and, for me, that was really thrilling, as I had hated to see it the way it was in 2007.

Archie was well placed after dressage, on a score of 40, and I was looking forward to taking him across country, because the track had gone back to being a good old-fashioned meaty course again with new fences and serious questions which would make it difficult to get the optimum time. Although it may sound strange to be wanting a difficult course, I am always disappointed when a cross-country course doesn't present enough of a challenge. Success in eventing is much more valuable and rewarding when the cross-country course has been influential.

I was first to go on Caffrey, who went very well and even managed to ignore a persistent dog which yapped at our heels for a while. I was thrilled to bits with his round, but at the end of the day when the course had proved more influential than expected, I was to realise it had been a seriously good effort.

The competition then began to build up excitingly, because several of the top contenders came surprisingly unstuck. Andrew Hoy, the dressage leader, and Pippa Funnell both fell early on at Huntsman's Close; Ruth Edge landed in the water off Muschamp Impala, and Clayton Fredericks was unshipped when Nullabor refused at the ditch at the Vicarage Vee. Only one rider, Polly Stockton on Regulus, had achieved the optimum time.

William Fox-Pitt and I were right at the end of the day with our second horses, and were the only riders with any hope of overtaking Nicolas Touzaint, who was by now in the lead on his Pau winner, Hidalgo d'Ile, so a thrilling finale was expected.

Archie felt fantastic, answering all the questions I was asking of him. He became a little tired on the way home but we were pretty much on time, so I was beginning to get quite excited as I knew we could go into the lead. Heading for the finish, I felt I'd jumped the last of the difficult fences, the awkward little houses up on the bumpy ground, and – prematurely, as it turned out – was thinking, *This is it!*

Archie was labouring, and not quite as responsive as he might have been, but all that was left was two little logs before the final fence in the main arena, and I was sure it would be all right. Unfortunately, in my excitement, I made the mistake of pressing him forward to the second log, thinking he needed my support, which he didn't. His stride opened up, getting him too close to the second log, and he caught his knee and skewed over the fence.

I had been too forward with my upper body, something I constantly tell people not to do when I'm teaching, and I fell off ridiculously easily as a result. I had time to think, *Oh please no, no, no!* Then gravity took control and I hit the deck as Archie cantered on up towards the finish by himself.

I was furious with myself. There was £60,000 gone, just like that. Money is always tight at the best of times, but with this house-building project I needed every penny I could get. Bernie Shonk, my groom, and Emily came running out and caught Archie. They were going to take him away, back to the stables, but I ran up to get on him and jumped the last fence.

The crowd was so supportive, cheering me like mad, but I was incredibly frustrated. It was such a silly, disappointing mishap – a split-second error that changes your life – that you can't really take it in at first. When you've been at this game as long as I have, though, you learn to cope.

Unbelievably, after my blunder, William, following me, was taken by surprise when Tamarillo decided not to jump one of the houses. It was just one of those days.

The owners were great about it, considering how disappointed they were. Irritatingly, Archie was one of only two horses to show jump clear next day, so we might easily have won. The only upside amid the hideous frustration was that Archie had at least proved that he was a good horse, consolidating the promise he'd showed at Pau.

Next, I took Gemma and Nancy to Saumur. Nancy had a run-out at a horrid pair of angled hedges and, deflated, I retired her and re-routed for Bramham, where we finished a thrilling second behind William. Gemma, however, finished ninth – the best of the British horses.

From the point of view of finance and space I knew that I must part with three of the home-bred horses which I still owned. Although it was obviously going to be hard to see them go, I had known right from the start that I had to be commercial about this venture. And so I advertised them, stating in the advert that if any owners needed a rider I would be happy to keep on the ride. I wasn't prepared to sell them to just anyone, and was really lucky to find Gemma a great home with a rider called, by coincidence, Gemma Tattersall.

Gemma is a talented up-and-coming young rider and her

owner, Chris Stone, bought her Gemma (the mare!) because she was just what they were looking for: a useful horse for a young rider to gain experience with. Being a proven advanced mare, who had already had one foal (Albert), she would also be suitable to put to Chris's stallion Chilli Morning. She had the fullest vetting I've ever seen, with ovary swabs and cardiology tests, but fortunately passed with flying colours.

I sold Kings Command, the six-year-old first son of Lily (Kings Mistress, mother of the three mares), to Charlotte Martin to event. King Albert, Gemma's six-year-old son, was bought by Patsy Mason, and she asked if I would ride him for her – so luckily he stayed with me.

Due to quarantine restrictions, the equestrian Olympics would be held at Sha Tin racecourse, Hong Kong, instead of in Beijing. We knew we would be better off there, where there'd be state-of-the-art facilities, veterinary expertise and wall-to-wall air-conditioning to help us cope with the high humidity, but I was glad that I'd experienced four 'proper' Olympics, as I anticipated this would feel like a glorified world equestrian games.

Under the guidance of Jon Pitt, a sports fitness expert who was employed by the British Equestrian Federation to help riders prepare, I started to concentrate on getting fit for Hong Kong. Jon let us choose a piece of gym equipment to have at home. I chose a cross-trainer because it was a machine I quite enjoyed, and I knew David liked it too. It was a huge bit of kit which I had planned to put in the little office with my computer, but it ended up dominating the sitting room and was quite a talking point with visitors.

I also did some running, which I'm not that good at, enjoying

Being rescued by David Green at Bramham.

David and I went to our friend Greg Stones's 40th birthday as Marc Bolan and Cruella de Vil

Tennis party on tour in Greece, 1999: me, Penny Dart, Zoe and Reggie House, Will and Jackie Michelmore, David, and Paul Dart.

New generation – Emily with our homebred King Albert, 2002.

Call Again Cavalier in typically exuberant fashion at Badminton, 2004. (*Mark Hawksworth*)

King Solomon at
Badminton, 2003.
The first horse
to win me an
Olympic medal
– Silver, Athens,
2004. (*Fiona Scott
Maxwell*)

Belated medal
ceremony
following Athens,
2004, with all its
controversy;
we received
our Team Silver
medals from the
Princess Royal.

Kings Gem, my second homebred, at Gatcombe, 2006.

First foal Kings Fancy at Boekelo, 2007.

Second chance – I was incredibly lucky when Eddie and Sue Davies asked me to ride Call Again Cavalier and subsequently bought me Imperial Cavalier. (*Barry Gomer/Rex Features*)

Emily on Patsy Mason's Mr Hiho. (*John Britter*)

Freddie on our family holiday in Thailand, 2010.

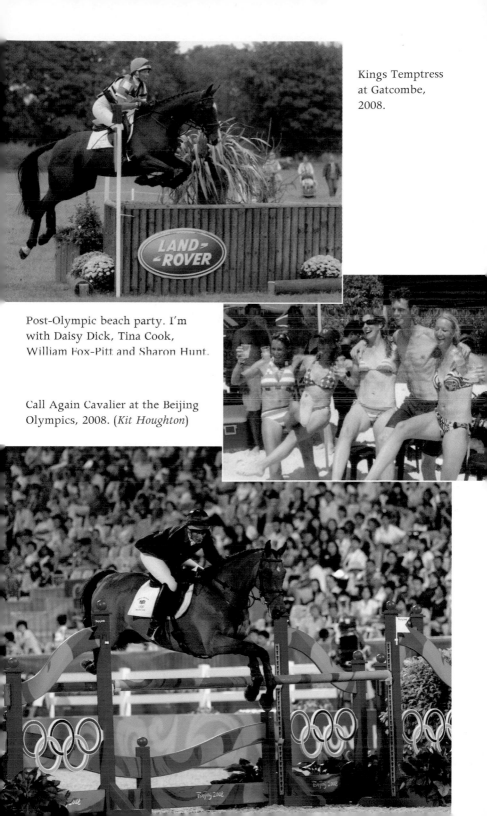

Kings Temptress at Gatcombe, 2008.

Post-Olympic beach party. I'm with Daisy Dick, Tina Cook, William Fox-Pitt and Sharon Hunt.

Call Again Cavalier at the Beijing Olympics, 2008. (*Kit Houghton*)

Apache Sauce
en route to
fourth place at
Burghley, 2008.

Hurrah, we did
it! Team Gold.
(*Kit Houghton*)

the cross-trainer more, and I galloped the horses in rugs to prepare them for the sticky atmosphere.

Even though I'd fallen off Archie, he was still in the running for Hong Kong, and in one way he was more suitable because of his placid temperament and the likelihood that he would cope better with the long flight. Cavvy had been a bit twitchy flying to Pratoni, though as it turned out, he was fine on the flight to Hong Kong. As far as I was concerned, he was definitely the right choice because he was more experienced, lighter in build and more likely to cope with the climate, but it was wonderful to have the choice.

All team prospects were asked to run in a low key advanced intermediate class at Salperton in Gloucestershire, where my two boys finished third and fifth. They were in good shape and I decided to enter them for the CIC at Barbury Castle. I took Cavvy semi-steadily and finished eighth, but I was planning to be properly competitive on Archie and speed on across country. Unfortunately, we had a run-out at the sunken road fence, which was my fault. I rode him badly, and as a result he didn't quite lock on to what he had to jump.

Up until this point, the selectors had been edging towards Archie for Hong Kong, but this made them realise that mistakes were more likely to happen with him because he was younger and less experienced.

Sadly, after the year had started so promisingly, the wheels were beginning to fall off our team effort. Lucy Wiegersma and Shaabrak, who were excellent runners-up at Badminton, didn't turn up at Salperton, which led to a certain amount of speculation. It turned out that Shaabrak had an abscess in his foot, which didn't seem to be settling. In the end, the selectors had to make the decision to drop Lucy from the squad. It was an awful blow for Lucy, who had been so focused and had put her all into Olympic selection, and she found it terribly hard to cope with.

Then came another shock. We were all at team training at the Unicorn Centre in Stow-on-the-Wold where a mass press conference was called. Zara was, obviously, the centre of attention – no one was really interested in any of the rest of us! – and she coped in her usual calm, good-humoured way.

It wasn't until afterwards that we realised what she was going through, as we were told in confidence that Toytown had injured himself at home. It transpired that he had escaped from the indoor school at Gatcombe and galloped back to the stables, slipping on the way, the sort of thing horses unfortunately do to annoy you, usually at the least convenient moments.

Twenty-four hours later, it was publicly announced that Toytown would not be going to Hong Kong, hitting the BBC news in seconds. This was particularly cruel for Zara because the horse had been injured before Athens as well. Zara will undoubtedly get an Olympic place one day, but it's unlikely to be on this horse, who clearly would have given her the best chance of a gold medal. She put a dutifully good face on it, but we all knew that underneath she was very low and found the next few weeks hard to get through.

During the team training at the Unicorn Centre, we had a King family sporting success. Emily has taken after me at school, and is keen on sport, particularly the high jump. She had qualified for the national under-12 finals at Birmingham, and I got Yogi's permission to take time off to watch her. To my great pride, all

Emily's hard work in juggling riding with sport and school work paid off and she won a gold medal and became the national champion.

Back on my sporting front, the only upside to all the team upheavals was that Daisy Dick and Tina Cook, who were competing to replace Lucy, now both got a place. Daisy had had a rough time with Springalong, falling in the water at Badminton, and Tina, like me in 2004, had been horrified that missing Badminton nearly cost her an Olympic place on a horse that had done well in three three-star competitions in 2007.

The other two places in the team of five were filled by Sharon Hunt, who had a brilliant Badminton on Tankers Town, and William. He had been in the enviable – and confusing – position of having three horses nominated for Hong Kong: Ballincoola, who was third at Badminton, Tamarillo and Parkmore Ed, his 2007 Burghley winner. Though he was clearly agonising over it, we all knew William's heart was with Tamarillo, who, like Cavvy, was a light horse, but in the end the selectors relieved him of the decision and gave the nod to Parkmore Ed.

In hindsight, the team began to weaken at this point. Tamarillo could be naughty, but he was arguably more physically suited to Hong Kong. Shaabrak and Toytown were both good dressage and cross-country horses, and we needed Zara's star quality and ability to pull a great performance out of the hat when it mattered. This was the start of a number of things that went against us.

I'm not a city person, but I found Hong Kong a really exciting place, and so different from anything I'd seen before with its amazing skyscrapers against the mountainous backdrop and the atmospheric harbour.

I was impressed with the facilities at Sha Tin as well. The stables had air-conditioning, as did the warm-up arenas, and there were rubberised stable floors and walkways. There were lots of procedures to do with sterilisation, but the Chinese volunteers smiled endlessly and everyone was helpful.

The horses all looked content – except Parkmore Ed. He wasn't eating or drinking much and didn't look happy, which was a concern because he was a strong member of the team and we didn't want any more problems. We also had no reserve horse as, with a team of five in the Olympics and the best three scores counting, that is considered a built-in safety net.

The organisers had created an Olympic Village in a hotel, but it was very different from the real thing. They did their utmost to give it an Olympic feel, and they tried hard with our opening ceremony, but it was nothing compared to the real thing in Beijing. We all told ourselves that we were in the best place for the horses but I found it sad that some of the first-time Olympic riders would miss out on mixing with the world's best athletes and seeing some of the other sports, and I was heartily glad that I'd had that experience.

There was no drink in the village, but we could go to a nearby bar, and there was a swimming pool. Some of the officials and owners were staying at the Sheraton, and that was a relaxing retreat as well.

Mum, David, Freddie and Emily all had tickets to each day's competition, and I could meet up with them in the international tent organised by Rosemary Barlow. They stayed at the Sheraton and I joined them on the first night. Emily and Mummy shared, and Freddie was in with David and me. He spent most of the night saying, 'Mummy, I can't sleep.' I told him not to worry, just to lie there and shut his eyes and that he'd drop off to sleep.

Unfortunately, this didn't work, as his personal clock had been upset by the flight, and he started on a repetitive moan of 'Mummy, I don't like Hong Kong. Can we go home?!' This built to a crescendo and, what with that and David snoring, I was quite thankful to retreat back to the village.

As the first horse inspection approached, it was evident that Parkmore Ed wasn't himself, which meant that William couldn't give him much work. It was a far from ideal scenario, made worse when a haematoma suddenly appeared behind his girth area. The vets had a good look at that and William was sent to the holding box before being passed, which was an unpleasantly tense moment. The haematoma didn't affect the horse's soundness, but it didn't look good and, as a team, we were further demoralised to hear that commentators had criticised us for looking downcast.

Then the dressage got off on the wrong foot for us. Springalong was really naughty, which was disheartening for Daisy who had put so much work into him.

Parkmore Ed, who was second to go because it was deemed more suitable for him to get the cooler part of cross-country day, had by now missed a lot of work, including the opportunity to be taken into the arena to get accustomed to the big screen. Underneath his solid exterior, Ed is a sensitive soul and he needed to be in form. Poor William couldn't do much with him and said afterwards that he'd been lucky just to keep him in the arena.

Sharon did a good test but in comparison to the sparkling Australian and German horses, her mark was quite ordinary. Suddenly, Britain was alarmingly off the pace.

Tina rescued spirits with a good test on Miners Frolic (Henry) and did a personal best – the right time to do it!

Fortunately for me, Ferdi was out in Hong Kong, helping the dressage team and also with his daughter, Maria, who was reserve. I was thrilled to have my own personal trainer there, which took some of the weight off Tracie Robinson, the British team trainer. She is always great about Ferdi helping me and has even been to sessions to listen to him so she could be on the same wavelength when looking after me.

On a personal note, I was thrilled with my test, which put me in ninth place. Flying changes are always my Achilles heel, but they went rather well this time and Cavvy stayed quiet so I could ride him positively forward. Afterwards I was bubbling with happiness, high on Olympic buzz and just feeling so lucky to be there.

The team, however, was not in a medal position at this point, which was not what we had anticipated at all. The Australians and Germans were running away with the competition, and the Americans were in front of us as well. There was a sense in the camp that it was not going to plan, but we also knew there was a lot to play for. We all got on well and felt united as a team.

Cavvy was amazingly calm, considering that he can be quite excitable, and seemed to be thoroughly enjoying the whole experience, especially hacking around the racehorse tracks with other horses. Perhaps it was his relaxation that was our downfall on the last day.

All of us – even 'hard men' like Mark Todd and Andrew Nicholson – poured with undignified sweat. But even though it flowed in rivulets after riding and stuck my hair to my head in a rather unflattering style, I was not particularly bothered by the heat and humidity, which, in any case, was not as bad as had been feared. I was feeling good, and I have always enjoyed the heat – I hate being cold – so I didn't give it much thought.

Each day we would be taken up by a shuttle bus to walk the cross-country course, which was on a golf course at the opulent Beas River Country Club about a forty-minute drive away. I always fell asleep on the bus, so I would try to get a seat where I could lay my head against the side and have a snooze.

The course, designed by Mike Etherington-Smith and beautifully presented by David Evans, his builder, gave the impression of being intense: a lot of fences in a short time, lots of fences off turns, and very few straight lines. I thought the first water complex was quite strong, even though in the end it rode well, and the second to last fence – two angled narrow brushes – made me go cold. Generally I was quite happy with the course for Cavvy because he was nimble, but knew that with all those jumping efforts the time would be difficult.

There was some controversy because at the riders' briefing it was suddenly announced that the course was only eight minutes long. We were expecting it to be ten – still shorter by some way than a real four-star course, but to be expected in the conditions.

Those extra two minutes could have made a difference to us as, generally, our horses were fit and could go on, but the last thing anyone wanted was for horses to be put under such pressure that they'd get injured. We were also mindful that, if there were any unpleasant sights of exhausted horses, eventing's place in the Olympic movement would have been jeopardised.

The horses travelled to Beas River the night before, in a very organised convoy. We went to visit them that evening and to check they were all happy. The only daunting thing was that every stable had a hook arrangement ready for a horse to be on a drip, which made us all think, *Oh no, what are we doing to our horses?*

In the end though, we were so lucky. The morning dawned dullish, cool and drizzly. As the last to go for the team, I knew I was in for a nervous wait, but I made myself sit and watch. It was comforting to see Mark Todd, first out on the course, do such a great job, but he was slow and we realised how tight the time would be.

Daisy went as fast as she could, but racked up a disappointing amount of time faults, as did many people. William then rocketed off on a mission. I think he was so depressed by his dressage performance that he felt he'd got to do something to contribute to the team's fortunes.

Apart from a rather alarming long stride to the last fence, he was foot perfect and finished with the second fastest time of the day. It was an amazing feat of horsemanship to conjure a performance like that out of a horse that had been below par and wasn't cut out for the weather.

Poor Sharon did a good job on Tankers Town, but the horse got tired and it all fell apart with a run-out at the penultimate fence. Tina, however, did a great job, and looked really classy.

Meanwhile, the Germans had steamed ahead with some inspired performances. The Australians, to their supporters' horror, incurred too many time penalties, and the Americans had rather fallen apart, which meant we had a chance of overtaking them and moving into bronze medal position.

By the time it was my turn, I was pretty nervous and my stomach churned. I just longed for it all to be over. Although it's a great honour to go last for the team – and it's the position everyone would like to be in because, of course, competitively, there's an advantage – it did seem like a very long morning.

A fine, blinding drizzle began as I was warming up, but I knew I'd got to ride forward, see forward strides, keep close to the string and stick to tight lines. Cavvy felt magical, lovely and smooth.

In hindsight, perhaps I should have taken a few more risks, and when I look back on my round, my turn to the second water was a bit slow, but there weren't many places I could have gone much quicker. The rain became much heavier but, although people kindly said that I'd gone around in the worst conditions, you don't notice it when you're galloping along.

We were travelling well and, as I came to the dreaded second last fence, which had been proving so influential, I remembered the time Cavvy ran out to the left at the World Games. I got my whip ready in the left hand and, in my anxiety, slightly overdid tightening the right rein, which meant I ended up heading straight for the highest part of the scalloped hedge. Thankfully, Cavvy was brilliant and sprang over it, as I said, 'Thank you, God.'

My relief at not making a mistake when the team needed my score so badly was huge. It meant I pulled up to sixth place and the team to bronze medal position. Suddenly there was everything to play for. After all, in Athens, we'd pulled up from fourth to silver, so anything was possible, and with Cavvy's great jumping record, I secretly nurtured dreams of moving up to an individual medal.

All our horses seemed in pretty good shape that night, even Ed, who had made an amazing recovery. William had been so brave because he hadn't been able to warm up that much. In fact, he'd gone pretty much from the stable to the course, but, if you think about it, horses in the wild go from standing still to sudden flight – they don't warm up before galloping off.

There were two show jumping rounds, the first to decide the team medals, and the second, under floodlights, for the individual medals, with the first round counting towards our final individual scores. The course wasn't particularly influential and a lot of people were jumping clear, which meant we weren't going to make much headway on the team medals but, obviously, it could put me in good shape for the final round.

We went clear around nearly all of the course and I was feeling calm, relaxed and pinging with excitement. We turned to the last line of plain fences, which were quite small: a double of verticals and then an oxer at the end. Cavvy hit the first fence; I heard the crowd groan and so did I. I didn't expect him to hit the last fence either, but he did.

I have analysed over and over again what I could have done riding-wise to help Cavvy. Perhaps he hadn't had enough fluids; perhaps I should have wondered why he was so good and quiet all week. He hadn't hit a single show jumping fence for two years, but it had to happen here.

We did well to win the team bronze medal, really, but I was heartbroken. My first thought was, there's another Olympics gone, and still no gold medal. Will it ever happen? I felt, at that point, that there was no hope.

Both Cavvy and I were flat when we went in for the second show jumping round and he had another two fences down, so we were well out of it. Ironically, the main worry had been Tina's horse in the show jumping, but she produced another immaculate clear round and won the individual bronze medal.

Tina rode beautifully and, out of all of us, was the only one who had really raised her game. She has been trying to ride at an Olympics since 1996 and, as the last-minute addition, had done the best of all of us. She also rather rescued the British effort, because our tally of two bronzes – the show jumpers and dressage riders failed to deliver – was below UK Sport's expectations and, in the press, our effort was completely swamped by Britain's brilliant tally of gold medals in Beijing.

The next day, Alice Fox-Pitt had organised a great consolation which meant I couldn't be down for long. Alice is amazing. She's so kind and thoughtful in sorting everybody out and she was determined to organise a boat trip for the team and close British supporters.

We had an idyllic day on a junk, motoring out to one of the islands where we anchored off it, swam to shore, had a wonderful barbecue on the beach, played volleyball and stood around in the water drinking and chatting. Freddie and Emily were jumping off the top of the boat, and encouraging the grown-ups to follow suit. I don't like to be beaten, so I had to do it as well, as did David.

We made a pact that some of the older generation didn't have to jump off the highest part of the boat, but Freddie was going, 'Come on, Granny, you know you can.' Mum is a very proficient swimmer, so she just climbed up to a high point and leapt off; everyone was amazed.

By the time I got home, I had recovered some of my spirit. I told myself that I'd got silver and bronze medals, and all I'd got to do was keep going for another four years and I might complete the set.

CHAPTER 25

The Hardest Loss

Three weeks after Hong Kong, I took Archie and Caffrey to Burghley. By way of preparation, we went to William Fox-Pitt's yard and met up with Yogi to share a jumping lesson. Being an offshoot of Lars Sederholm, who had helped me so much in the 1990s, Yogi is a good jumping teacher, and watching William is a fantastic lesson in itself.

Most of my jumping technique has been learned from watching others, and William would be the person I'd watch most. He's so soft and free with his horses and they have a lovely life with him, spending lots of time relaxing out in the field.

Burghley was on a knife-edge; the rain was so relentless that no one was sure whether it would go ahead. I was hoping desperately that cross-country day would happen, because both my horses had gone well in the dressage. Thanks to Ferdi, Caffrey had really improved, with more relaxed changes, and Archie was coping really well with the conditions. He'd been one of the last to go and by the time it was our turn, the arena was a mass of brown stodge. Archie must have been longing to avoid the deep, ploughed lines created by previous horses and canter on the grass, but he was very good and went where I asked.

On the Thursday night, as the rain poured down, part of the *Masterchef* final was filmed at the Event Riders Association dinner. We had the most delicious food and it was a fun atmosphere.

Perhaps if it had been my first four-star event, I might have been reluctant to go across country in the mud, but I knew my two horses were fit and brave and strong, and I was quite happy. Many others, however, struggled and a number of riders withdrew after one refusal. It turned into a bit of a survival of the fittest, and at the end of the day William was lying first and second with Tamarillo and Ballincoola, the American rider Phillip Dutton was third, and I was fourth and fifth on Archie and Caffrey, who both felt fantastic.

William thanked me profusely for clocking up some time penalties, but I was a little annoyed with myself. Even so, I don't think I could have gone much faster. Only two horses were within the time: Tamarillo and Barry's Best, ridden by Rosie Thomas, who was first to go on the course and really boosted everyone's confidence with her gutsy performance.

Next morning, Phillip withdrew, and I had the same fence down on both horses, which moved me up to third and fourth. A part of me thought it was a shame William didn't have flu that day! However, it was lovely for him to win on Tamarillo after all the bad luck they'd suffered.

On a personal note, I felt satisfied. It had been a tough event and I knew inside that I'd done a good job on this occasion. On a financial note, my placings also gave me a boost in the new HSBC Classics series, in which riders accrued points in the four-star events that would enable them to win substantial sums of money at the end of the season. This meant it was worth me going out to Pau again and having a crack at gaining some decent prize-money. As Cavvy had, in reality, had a quiet year, with hardly any pre-Hong Kong outings, I decided that he could cope with another run. After speaking to the Davieses, we agreed that it was worth returning to France for a bit of fun.

In the meantime, Blenheim, where I had taken Nancy and Tessa, was cancelled at the halfway stage due to the appalling weather, and I re-routed them to Boekelo, where I had another unfortunate mishap.

Perhaps because she hadn't done enough work, Nancy set off across country like a lunatic, producing a new and disconcerting head-wagging action when I tried to control her. Unsurprisingly, we came unstuck early on, at a complex with a log on top of a bank, followed by a downhill slope to another log on a right angle.

It all went wrong as we whizzed towards the fence with Nancy shaking her head. Going on an awkward four and a half strides instead of five, we went splat on the ledge. I lost my stirrups and reins but felt momentarily rather pleased to be still on the horse. This smug feeling didn't last long, though, as I couldn't stay with her. As she launched off, I fell backwards and landed with a thud on my back.

Ruth Edge caught Nancy, and the jump judge rushed over to see if I was all right. Once they had established that I still knew who and where I was, they let me walk back towards the stables with Ruth and Nancy. The problem was that later I had no recollection whatsoever of getting back to the stables.

It made me realise that the controversial new rule of one fall and elimination, which was introduced from August 2008, is a good one, because although I thought I was fine, and apparently appeared fine to other people, I was obviously concussed and not with it, and shouldn't have been riding across country and making judgements that might not have been safe.

The doctor checked me out, by which time I was OK to show jump next day with Tess, who finished seventeenth. I was a bit annoyed with myself about Tess's dressage because I didn't ride her forward enough, but I think one day she will do a good test. Her jumping, however, was really satisfying; as a novice she was hopeless and, unlike her sisters, she doesn't have a natural technique.

She is a tubby horse, who has to be kept on a diet – again unlike her sisters – but has the calmest temperament out of the three mares and I have high hopes for her in the future. I am keen that at some stage she provides a just reward to Derek Baden, who is one of my most loyal owners.

Nancy was less straightforward. Although I didn't want to end her season on the Boekelo note, she can become fretful when travelling. At home, she shows a loving and devoted nature; she likes to be near you, and will stand with her nose resting on you or walk with her head near you. However, she is also very much a blood horse and has something a little strange in her make-up.

She has a tendency to get stressed and finds stable life quite difficult. When horses are being led out of other stables, she gets worked up, so she lives out as much as possible. I have learned that she copes better with life if she's out with Emily's horses; that way she remains relaxed and content and maintains her weight.

After a lot of umming and aah-ing I decided she would

accompany Cavvy to Pau for her first four-star. I had an open mind as to how she'd get on, but her owners, Gilly Robinson and Hazel Fastnedge, were very supportive.

Nancy did a good test for her first four-star attempt, and kept her cool, appearing to cope well with the change of atmosphere. There were a lot of places to make a mistake on the cross-country and, while trying to be positive, I decided not to be too competitive and to opt for some slower routes.

The danger of deliberately being uncompetitive is that you'll fiddle along and not ride well. However, Nancy went really well, only running out at a pair of angled hedges, perhaps remembering what had happened at Saumur. She finished twentieth, which was a perfectly acceptable result in what was a strong field, and I had a great feeling of pride at having got my first home-bred horse to a four-star.

Cavvy was supposed to be the real banker, but due to an annoying error on my part, I missed out on that useful extra money.

Our dressage took place in early-morning fog and a quiet arena, and he produced a lovely test which had us right up in the placings. I knew the cross-country was well within his capacity, as long as I rode him correctly. Ahead of us was a plain log pile on an easy line, followed by three strides to an angled trakehner and five to a corner. At the last minute, something made me steady him and add another stride. I'd been conscious that we were going a bit freely, but wasn't organised enough to correct it sooner.

Cavvy's head came up and we skewed over the first log pile, and we became so unbalanced that he was approaching the trakehner sideways on. I had a split second to decide whether we could jump this huge fence off one stride and decided instead to circle and give ourselves more room. Unfortunately, I managed to cross my tracks while doing so and incurred 20 penalties.

The next day Cavvy was foot perfect in the show jumping, ending up eighth, and I later worked out that we could have won. Apart from Burghley, it seemed that all my major competitions that year were blighted by ridiculous expensive mistakes, but it's something you just have to shrug off.

I had one more chance to win some serious prize-money to put towards my new house. Earlier in the year, Stuart Buntine, an innovative and energetic event organiser who runs Belton, had approached me, plus several other leading riders, about a new concept called Express Eventing.

The idea was a 'one seat sees all' eventing-based competition to take place in Cardiff's Millennium Stadium in November. There would be freestyle dressage to music, followed by a timed show jumping round, a timed 'pit-stop' in which we changed into a different shirt, and then a timed 'cross-country' course. The prize-money was massive – £100,000 to the winner.

It turned all our heads. Riders simply don't have the chance to win that sort of life-changing money very often, and I'm sure all of us were dreaming of paying off our mortgages when we signed the contracts so many months in advance to say that we'd turn up and do things like cooperate with the media.

Cavvy was sixteen by now and the plan was for him to be a fun horse in 2009, with Archie taking over the top spot. His owners therefore agreed that I should take him to Cardiff for what promised to be a fun and lucrative weekend – everyone was guaranteed to take home £3,000 even if they finished last.

My last month with Cavvy was so enjoyable. The girls were off for November, and the other horses turned out, so it was just him and me, and he'd always been a joy to look after.

I had a couple of lessons with Ferdi, as we practised the more difficult movements, such as canter pirouettes and tempi changes, which Cavvy took to easily. I also got a tape of music sorted out. I did a rather cheesy thing and used Andrew Lloyd Webber's music, because I knew he would be a judge, along with Arlene Phillips from *Strictly Come Dancing*.

The *Phantom of the Opera* music suited his powerful trot, we used 'King Herod's Song', a slow, swanky piece of music from *Jesus Christ Superstar*, for the walk and Julian Lloyd Webber's 'Variations on a Theme of Paganini' for the canter work. It was an exciting build-up, as all over the country riders were rushing off for dressage-to-music lessons.

All the riders and their partners were put up at a posh hotel the night before, and David and I attended the smart dinner. Jodie came back to help me as a groom for the weekend and she and Mum and Emily brought Cavvy up in the lorry next day. Mum had loaded the lorry up with friends from the village, including Daphne Sleight, my old Pony Club district commissioner.

The competition had received a lot of publicity, and the *Sidmouth Herald* was following my progress. The organisers had sold 14,000 seats; that might have been a drop in the ocean in the 90,000 seat stadium, which was very cold and echoed, but was nevertheless pretty good for a horsey event. There was a terrific buzz surrounding the competition, and the arena, with its special green surface, looked fantastic, like a model of a course.

Everything became very rushed, though. There was limited warm-up space at the back, and it was on a slope. Before going into the arena, we had to warm up by trotting round concrete pillars in what was essentially an underground car park.

Cavvy did a great test though, and we lay second to Bettina Hoy on Ringwood Cockatoo, who had won at Pau. I was pleased with this, as Bettina is a great dressage rider and she did a beautiful test.

When I first saw the course, I was quite happy with it. The main problem was that the schedule was somewhat frantic, and riders' time to walk the course and take in the enormity of having to remember forty jumping efforts, was limited. It had been built overnight, after an Australia–Wales rugby match; stadium ground staff and officials had literally stayed up all night to do it, unsurprisingly running out of time and only finishing at 9.30 a.m. that morning.

I walked round and round it as fast as I could, keeping going so that it became fixed in my mind. There was a false bank which I didn't like the look of, and it turned out to ride badly, but other than that I didn't think it was too bad, just rather over-technical.

The first rider on the course was Rodolphe Scherer, who had been persuaded to come over from France. His horse shot across the false bank and Rodolphe came off, landing hard on his hip. That, in hindsight, was the moment everything started to go wrong. Instinctively, I didn't like what I saw, and decided not to watch any more.

The competition descended into chaos, as rider after rider either got eliminated for three refusals or simply lost their way. Nicolas Touzaint, and the two Americans, Phillip Dutton and

Buck Davidson, got lost. Tina Cook was eliminated on her Olympic horse, Henry, and was in tears afterwards because the horse was so upset. Then there was a long hold because Mark Todd's horse, Gandalf, went through a corner. This could so nearly have been a bad accident but mercifully wasn't.

A handful of riders did really well to complete, most notably Lucy Wiegersma who did an immaculate round, but they were all pretty flustered and it had become a bit farcical with the commentator, John Kyle, starting to say things like 'And now she's turning left to the wall' in order to help riders remember their way.

Oli Townend went really fast and, as he wasn't far behind me in the dressage, I knew I couldn't catch him, I'd just got to go as fast as I safely could in order to pick up some prize-money.

Cavvy jumped one of only two clear show jumping rounds, and then we were in the pit-stop. This was panic-inducing. The noise and chaos were overwhelming and what seemed such a straightforward thing – pulling on a stretchy branded shirt and putting my crash hat back on – took far too long. Emily was my helper and we both became flustered.

Cavvy went clear until we came to a double of corners, which I knew hadn't been riding that well. For some reason, we drifted to the right over the second corner, I hope not due to me using too much right rein. He dived at it, half banked it, took the red flag with us, and caught his hind toe on the back edge of the fence. This meant that his hind leg extended as he went over the fence, which is how he broke it.

As I hit the ground, my first thought was that I'd blown it. Then I looked up and realised something far more serious and awful had happened than my losing some money. Cavvy was on the ground, struggling to get up, and I knew instantly what had happened. I put my hands to my face as he got up, with his hind leg just hanging at a terrible angle. He knew something was wrong, and gave a heart-breaking whinny, which will haunt me for ever.

Fortunately, he stood still while I ran to him. The arena, which had been full of roaring, screaming noise, went silent. People rushed up with screens, and the trailer arrived to take him out of the arena, but everyone could see what had happened because they were sitting high up in the stadium. People were crying and walking out; others were just frozen to the spot, horrified.

I was just praying for it to be over. Cavvy somehow hobbled into the trailer, I got in and held his head, stroking him and trying to comfort him. John Killingbeck, the vet, was at the other end, pushing against his hip and trying to give him some support while the trailer left the arena.

Cavvy was pouring sweat, so much so that it was like a sauna in the trailer. The air was so thick that I could hardly see John. Agonisingly, the trailer got stuck on some sand as it was leaving the arena, and the couple of minutes we were waiting to move off felt like hours. It was the final straw.

I was asked if I wanted Cavvy to be taken to a veterinary centre to be examined, but I begged them to put him down as quickly as possible. I knew it was no good, and I couldn't bear him to be suffering.

CHAPTER 26

Looking Forward

I have had many traumas and disappointments in my career but, with the exception of Ryan's collapse at Weston Park, Cavvy's death was easily the worst thing that has happened to me with a horse, and it was much worse because it was so public. Perhaps that was why I didn't cry until I spoke to Janette Chinn, who had been watching helplessly. I had to compose myself because a big crowd had gathered around the stables and everyone was looking down on me, asking how Cavvy was. Instinct made me pull myself together to reply to these poor shocked people.

My immediate concern was for Emily and Jodie, both of whom were distraught, and for Mum and her friends who would have to make the saddest journey home with an empty lorry. David and I were due to go away for our annual holiday the next day, but I felt terrible for the owners, and for everyone who had bought tickets and had to witness such a tragedy.

However, the public response was extraordinary. While I was away on holiday, Mum dealt with the flowers – we got masses and masses of bouquets. And I came home to five hundred letters of sympathy, plus many emails and texts.

*

David and I spent three days in Oman but we didn't see very much. Perhaps because of all that had happened, I felt very tired and we didn't get to explore the country with its valleys and hills and inland lakes. Some day I'd love to go back because it's quite different from the only other place I've been in the Middle East – Dubai. We then flew to Sri Lanka where we had a wonderful holiday travelling down the west coast.

On Boxing Day, we went on a family skiing holiday with Stephen and Fiona Joyce and their daughter Molly, one of Emily's best friends, and her sister Katie. We took an apartment near Montreux on Lake Geneva, the plan being to drive to a different resort each day. Unfortunately, on the first hour of the first day in Avoriaz – poised at the top of the Swiss Wall, a famous black run down into Switzerland – Freddie, who is quite fearless on skis and was doing some bumps beside the run, fell over on a patch of ice and broke his humerus. He was taken off in a blood wagon and airlifted to hospital in Aigle. This rather curtailed our activities and we came back on New Year's Eve.

Meanwhile, progress was being made on the new house. Because the yard where we wanted to build came within a designated Area of Outstanding Natural Beauty, we had to conform to strict planning regulations. My first plans were rejected, as were the second lot, but we went to appeal and opted for an informal hearing. This took a whole year, but in the end we won, and I got permission to convert part of the old stone yard and build new stables.

Needless to say, the new stables happened much faster than the house, which turned out to be a slow process. The local building company discovered that the mortar in the old flint walls was too powdery to save. The building inspector came and condemned the barns, so they had to be flattened. I then had to reapply for planning as it was now going to be a 'new build'.

I had always dreamed of living beside my stables. The thirty-minute journey between home and the yard had become part of my life, but it was very hard work. Sometimes that last half-hour felt like the final straw after driving all the way back from an event at the other end of the country.

It also involved a lot of work and organisation with small children, and I was constantly packing the car and having to remember everything. It's been awkward for them, at times, too, having to go via the yard on the way to and from school.

Now David will have to drive! Initially, the house was entirely my project, but this year he has taken over financially and has become interested. It will have views of the sea, and lots of light, and I think it will be wonderful when it's finished. My good friend Jackie Michelmore has been a great help with the interior and exterior design.

Unfortunately, the prize-money I'd hoped to be putting towards the house hasn't been forthcoming this spring. In fact, apart from the foot-and-mouth year and my broken neck, I can't remember a leaner time.

Despite the loss of Cavvy, things had still looked promising before Christmas. I acquired an exciting new horse, Hobby du Mee, who is owned by Eddie and Sue Davies with Janette Chinn and was ridden for Ireland by Austin O'Connor.

He is a horse I have always admired, having first spotted him as an eight-year-old at the Punchestown Europeans in 2003. At the time, he was being ridden for the silver medal French team by Jean Teulère, and the way this young horse handled such an imposing course was really eye-catching. Austin was thrilled to get the ride later, and I was impressed by their double clear in Hong Kong.

However, the decision was made to move him from Austin, so he came to me. We didn't have much time to get acquainted, as I soon realised that he wasn't very sound. Having started top-level eventing early in his career, he'd done a lot of mileage, and he felt like an older horse than his fourteen years.

As soon as I increased his work, I could feel there was something wrong, and I told his owners that he needed to be examined. It turned out that he was lame all round, with suspensory ligament damage in his hindlegs and worn coffin joints in front.

There is an operation which can relieve pain successfully, but I wasn't sure it was worth it at his age. However, the Davieses have had it done, so we shall see what happens this autumn. Hobby is a petite horse in comparison to Archie, but he is a lovely polite ride and real quality.

The first event of the season was Stilemans, where I took Kings Albert and Rock to do novice sections. Four days later, Albert started to show a snotty nose; he was coughing and had a temperature. A few days later, Rocky followed suit.

I isolated the pair of them, disinfected everywhere and hoped I'd got away with it as I continued with my plans to go to Fontainebleau with four advanced horses.

As Fontainebleau was to be the site of the 2009 European Championships, and I'd never been there, I thought I'd go and get a feel of the site. A three-star CIC takes place there each year in March.

I was imagining a beautiful, typically French eventing site, with a chateau and parkland, something along the lines of Chantilly or Le Lion d'Angers. In fact, Fontainbleau is on a rather scruffy little racetrack and the cross-country is almost all wooded, like Tweseldown but without the view. The town itself is beautiful, but the event is two kilometres away from it.

It was too early in the season to be really competitive, and they were all a bit too jolly in the dressage, but all four horses went well, although I wasn't sure that the Championships were going to be Imperial Cavalier's (Archie) forte because it was a twisting course rather than the galloping track he liked.

Kings Fancy (Nancy) jumped a double clear and I decided that this would be a good time to sell her because I didn't visualise her getting a top three finish in a four-star, although she could be a very good horse for someone else.

No sooner had I put the advertisement in *Horse & Hound* than she became ill, too. The yard ground to a halt – I had my first Easter at home for twenty years – and, disappointingly, I had to withdraw Archie from Kentucky, a venue I feel would have suited him. Badminton came down to just good old Apache Sauce (Caffrey).

The only cheering thing on the horizon was that my '2012 back-up horse' arrived! The Davieses and Janette had spotted an eight-year-old called Fernhill Urco winning Barroca d'Alva CIC in Portugal under the young Portuguese rider Duarte Seabra, riding for the Irish-based producer Carol Gee.

Urco is more 'foreign' than my usual stamp, a workmanlike steel-grey gelding, Holstein cross Thoroughbred, with big movement. Frustratingly, my first chance to see what he was made of, at Chatsworth, was called off due to heavy rain. So, the next weekend I got up at 3 a.m. to go to Aston-le-Walls, where he finished third in an Open Intermediate section. He made a lovely shape over a fence and was brave, but he also had a tendency to run on naively at everything, even in the show jumping, and I remember thinking, 'Blimey, I can't stop.'

Our next outing was at Tattersalls, where he was sixth in the CIC World Cup qualifier. Archie, who was thrilled to be out, was third, which was good enough to earn us a listing for the European Championships at Fontainebleau, and Tess thirteenth. In addition, Albert and Kings Rock went well at their first one-star competition, at Houghton, so I felt I was back on track.

I was very proud when Tess was added to the European list as well, following a fourth place at Luhmühlen, her first four-star and a pretty good result for a nine-year-old, especially as there were a lot of problems on the course. Her achievements during the season won me my third consecutive British Breeders' award for the best British-bred young event horse.

I rode Urco in the concurrent CIC at Luhmühlen, where he began to show his greenness. We came to a coffin (rail – ditch – rail), where he jumped in boldly but then suddenly saw the ditch, dropped his back legs and caught his stifle. I leapt off, realising he wasn't right, and there was a nasty moment with him standing there, quivering and holding his hind leg up, but, fortunately, he'd only banged a nerve.

Tess's good result spurred me into doing an embryo transfer with her. I'd been dragging my heels, because it's an expensive process, and I was only going to consider doing it once she had proven herself at four-star level. I decided to send her to the Beaufort Embryo Centre, and chose the advanced event stallion Chilli Morning, who is owned by Chris Stone, who bought Kings Gem the previous year – I had seen Chilli Morning competing with Nick Gauntlett.

Fortunately, Tess came into season a couple of days after arriving there. She double ovulated and when she was flushed eight days later, there were two embryos that were good enough to be implanted into surrogate mares. I'd also decided to try and get an embryo from Kings Fancy before I sold her – she is now with Laura Shears. For her I used the advanced event Stallion Mill Law. It worked very smoothly so the following summer I had a whole new dynasty of three foals!

Meanwhile, Archie was very much on track for what I hoped would be my sixth ride at a European Championships. His big summer event was the CIC at Aachen; it was a lovely sunny weekend, the prize-money was good and we finished fourth – it was all looking good. My first suspicions that it was all about to go wrong came at Gatcombe, where I was lungeing him before his dressage test to calm him down. There was something that didn't look quite right, but I got my farrier, Clive Evans, to take a nail out of one of Archie's shoes, and he seemed sound after that, so I carried on.

Unfortunately, I blew our chances of a British Open title with an incredibly silly fall, having had a commanding lead after the dressage. There was a tyre fence off a turn, which you could either take on a long one stride or a short two. Tess popped in a neat two strides and did it perfectly, going on to finish seventh and win the best-young-horse trophy for Derek Baden, but I thought that Archie, as a bigger horse, would be better off on one.

Fatally, I changed my mind. I'd been chatting at the start to Joe Meyer and William Fox-Pitt, who both told me they were planning to go on one stride and both subsequently ran out at the second element so I decided to hold for two strides, but there was no way Archie could fit in two, so he tripped over the side of the fence, and I fell off. It was so embarrassing, and I felt I'd really let him down.

Our final pre-Fontainebleau run was at Highclere, where, again, I lunged him before the dressage to settle him. To my shock, he again looked unlevel. The team vet, Liz Brown, agreed – he looked sound when trotting on a straight line but not so great going on a circle.

A trip to Sue Dyson in Newmarket confirmed my fears: Archie had inflammation of the hind suspensory ligaments, and although he could have run at Fontainebleau, it might have damaged him further. Remembering that he hadn't really enjoyed the deep sandy going there in the spring, I reluctantly decided that it wasn't meant to be. My overriding ambition for him was the World Equestrian Games at Kentucky in 2010. I'd always thought that would be the course for him, and I didn't want anything to jeopardise that.

So my end of season was unremarkable but satisfactory: Caffrey was twelfth at Burghley, and Tess went beautifully to finish eighteenth and win the embryo transfer prize as best mare; Urco continued to progress with placings at Blenheim and Boekelo, Rocky spent the autumn in Justin Tuffs' show-jumping yard to try and improve that phase.

By that stage, however, I had far greater worries than competition records. Emily had not had a good year. Her troubles began in the spring with a broken patella while playing hockey. Then, in June, she had a nasty fall at West Wilts. I'd left her there with Mum while I went to speech day at Hartpury College, where I was guest of honour. As I emerged from the ceremony,

I saw a missed call from Mum: Emily had been taken to hospital in Bath.

I found her to be in a real state, concussed, with broken ribs and torn cartilage between them, and her whole body in shock and pain. Apparently, the horse had spooked, and she'd come off backwards, falling heavily on her back.

A couple of months later, at Burghley, she shut her thumb in a door and broke it. This third accident seemed to break her spirit, and in front of David's and my horrified eyes she quickly slid into a frighteningly hopeless, lifeless state.

Tests revealed that Emily was suffering from chronic fatigue syndrome, for which the cure is rest, calmness – and hope. Emily's symptoms were that of flu, but with no temperature; she couldn't get to sleep at night and would eventually drift off in the small hours, sleeping heavily until waking, not refreshed, at lunchtime. Then she would lie in a glazed state in front of the television. She became hyper-sensitive, not bearing to be touched, and even her clothes made her uncomfortable. You couldn't even hug her to comfort her because she'd cry out in pain.

It is heart-rending and bewildering to watch your child suffer like this. You feel both helpless and, I'm sorry to say, occasionally impatient, but the overriding feeling is that you would do anything in the world to make them better. However, it wasn't until I Googled her symptoms that the real seriousness of the situation sunk in; chronic fatigue syndrome is the new name for ME, an illness I knew could be a life sentence.

CHAPTER 27

Lightning Bolt

The thought of my daughter ending up in a wheelchair or bedridden, which is what happens in the most serious cases of ME, was unbearable. As a family, we knew only too well what could happen: I have an uncle who had been severely disabled as a result of ME.

Just as I was weighing up the options of what we could do to help Emily, I got a call from Neil Gibson, a reiki practitioner. He had got my number from Lucinda Fredericks, whose horses he helps, as he wanted permission to use a picture of me in his leaflet.

I told him truthfully that I wasn't a great believer in alternative medicine but to send me his leaflet to read. Then, when I saw that reiki can help with ME symptoms, I rang him up and asked if he would come and see Emily. Neil explained that he couldn't cure her, but he could help; even better, he said that he knew of a person who had been helped by something called the Lightning Process.

I immediately looked it up on the Internet and was impressed by the high-profile backing the course had attracted from people such as Esther Rantzen, whose daughter had been extremely ill, and the rugby player Austin Healey, whose wife had suffered from ME following post-natal depression. The website was easy to use, and I found a local practitioner, Jan Oakley, at Bideford. She sounded lovely on the phone and said she had a 100 per cent success rate with teenage sufferers. But she pointed out: 'Your daughter needs to come in the right frame of mind.'

Thankfully, Emily was willing to give it a go and answered all the preliminary questions positively, because the process doesn't work unless you give it complete commitment and belief. Where perhaps we were luckiest was in the speed of Emily's diagnosis; she had only been suffering the symptoms of ME for about three months – often it takes five or six months just to diagnose it.

If I hadn't seen the Lightning Process with my own eyes, I don't think I would have believed it. Emily joined five fellow ME sufferers for a three-day course of four hours a day. At the start they all looked awful and were suffering, like her, from 'brain fog' and lethargy; it had been a Herculean task just to get them there in the first place. Jan captured them all from the start. She explained that the brain is slow to recognise changes: for instance, if you stop wearing a watch, you will continue to look at your wrist to tell the time. ME begins after you've had a virus or a trauma; your body appears to have recovered, but your brain doesn't recognise the fact. You then get the side-effects, such as hyper-sensitivity and aching, and you fall into a seemingly inescapable loop of illness.

At the beginning of the course Jan asked her patients how they felt on a scale of one to ten – most replied three at most. Then she asked them to remember the feeling of being well, and what action most summed up feeling well and happy. For Emily, it was galloping across a field. Jan asked them how they felt after visualising this moment of happiness and good health, and immediately they all started to feel they were improving. She taught them a brain-training process involving visualisation, positiveness and a belief that they could feel better. Jan made them repeat the process over and over again during the three days. I even began to do it myself, and immediately felt energised. It was extraordinary.

At the end of the first day, the group were all told to do something they hadn't done for ages. Emily took our collie, Tommy, for a walk, something she hadn't done for months. The following day, she took Tommy a bit further, which made her faint, but he licked her face and she got up and kept going. Excitingly, she was looking brighter, and that night she slept a little better.

By the third and last day, I was feeling desperate, because Emily seemed to be taking such small steps. But at the end of the third day's session she was suddenly bright-eyed, and you could see there was a lot of positive reaction in the group, which made me feel choked with emotion.

On the way home, she asked for fish and chips, and when we got back she went onto the British Eventing website to look for events to enter. The next day, she came into our bedroom wearing a tracksuit and asked me to play tennis with her. I could hardly see the ball for tears. She explained that she felt as though she'd been let out of a cage.

When she asked to go hunting on Boxing Day, I was unsure whether to allow her to go. Having being doing nothing for three months she was so unfit. I phoned Jan Oakley, and her reaction was, 'Yes, you must treat her as a normal, well person.

She said, OK, Emily might be very stiff and get sore muscles after hunting but it would be a healthy stiffness ... and how right she was.

I was torn between elation at her recovery and fury that we'd been so lucky when other children were still unable to drag themselves out of bed. It turned out that some doctors were unaware of the Lightning Process and that it was not officially recognised, due to it being considered hypnosis, which is not necessarily a good idea for teenagers.

However, the first thing I did was ring up Neil Gibson and thank him, for without him contacting me, none of this might have happened. The second thing was to contact my uncle, who had been an ME sufferer for twenty years and was in a wheelchair. It took a lot of persuasion to get him to attend a course. He was sceptical and nearly didn't complete the three days, but then he realised that he wasn't aching any more. He hasn't used a wheelchair since and went on holiday for the first time in years without it.

I managed to get publicity for the Lightning Process in local papers, on BBC *Spotlight* and in *Horse & Hound*. I was inundated by phone calls from interested and grateful people, and I'm thrilled to report that the process is now going through trials with the possibility of it being accepted by the British Medical Association and allowed to be an NHS recommended therapy.

After what was a much happier Christmas than anticipated, my twin preoccupation was the house move and the build-up to Badminton and the World Equestrian Games. Sadly, however, there was more family crisis to come.

Emily had another serious fall, this time at home when schooling King Casper. She'd gone up the road on her own to work him, and I was just beginning to wonder where she was when I heard a tractor approaching at high speed. It was our neighbour Andrew, who had spotted Emily lying on the ground and the horse loose.

I rushed up to find Emily looking terrifyingly still, but as I got closer I could see movement: her shoulders were shaking with sobs. She was concussed and in so much pain that she couldn't move her legs, though, thankfully, she could feel them. Her body was shaking with cold, so I tried to keep her warm until the air ambulance landed in the field.

The hospital diagnosed heavy bruising, but she was in so much pain that we had to bring a mattress downstairs for her to lie on – she could barely get down on the floor to lie on it. She cried and groaned so much with every movement that it was agonising to watch; I just wanted to take the pain for her.

Emily came to watch me ride her horses for her at Larkhill, but she could only creep around, and I didn't like the thought of her being on such strong painkillers. By Belton, she was more enthusiastic, because my horses were going well, but she was still limping, and, as we were parked next door to Andy Thomas, the British team physio, I asked him to look at her. He thought that she might have fractured her pelvis, and by the end of the day I noticed that she was grey and listless with exhaustion and pain.

I took her back to hospital, where they did more X-rays, but they didn't find anything. I persisted, because she clearly wasn't improving, and finally they did an MRI scan, which showed she'd fractured her pelvis in two places. It was a relief to have it finally confirmed, but we weren't out of the woods. After a few weeks of healing the hospital tried to get Emily mobile, encouraging her to walk and use the hydrotherapy pool, but, to my horror, she seemed to be deteriorating instead of recovering. I consulted a physiotherapist, who suggested that her sacro-iliac joint might have become displaced, and, sure enough, it had slipped out of line. This was simple to fix, and after that her progress was rapid.

This was a relief, as home life was becoming chaotic. We'd hoped to move into the new house at Christmas, but, inevitably, the finishing touches took longer than expected, and I'd been struggling to raise the funds due to a lack of prize-money income. I was juggling sleeping at the hospital with shifting all our possessions, which I'd been doing by filling up Emily's trailer each day and transporting them bit by bit on my daily drive from our farm to my yard.

I hadn't realised that over the five years of building the house David had never really taken on board the fact that we were actually moving. Farming is his life and he is very focused, dedicated and successful at his work. I had been the driving force in getting the new house built, because it was what I wanted, and I hadn't stopped to consider the impact that moving away from the place he'd lived in all his life was having on him.

I felt desperately guilty for not noticing how anxious he'd become and for being impatient when he seemed so demo-tivated. His mood was utterly black, he was unfocussed and was losing weight, which was terrifying him. It was all so unlike the outgoing, friendly, jolly, dependable man I'd married, but with Emily stretched out on one sofa and he on another, the house to sort and horses to ride, I maybe didn't give him the attention I should have.

After a dire period, David was diagnosed with clinical depression, something I knew very little about. It hasn't been easy, but we've both learned a lot, and I admire him for the way he has tackled the illness and been so open to getting medical help.

We are all now very happily settled into our beautiful new house. I have to keep pinching myself to believe that I live in such a lovely house. It's certainly a far cry from the verger's cottage of old, with its outside loo and no heating. To be able to see the sea and roll out of bed each morning and actually be at my work place is sheer luxury!

CHAPTER 28

The Road to Kentucky

After a working winter holiday with his owners, Archie's inflammation settled, and he was given the all-clear to be prepared for Badminton 2010. By the time we got there, he was popping with energy after a winter of anticipation, and our dressage was not as good as I'd hoped. We were fourteenth at that stage, and I knew I was going to have to work harder at subduing him at a championship.

He was equally full of beans when we set off across country, and it didn't do our cause any good when we got held, just before the big Giant's Table fence in front of Badminton House. I ended up chatting with the crowd, as you often do on these occasions, and perhaps allowed myself to get distracted, as we had a couple of hairy jumps down the Vicarage Vee line. However, he went beautifully the rest of the way, and it moved us up into second place, behind Paul Tapner.

I was lucky to have only show jump down, because by that stage he felt very strong and forward, and we slipped to fourth place, but I knew it was good enough to earn a place at the World Games.

The announcement of the squad caused quite a stir. The six selected were me, William Fox-Pitt with his Kentucky winner

Cool Mountain, Tina Cook and Miners Frolic, the reigning European Champions, Nicola Wilson, who had gone so beautifully as pathfinder in Fontainebleau on Opposition Buzz, Pippa Funnell on her fabulous Bramham winner Redesigned and Piggy French with a new ride, Jakata.

There was a lot of talk about the fact that neither Redesigned nor Jakata had four-star form, and that people such as Lucy Wiegersma, Oli Townend, Daisy Dick and Sharon Hunt, who had won Luhmühlen on Tankers Town, were only reserves. The chatter came to a crescendo at Barbury, supposedly our main competition outing, when Miners Frolic was absent and Piggy had to withdraw Jakata. But the selectors stuck to their guns, and, as it turned out, all their choices were totally justified.

We probably added to the rumour mill when Archie pulled off a shoe, and quite a bit of hoof, a few days before Barbury. A local farrier came to reshoe him, but the horse was alarmingly sore afterwards. I quickly removed the shoe and poulticed the foot, travelling to Barbury minus the shoe. I called in to see Clive Evans, my farrier, on the way, and he did a great job.

Archie actually led the dressage at Barbury with a lovely test, but I felt the ground was too firm for a horse with a sensitive hoof and withdrew him. Instead, we had a useful run at Aston-le-Walls, finishing seventh. He was also well placed in the British Open at Gatcombe a few weeks later, but I decided it was sensible not to run across country there either, and we finally had a pipe-opener at Highclere, where he felt super and finished second in the advanced.

Kentucky would be Archie's first flight and also my head girl Jodie Summers' first time at a championship as well as her first trip to America, so there was excitement all round. Emma

Moore, my other reliable groom, was resigned to looking after the horses at home, having had the pleasure of being head groom at Burghley with Caffrey and Tess a few weeks before. I volunteered to be one of the drivers to take the horses to Liege in Belgium, from where they were flying on to Kentucky with William's head girl Jackie Potts and Liz Brown. Whenever William and I travel together we have a regular meeting place in a service station on the A303. As the 3 a.m. rendezvous approached, I realised to my horror that the lorry was getting slower and slower.

The next stop was Tina's yard in Sussex, and I rang to warn her that I was getting behind. I arranged for the DAF break-down team to meet us there, and they found, to my relief, that the problem was that the speed limiter cable had seized up, which is why we couldn't go any faster than 40 mph.

This was soon sorted, and we reached Liege without incident, where we all kissed our horses goodbye. I drove home, turning round two days later to pick William up again and drive to Heathrow.

We'd heard that Kentucky was a bit disorganised, and I know that our chef de mission Will Connell and his team put in a lot of work before our arrival, but, having expected the worst, it appeared to us to be perfectly under control.

There was a great team spirit between the six of us. Yogi has a system whereby we each get paired up with a 'buddy' who we look out for. This time mine was Nicola Wilson, and I really enjoyed her company – she is definitely a great asset to the team, very level-headed and good fun.

One fun event was a Land Rover off-roading challenge with the Americans. Each of us had to drive through an obstacle course, and if you touched the markers, you lost seconds. Our chefs, Yogi and Mark Phillips, were sitting in the passenger seats directing operations, and Yogi became incredibly competitive. We won, but we couldn't decide if this was a good or bad omen.

It was interesting to watch the other equestrian disciplines. We went out early one cold morning to watch the endurance teams start; grey Arab horses seemed to be popping out of the fog everywhere, and the sound of crews shouting to each other carried in the misty, still air. It was an exciting atmosphere and was fun to watch.

I'd never seen reining either, which is an extraordinary affair, but interesting to watch. And we were able to watch the dress age and had a chance to support the British team, which we often don't, as the dressage is usually after the eventing. I think that their amazing success, team silver and two individual silvers for Laura Bechtolsheimer, was a factor in our success; we were so enthused watching them and felt so proud to see them doing well.

Laura's tests on Mistral Hojris brought tears to the eyes, and it was a real treat to see the Dutch gold medallists Edward Gal and Moorlands Totilas. I'd never seen the horse in the flesh before and loved watching him work, something that seems all the more special if we're not going to see him compete with Edward again, now that he's been sold to a German rider.

On the first day of the eventing dressage, Nicola did her best with Opposition Buzz, who got the unlucky draw of being first into the arena, and William did a very accurate test on Cool Mountain, which kept us up there. But there were a lot of polished performances from people whom we perhaps hadn't taken into account, such as from the Italian and Swedish teams, and with the Germans earning a raft of brilliant marks, it looked alarmingly like Hong Kong all ever again. We began to fear that they would run away with the gold medal and leave us standing, unable to close the gap.

But then on the second day there was a good test from Tina on Miners Frolic, and from the two individuals, Pippa and Piggy, on their young horses – Pippa's was particularly amazing on a nine-year-old – before it came down to me to clinch our team placing.

I had been fairly hopeful that I would be picked for the team, but it's always a very satisfying feeling when it's confirmed, and then I was thrilled and honoured to find myself in the anchorman position, even though I knew it would it would be a test of the nerves. My main problem was that Archie had arrived in Kentucky ridiculously excited, and there was nowhere for him to let off steam with either a hack or a gallop. Even the canter track had hard ground. There were beautiful working arenas, but just going round in small circles doesn't suit him.

He would burst out of his stable every day, with ears pricked and eyes bulging, and everything made him excited; he jogged everywhere, wanted to run forward the whole time and would stare at all the unusual looking horses, like the endurance ones in their coloured bridles, as if they were monsters. As the start of our event got nearer, Archie was still being ridiculously enthusiastic.

Ferdi and I decided that the only thing was to work him really hard. The two days leading up to my test we worked him really thoroughly and he started to produce some lovely work. On the day of our test, I had a jumping lesson with Peter

Murphy, our team jumping trainer, lunged him and had two separate sessions with Ferdi, but when I got on him for the fifth time that day, for the actual test, he felt as if he was going to the cross-country start. He seemed distracted, which makes him hard to ride in a test; he couldn't contain his walk, became fixated by the judges' boxes and wouldn't listen for the flying changes, but, in reality, it could have been much worse. I came out worrying that I hadn't helped the team effort enough, and knowing that I'd probably blown my chance of individual success, but it turned out that it was a good enough mark to move the team up to second place behind the Germans.

The weather was extraordinary: hot and humid when we arrived, in the 90s, then stormy. There was torrential rain and bitter cold, reverting on cross-country day to pleasant, sunny spring-like weather.

When we first walked Mike Etherington-Smith's cross-country course, a lovely galloping track where you could keep the speed up, we all came back feeling very positive about it; it was big, though not overly so, and very fair to the horses. There was a variety of obstacles: the water fences stood out as being serious questions – the first came early on a curving line, and the second, where the brave decision had been made to put a Normandy bank in the middle of the pond, was magnificently built. Horses seemed to read this well, and it provided a good spectacle.

There was also a coffin with a very acute corner and a double of hedges at the end at which my initial reaction was that I'd like to be up on the clock and able to play it safe. At a one-day event, you wouldn't think twice about taking on a fence like this, but it looked a risk in a championship situation especially as the easier alternative was not too time consuming.

As I was near the end of the day, I had time to watch and make decisions. I could see that people were able to take the long route at the hedges and still make the time, which was reassuring, and some of the pressure was taken off when members of the German team made some surprising mistakes and dropped out of the reckoning.

Nicola got the team off to a fantastic start, clear inside the time with a really bold round, and William also did an amazing clear, as did Pippa and Piggy. But Tina had a sticky moment when Miners Frolic jumped into the first water boldly, and she was forced to take avoiding action; agonisingly, she crossed her tracks in the process and incurred 20 penalties, which was very hard for her, having been the star of the team in the last two championships.

Despite the German team effort falling apart, we still had the Americans, New Zealanders and Canadians, who were the dark horses of the championship and went brilliantly, hard on our heels, and I had to go clear to keep us in the gold-medal position. I had to remind myself not to think about the pressure and to stick to what I wanted to do, which was to be brave, forward and positive. But Archie was so easy to ride. He was a changed horse, as if to say 'at last we can get on with the best bit'.

We had one little slip at the quarry, as I turned tightly to go to the palisade and drop, and he lost his hind legs for a moment, but otherwise he was fantastic, giving me one of those memorable rides that feels so assured and powerful. We were easily up on the time, which gave me the opportunity to take the long route I wanted at the hedges and also to set up properly for the last two fences, where there had been some messy jumps as previous horses and riders spied the finish line.

There was huge relief and excitement at being in the team gold-medal position, but it was the tightest possible situation, because we didn't have a fence in hand over the Americans, who definitely had a home victory in their sights. It's also quite a hard position to be in psychologically, because the cross-country feels, to me anyway, like the most important part, and it's hard to get out of the mindset that when that's gone well, you've done your best already.

It was probably almost more nerve-racking for those watching, because when you're riding, you can only do what you can do. I didn't know what would happen, whether Archie would be strong and run at the fences or be more respectful and jump cleanly, and I couldn't help remembering what happened in Hong Kong when Cavvy, who was normally such a clean jumper, had two fences down. All you can do is pray that it will be your turn.

Peter Murphy had given us all some good exercises to get the horses jumping up in the air, and I fitted Archie out with ear muffs – you can't put anything in them, but it does block out some noise – jumping boots on his hind legs to encourage him to be more careful behind and I changed his bit from a plain snaffle to a MacGenis loose-ringed snaffle.

The time was tight, so you had to ride the corners economically and keep tight lines without upsetting the horse's rhythm. Tina had two fences down, which was tough for her but fortunately didn't affect the team score. Then Nicola gave us a wonderful boost with a clear round.

Archie felt in control, although he did run through the bridle before the gate and ended up rather deep to it, but did a good job to get himself out of trouble. Jumping the last fence clear was a wonderful feeling; I was ecstatic.

A little of the pressure was eased by the Americans having fences down, but in the end we didn't need the margin because William rode the most brilliant clear round to clinch the gold medal and, deservedly, an individual silver medal behind Germany's Michael Jung.

The feeling of getting team gold was indescribable: relief at not letting anyone down, sheer happiness and overwhelming emotion all rolled into one. The crowd went mad, it was great for Yogi to get his first team gold on the world stage and everyone was in tears of joy. For me, too, it was lovely to see David looking so happy.

The party after wasn't that wild, as, unbelievably, the bar closed early at our hotel – the owners were leaving early the next morning – but what a feeling. We could feel so proud as a nation, because we knew we had been the outstandingly consistent squad in the jumping phases, and we had the prospect of six top-class horses for the 2012 Olympics. It was a great feeling that was set to keep me going for a long time.

CHAPTER 29

Can We Do It in 2012?

The months after Kentucky were tremendously exciting, because we knew that if – and it was a big if – we could maintain form as a team and keep our horses sound, Olympic gold at London 2012 was a real possibility. That was a fantastic feeling, but a terrifying one as well.

Part of you feels that the climb back to being on top of the world has been so hard fought that you want to preserve the moment – and your horse – in aspic and not emerge for two years, so precarious is success in eventing. But doing nothing isn't really an option; you have to live normally, and do your best.

The 'normal' side of my 2010 season was actually pretty successful, too, and with the early months having been so stressful on the home front, competing my other horses felt like a holiday and was really enjoyable. Caffrey, in particular, had a good season. He can be so naughty and frustrating, but he did me proud with second place in the World Cup qualifier at Tattersalls, seventh at Luhmühlen, fourth at Gatcombe and fifth at Burghley. Tess was disappointing in the spring – I retired her after she ran out at the influential open corner at Badminton and rerouted her to Luhmühlen, where I overrode a hedge combination and she ran out again — but I was very pleased with her seventh place at Burghley. Her two embryo foals were born in June, along with Nancy's foal. Silva Bedding, a lady who lives nearby, foaled them for me, as I was away at Tattersalls at the time. We had three gorgeous colt foals — it was funny to see these beautiful quality foals next to their big, heavy, common surrogate mothers, who I had rented from the Beaufort Embryo Transfer Centre.

That summer I used the Twemlows Stud embryo transfer prize that Tess won at Burghley in 2009, where I put her in foal to Grafenstölz. He's a fashionable sire with excellent jumping and dressage lines, and I hope that his breeding will improve her technique over a fence. One embryo was flushed and implanted successfully.

I was thrilled to see my first two home-breds, Kings Gem and Kings Fancy, doing their first four-stars, at Pau, with their new owners and I didn't even mind being beaten by the two 'Gemmas' in the British Open at Gatcombe. Kings Gem finished third with her new jockey, Gemma Tattersall, who is excellent at riding at speed and has an accurate eye. Most of all, it is very satisfying to be able to produce horses that other people can do well on.

Albert continued to impress; he progressed to advanced, winning a couple of intermediates on the way. Urco, after having a successful start to the season with high placings at Belton advanced and the World Cup qualifier at Chatsworth, was found to have a slight tendon strain, but was expected to be back to full work in 2011 — as he upgraded so quickly, the rest would do him no harm — and I was very lucky that the

Davieses bought me another youngster by Cavalier, a four-year-old who is very much in the stamp of Archie.

After all her problems, Emily got back into her stride and now has three horses and three sponsors. She felt King Joules was getting too strong, so he was sold to Jo Chipperfield, which is proving a great match, and we have found a youngster who will run under the Joules banner in 2011.

Everys, a local solicitor, is supporting her with King Casper, who is now called Everys King, and Hiho Silver, a West Country jewellery company, for whom Emily has designed a teenage range, has Mr Hiho. He is a big Dutch-bred horse we found in Vicky Tuffs' yard in South Wales. I felt he was too big for Emily, but she loved him, getting into cahoots with Patsy Mason, who owned Albert. I suggested to Patsy that she might like to look at the horse competing at a novice event; without hesitation, she fell madly in love with Mr Hiho and bought him there and then, so quickly that we had to have him vetted *after* purchase, which isn't quite the right way round!

Mr Hiho went through a nappy phase, but I'm proud of the way Emily has turned him round. She won her first novice on him, at Bricky, while I was away at Kentucky and finished thirteenth and sixteenth at Aldon CCI*, her first three-day event, on him and Lenamore Famous Freddie, a lovely little dun horse that we had to sell for Hylda Mills. I'm relieved to say that I still beat her!

Emily received some good news when she was put on the junior 'A' list for 2011. She is the youngest of the twenty-five and has dreams of getting a place on the junior squad as soon as possible.

Our new house, the cause of so much pain and anxiety to David, now looks wonderful, and I'm happy to say that he has become much more interested and positive about it.

Freddie, meanwhile, is becoming a successful sportsman in his own right and has been spotted by Exeter FC. He keeps asking me when I'm going to give up and advised me that perhaps 2012 would be a sensible time – until he found out that the 2016 Olympics are in Rio de Janeiro and thought he fancied a trip there!

If I make it to the 2012 Olympics, it will be a British record, as Ian Stark and I are on level pegging with five Olympics each; only the Australians Bill Roycroft and Andrew Hoy, and the Americans Mike Plumb and Bruce Davidson, have done six.

I feel strongly that I want to be at London; I've won Olympic bronze and silver, and I still want a gold medal. I don't know why I'm so motivated after all this time, but I think it must be in the genes. I never knew my father in his competitive sporting days, but I suppose I must have inherited it from him.

I do think more carefully now about what horses I ride; I couldn't go back to the days of taking risks on horses that don't jump well, and I don't feel that I need to go for it at every one-day event any more, as I did thirty years ago when every point and every pound won counted in my struggle to prove myself and earn a living. However, I think I am as competitive as ever to win at the top level.

London 2012 will probably be a watershed for many people, both riders and officials, but I can't imagine a life without eventing. None of the alternative options with horses really appeals at the minute, so while my drive is there, and while I have such lovely horses, owners and sponsors, I will continue. Maybe I'll hang on to ride in a team with Emily! But, in the meantime, I'll wait for the horses to tell me when it's time to stop.

HOW OTHERS SEE MARY

Alan Smith

Equestrian correspondent of the Daily Telegraph *for forty-eight years*

If ever a rider was the archetypal hero of Kipling's poem 'If', treating 'triumph and disaster just the same', then surely Mary King is that person – though, contrary to the ending of the poem, no one would ever mistake her for a man! In more than two decades of writing about her exploits, her tremendous successes, and the occasional dramatic setback, as when she and King William had five show jumping fences down in the Barcelona Olympics and dropped from fourth to ninth, Mary has never been less than open, frank and friendly.

Perhaps because she had to make her own way in a competitive world, first with Sheila Willcox, which taught her a lot but was not an easy time, and subsequently taking one inexperienced horse after another through the grades, Mary has never taken anything, least of all her publicity, for granted.

That she has had a succession of supportive owners and sponsors – essential for all but the richest of riders – is in itself an eloquent tribute to her open, warm personality. But running through it is, and clearly remains, a steely determination to stay at the very top. Despite having two children and the odd accident, like breaking her neck in 2001 – something she dismisses with a smiling shrug – and although having finally achieved the Olympic medal she so coveted in Athens, Mary has lost none of her enthusiasm.

And the superb cross-country ride she gave Call Again Cavalier in Hong Kong clearly demonstrated that the skill is equally undiminished. Then, hitting two of the last three show jumps – the horse's first such mistake for two years, which robbed her of the chance of an individual medal – was treated with characteristic composure. His fatal accident at Cardiff a few weeks later was much harder to take, but she never shied away from it.

My sojourn as a reporter ended in 2008, but if Mary, who brought so much pleasure, and good copy, to that career, as well as delighting my readers with her achievements, can win a gold in London 2012 I might have to come out of retirement to write it up.

Bridget Parker
Chairman of selectors (1993–96) and breeding mentor

Mary was always absolutely excellent in a team. She was a real team player who worked well with everybody and was very obliging about going either first or last. This was especially true at the 1994 World Games when we asked her to go first, on the premise that it would throw the judges to see a really good dressage test so early, and this was to work to our advantage. She was never more masterful in nursing King William home in the hot weather across country or in staying calm during the following day's show jumping, upon which the team gold depended.

I was so pleased for her when she won her individual medal the following year in Pratoni, but I have to admit that, if I'd known she was pregnant, she wouldn't have been in the team because I'd have wanted her to feel that she could pull up at any time.

I was very disappointed for her that she didn't have a good Atlanta Olympics, but even in moments of dreadful disappointment she never blames the horse. There she could so easily have said, 'The damn thing wouldn't turn the corner', but she didn't.

And here she is, more than a decade later, still a great team member and still smiling and enjoying it all. Her attitude to life comes through in her riding.

Gilly Robinson
Long-time owner

It was really the gosling incident that clinched our initial sponsorship deal with Mary, because she had the courage to be truthful and admit that the fluffy creature in the photograph in her sponsorship pack had been eaten. I thought if she was honest about that, she would be honest about other things.

The result that meant the most to me was darling Boris (the love of my life!) coming second and third at Badminton, closely followed by William winning. When Boris was in the lead and then fell in the lake, I went out to meet Mary when she weighed in. She came out of the tent, and we both said simultaneously, 'Damn!' and then started laughing, despite the fact that it was really a sad result. But you've got to get on with these things, and that's been the style of our relationship. She's taught me to say, 'Never mind.'

Olympics are not my favourite thing because they're not a great experience for owners – I'd rather win Badminton or Burghley – but it's not all about the owner and I know what it means to Mary, so I have felt for her so much when it's gone wrong.

I haven't got a competitive bone, but as an owner you have to respect the fact that it's the rider who is doing the dangerous bit, and it's they who want to win most; if something goes wrong, they're much more upset than you are.

As everyone knows, I'm a great one for a party, and I think our relationship has worked because Mary is never precious about having a good time. Once, when we were sharing a hotel room in Luhmühlen, we went down to a classic German buffet breakfast. Mary, who loves her food, went, 'Oh yum – chocolate spread!' put it all over her bread and then found it was pureed prunes.

After winning Saumur with Solly, she came back to England with me in the Winnebago. 'I'm starving,' she said. 'Can I look in the fridge?' She found a trifle, intended to serve eight people, and ate the lot!

That's why I have so much respect. She can stay up all night with the rest of them – she's particularly competitive at party games! – and then be so focused.

Mandy Stibbe
Former riding contemporary and present chairman of selectors

I first sat up and noticed Mary Thomson at Badminton way back in about 1985 when she casually appeared on the scene and blew us all away with an amazing performance on the lovely laid-back Divers Rock. She's never looked back and has had a remarkable record with owners, most of whom have stuck by her, which is quite an achievement in this competitive and fickle age.

She's had many horrible falls, especially the one with Boris at the Normandy Bank at Badminton, which frightened the hell out of all of us. Yet nothing stops her from perfection and winning, not even a broken neck! I think only an Olympic gold will satisfy her, and she truly deserves one.

As a team member, I can't think of anyone more focused. Many riders change at a championship because they're out of their comfort zone, but nothing causes Mary to take her eye off the ball.

It must have been particularly difficult when we asked her to be reserve for Athens; she agreed even though she knew that she would not even be stabled on site or accredited. Many people would have said no thanks, as the chance of getting in the team was slim, but we felt that she was so professional that she would be able to deal with her preparation wherever she was and not be affected by the lack of support or be fazed at seeing the competition venue at the last minute. Sure enough, when she was called up, she just got on with it and medals were won.

The sight of Mary in a bikini at a warm-weather champion-ships has made many a male team official go weak, and as far back as Barcelona she blew everyone off the tennis court, and still does.

Mary is a great ambassador. She always has time for people, whether it is at a press conference or with a waitress who wants to tell her that they once saw her on King William. I can't ever remember her losing her temper or being rude. She truly is an icon for the sport.

Lucinda Green
Former riding contemporary and chairman of selectors

I can't think of Mary without thinking of Riders for Romania. A lot of people just paid lip-service to it, but from Mary I got total commitment year after year. She was completely driven to help and she was fantastic with the children. She really loved them, and some of them, through no fault of their own, were hard to love.

We used to play cards in the lorry late at night, when pulled up in a lay-by somewhere in Eastern Europe, and Mary always had to win. She really wanted to. I didn't think any the less of her for it, but it was an example of a focus that few of us can really comprehend.

In between Romania and the tragedy at Cardiff, where her first thought was to comfort others, I've seen Mary in every sort of situation and she always behaves exactly the same. I imagine her faith helps her in that way. She has an enviable balance, which brings Kipling's poem to mind: people were furious with her for smiling in Barcelona, but she did that because she can 'treat both imposters the same'.

Yogi Breisner
World Class Performance Manager since 2000

My earliest experience of Mary, and one which shows her determination, was when King Solomon got injured at an early stage in preparations for the Sydney Olympics. Star Appeal, however, was going to Badminton and Mary asked me if we would be interested in taking him to Sydney instead.

I said no, not really, because we felt he was an older horse that had had his day. But, I said jokingly, 'Of course, we will be interested if he wins Badminton!' to which Mary replied, 'Well, I'd better win then!' At that point I realised the sort of rider she was and, when I was asked to tip a winner, I immediately named her.

That win encapsulates Mary perfectly. Her children had been ill and she'd been up all night. She managed to be both a mother and family person and a totally focused competitor, all at the same time.

Annie Corbin (née Collings)
Former groom

Badminton was a family highlight when I was young and I remember when Mary, whom I knew from Pony Club, first went on Divers Rock in 1985 and I was running from fence to fence to watch her.

Mary was good for my confidence, because I am a follower rather than a leader, and she introduced me to travels and sports that I would never have done normally, like going to Romania or South America and driving an HGV.

She tried to teach me to snorkel – Mary can do any sport well and she and Katie Meacham were particularly competitive with swimming races when we were on holiday – but I didn't like going out of my depth or wearing flippers. At one point, instead of doing as I was told, I insisted on going through a gap in some rocks; there was quite a swell and I got into trouble and nearly pulled Mary under before being thrown on to some rocks.

I was always a natural groom, rather than a rider, but Mary treated me like a friend and, thanks to Gill Robinson, who was particularly kind, always included me in meals and outings, really in the days when many grooms were much more seg-regated from riders.

As long as the horses were all right, Mary was keen for me to go out and have fun, and we'd have a good debrief on gossip the next day. At one wild Punchestown, I nearly got thrown out after some people – David Green may have had a hand in this – tied me up with ribbon and left me in the marquee.

My proudest moment was when Cuthbert finally behaved and, on his retirement run, finished second at Burghley, while I will always be grateful to King William for all the travels he took me on. There were a few lowlights, too, most notably when we waited and waited at team training in the hope of being taken to Stockholm with Boris and, then, at the eleventh hour, realised there was no hope.

Mary has worked so hard to get where she is and would never ask a groom to do something she wouldn't do, that, even now, I take it hard when things go wrong; I cried over Cavvy at Cardiff. And it isn't just Mary that's an amazing person; her mother, Jill, is pretty special too.

William Fox-Pitt
Team mate

I first got to know Mary on the Riders for Romania trips, when I was rather young and shell-shocked and she was great company and fun to be around.

We first rode on a team together in 1995 when, again, I was the new kid on the block and she was established with King William. She struck me then, as she has ever since, as being a confident, reassuring, unflappable presence, a good anchor on a team when emotions can run high. No one is more personally focused than Mary, and yet she is so supportive within the team.

She's flexible, non-precious and never high maintenance. She deals well with her feelings and doesn't inflict them on anyone else. In Athens, when Tamarillo was lame, the team was losing any chance of a medal and I was feeling pretty sorry for myself, Mary was nothing but supportive and upbeat even though her own longed-for Olympic medal was in jeopardy.

From the moment we got to Hong Kong, we definitely thought she was on a roll and would get an individual medal, but although nothing went drastically wrong, it didn't come off either. I knew, as a fellow competitor, exactly how she felt –

inwardly devastated – but there was not a trace of self-pity either then or in any subsequent conversation.

I've always admired Mary's approach to life and the way she's never let any of her successes affect the way she rides or how she loves her horses.

MARY KING – MAJOR RESULTS

1981	2nd	Osberton (national 3DF)	(Humphrey)
1984	2nd	Windsor	(Divers Rock)
	6th	Boekelo CCI***	(Divers Rock)
1985	7th	Badminton CCI****	(Divers Rock)
1986	1st & 2nd	Bramham CCI***	(King Cuthbert & Silverstone)
	4th	Breda CCI**	(King Boris)
	1st	Osberton	(King Arthur)
1987	1st	Windsor	(King Arthur & King Max)
	8th	Burghley CCI****	(King Boris)
1988	1st	Breda	(King Max)
	2nd	Bramham	(King Cuthbert)
1989	2nd	Badminton	(King Boris)
	5th	Le Lion d'Angers	(King William)
	2nd	Rotherfield Park CCI***	(King Cuthbert)

1990	3rd & 7th	Badminton	(King Boris & King Cuthbert)
	1st	Gatcombe British Open	(King Boris)
	2nd & 4th	Burghley	(King Cuthbert & King Boris)

1991	1st	Gatcombe British Open	(King William)
	Team Gold Medal	European Championships at Punchestown	(King William)
	1st	Osberton	(King Kong)
	1st	Loughanmore CCI**	(King Alfred)
	1st	Le Lion d'Angers CCI**	(King Samuel)

1992	1st	Badminton	(King William)
	1st	Windsor	(King Kong)
	2nd	Pratoni del Vivaro	(King Samuel)
	9th	Barcelona Olympics	(King William)

1993	2nd	Punchestown	(Star Appeal)

1994	World Team Gold and Individual 4th	The Hague	(King William)
	2nd & 4th	Burghley	(King Kong & Star Appeal)
	1st	British Novice Championships	(King Solomon III)
	2nd	Le Lion d'Angers	(King Solomon III)

1995	1st	Compiègne CCI**	(King Solomon III)
	1st	Punchestown	(Star Appeal)
	2nd	Gatcombe British Open	(Star Appeal)
	2nd	Scottish Open, Thirlestane	(Star Appeal)

	European Team Gold and Individual Bronze Medals	Pratoni del Vivaro	(King William)

1996	13th	Atlanta Olympics	(King William)
	1st & 2nd	Gatcombe British Open	(King William & King Solomon III)
	1st	Ladies' Open, Thirlestane	(King Solomon III)
	1st	Burghley	(Star Appeal)
	1st	Blenheim CCI***	(King Solomon III)

1997	1st	Saumur CCI***	(King Solomon III)
	2nd	Badminton	(Star Appeal)
	2nd & 3rd	Gatcombe British Open	(King Solomon III & Star Appeal)
	3rd	Blenheim	(King William)
	European Team Gold and 8th	Burghley	(Star Appeal)
	1st	Achselschwang	(King Solomon III)

1999	3rd	Blair Castle	(King Richard)
	5th	Burghley	(Star Appeal)

2000	1st	Badminton	(Star Appeal)
	7th	Sydney Olympics	(Star Appeal)

2001	4th	Burghley	(King Solomon III)

2002	3rd	Burghley	(King Solomon III)

2003	4th	Badminton	(King Solomon III)
	5th	European Championships, Punchestown	(King Solomon III)

2004	Olympic Team Silver	Athens	(King Solomon III)

2005	4th	Burghley	(Call Again Cavalier)
	2nd	Kreuth CCI***	(Birthday Night)

2006	2nd	Punchestown CCI**	(Kings Fancy)
	World Team Silver Medal	Aachen	(Call Again Cavalier)
	9th	Boekelo	(Apache Sauce)
	3rd	Le Lion d'Angers	(Kings Gem)

2007	9th	Lexington CCI****	(Apache Sauce)
	1st	Chatsworth World Cup Qualifier	(Call Again Cavalier)
	1st	Gatcombe British Open	(Call Again Cavalier)
	17th	Burghley	(Apache Sauce)
	16th	Blenheim	(Kings Gem)
	European Team Gold and Individual Silver Medals	Pratoni del Vivaro	(Call Again Cavalier)
	12th	Boekelo	(Kings Fancy)
	5th	Le Lion d'Angers	(Kings Temptress)
	2nd	Pau CCI****	(Imperial Cavalier)

2008	11th	Badminton	(Apache Sauce)
	2nd	Bramham	(Kings Fancy)

	Olympic Team Bronze	Hong Kong	(Call Again Cavalier)
	3rd & 4th	Burghley	(Imperial Cavalier & Apache Sauce)
	8th	Pau	(Call Again Cavalier)
2009	3rd	Tattersalls World Cup Qualifier	(Imperial Cavalier and Fernhill Urco)
	3rd	Luhmühlen CCI****	(Kings Temptress)
	4th	Aachen CIC	(Imperial Cavalier)
	5th & 8th	Barbury International	(Apache Sauce & Fernhill Urco)
	1st	Advanced at Aston-le-Walls	(Fernhill Urco)
	7th	Gatcombe World Cup qualifier	(Kings Temptress)
	2nd	Hartpury International CIC	(Apache Sauce)
	7th	Blenheim Young Horse CIC	(Fernhill Urco)
	13th	Boekelo	(Fernill Urco)
2010	4th	Badminton	(Imperial Cavalier)
	2nd	Tattersalls World Cup qualifier	(Apache Sauce)
	7th	Luhmühlen	(Apache Sauce)
	4th	British Open Championships at Gatcombe	(Apache Sauce)
	5th & 7th	Burghley	(Apache Sauce & Kings Temptress)
	Team Gold Medal and 6th	World Equestrian Games, Kentucky	(Imperial Cavalier)

INDEX